SCOTTISH VOICES

FROM THE SECOND WORLD WAR

ABOUT THE AUTHOR

Derek Young is a Research Fellow at the University of Stirling. He was awarded his PhD in History under Hew Strachan at the Scottish Centre for War Studies, University of Glasgow. In writing and compiling this book, Derek Young drew upon previously unused records in regimental museums, local history archives, university collections and national Scottish museums. He also made a national appeal across Scotland through the media for veterans to come forward to be interviewed and diaries to be sent in for consideration. His other books include the widely praised *Scottish Voices from the Great War*, also published by Tempus. He lives in Dundee.

Praise for DEREK YOUNG

£17.99
07524 3326 1

'Poignant and important' *THE COURIER AND ADVERTISER*

'A warts-and-all view of trench warfare' *THE SUNDAY POST*

'Derek Young has rescued a treasure trove of personal letters and diaries from the archives' TREVOR ROYLE

'A vivid picture of what it was like to be a Scottish soldier in the Great War... a powerful and emotional piece of work'
THE SCOTS MAGAZINE

SCOTTISH
VOICES

FROM THE SECOND WORLD WAR

DEREK YOUNG

TEMPUS

First published 2006

Tempus Publishing Limited
The Mill, Brimscombe Port,
Stroud, Gloucestershire, GL5 2QG
www.tempus-publishing.com

British Library Cataloguing in Publication Data.
A catalogue record for this book is available from the British Library.

ISBN 0 7524 3710 1

Typesetting and origination by Tempus Publishing Limited
Printed in Great Britain

Contents

Preface

Why do wars have numbers?

There is a flaw in human memory – the greater the distance from an event the less one remembers and the less bitter the memory. As a mother forgets the pain of childbirth so too does the collective national memory change from grief and mourning to one of national pride. Forgotten are the losses, the death and the suffering – in their stead a misplaced collective identity.

In 1918 the Great War, the war to end all wars, came to an untidy end. Some twenty-one years later it was no longer the Great War – reduced instead to a number as the expansion of the cancer that was National Socialism led inexorably to a Second World War in which over 50,000 Scots lost their lives.

Those who took the world into a second period of slaughter were, in the main, participants in the horrors of the first. Why? There are those who would say that I should already know the answer to that question. Indeed I know several answers, but not THE answer. Why?

War affects men in many ways. To survive, Ian Cameron divorced himself from the reality of war:

> I was in Malta for three years – I was away with the fairies when I came back.

Ewan Frazer took a more pragmatic approach:

> We believed in the survival of some of the fittest, with a lot of luck.

Jimmy MacKenzie echoes these views:

> I'm not glorifying war and I don't believe in it really, but I can't say
> in regret anything I did. Although war is a horrible thing, there must
> be times when it is the only option.

Others, like Ian Rintoul, who served five years in captivity, have a
different, but no less valid, point of view:

> I will never forget the hopelessness of it all – 5 years lost out of our
> young lives.

From the outset, National Service meant that Scots were conscripted
into regiments and units which had no relationship with Scotland.
Choice of true 'national' service was removed. This book looks at
those who did serve in Scottish regiments and those Scots who served
in regiments and units which were not designated as Scottish.

Once again, this book is not my words, not my story; I wasn't there.
Those of my generation were lucky, we had no war. The words in the
book are from those who were there – this story belongs to them.

Yet again we have taken to numbering our wars – First Gulf War,
Second Gulf War, Third… *ad nauseam*. As I sit writing this introduction the news comes that another two Scottish soldiers have been
killed in Iraq and, while the families of those men have my heartfelt
sympathy, I can't help myself asking – why?

Why do wars have numbers?

Acknowledgements

My thanks once again go to David Murphy at the Royal Scots Museum, Edinburgh Castle, and a special thank you goes to Anne Petrie for her invaluable help. I would like to take this opportunity to thank all those who contributed letters, diaries and photographs for inclusion in the book and especially those who put themselves through the process of being interviewed, prodded and probed.

Derek Rutherford Young

Note to the Reader

In some instances proper names have been replaced by the symbol ##### in the extracted quotations to maintain anonymity.

And then they were gone

Royal Scots	1633–2006
Royal Scots Fusiliers	1678–1959
Cameronians	
(Scottish Rifles)	1689–1968
King's Own	
Scottish Borderers	1689–2006
Royal Highland Regiment	
(The Black Watch)	1725–2006
Highland Light Infantry	1777–1959
Seaforth Highlanders	1778–1961
Cameron Highlanders	1793–1961
Gordon Highlanders	1794–1994
Argyll and Sutherland	
Highlanders	1794–2006

'And all around the young dead soldiers lay' *John Bell*

When you go home,
tell them of us,
and say

'For your tomorrow we gave our today'

Inscription from the Kohima memorial

No Requiem

Balmoral bonnet, Highland flash,
Rifle, grenade and haversack.
'Flowers o' the forest', No piper plays,
Where the Northern lads lie dead.
No longer afraid,
After the raid.

What shall I give,
Which they have not given.
For what must I strive,
Where they have not striven.
As I stand by the river alone,
Far more afraid,
After the raid.

John Bell

Part One

Once More into the Breach

Enlistment

Remembering the problems with enlistment in the First World War, the initial rush to the colours and the resulting shortages in essential industrial manpower, the pre-war government chose to introduce a process of conscription. In May 1939, with the onset of war looking increasingly likely, the Military Training Act was introduced in Britain. Men between the ages of twenty and twenty-two could expect to be called up for a period of military training lasting six months. Between May and the declaration of war on 3 September 1939, only one round of conscription was implemented. With the declaration of war all men aged between eighteen and forty became eligible for military service under the umbrella of the National Service Act. Although the government introduced conscription in May 1939, young men still had the opportunity to volunteer. Those who, like Stanley Rothney, chose to enlist had the opportunity to choose a branch of service with which to serve:

September 1939 I was in the employment of an oil company and we were all summoned and then the boss unlocked the safe and took out the sealed orders. All the oil companies amalgamated into one, controlled by the Government Petroleum Board. I was only temporary staff so I was paid off. I found a job with the forestry commission until I was 18 years of age at which time I volunteered for the army. I went to Aberdeen and enlisted in the Royal Scots. I wanted to join the Scots Guards but when I presented myself to the recruiting office the recruiting sergeant said 'how old are you'? 'Eighteen' I said. 'Too young, you've to be nineteen for them'. He says 'we've got something for you – 70th Young Soldiers Battalion – from 18 to 19 you're training then you get your regiment of choice'. Which it transpires was 100% fraud, because once you were in the army you went wherever the army put you.

The young Stanley Rothney was not alone. Thousands of young men took the opportunity to volunteer rather than wait for the inevitable call-up.

Willie Morrison saw the writing on the wall and chose to give up a good job in order to assure he had a choice:

I was in Edinburgh, assistant manager at the George Hotel there. Shortly after the war broke out, well I'd be called up in any case but if you didn't wait for your call up you could select what service you went into. I chose the airforce. The day came when I had to report. That was in Bathgate in Lanarkshire, where we were kitted out, did a bit of square bashing and so on.

If military service was inevitable, it was seen as preferable to have some form of choice. Ian Niven also took the opportunity to volunteer for the army when he was eighteen:

I volunteered for the Royal Scots in October 1942, I was 18 years of age. I joined the Lowland Regiment at Cameron Barracks, Inverness, and at 19 was transferred to the Royal Scots.

Volunteering for military service was seen by some as the lesser of two evils. Many saw military service as the preferred option when faced with unwelcome alternatives such as working in the mines. Charles Devlin was one such young man who was quick to make the choice:

> There was a prospect of being put down the mines – I said 'I'm not going down the mines'. I had an older brother who was in the RAF and although I was air minded, as a lot of youngsters were at that time, he was stationed down in England and he had never been abroad and used to come up on leave. So I says 'I wouldn't fancy going in the RAF and getting stuck in Middle Wallop or something'. I tried to join the Fleet Air Arm, I asked if I could specifically go in to the Fleet Air Arm but at that time they said 'oh you just go into general service then ask for a swap over'.

Both Stanley Rothney and Charles Devlin were victims of the recruiting sergeant's 'white lies' – both being told they could get a swap 'just for the asking'. Understandably, as in the First World War, there were a number of grey areas when it came to getting the recruits in. Recruiting offices were given the current manpower priorities and recruiting staff directed their efforts to fulfilling these requirements.

For others, the impending prospect of military service presented an opportunity to continue civilian trades within the umbrella of the armed forces – serving their country to the best of their ability and skills. It made sense that, even in uniform, many would aim to maintain some form of normality. A.L. Forbes was keen to avail himself of this opportunity but his gallant attempt backfired through no fault of his own:

> It was obvious that there would be war again with Germany. We men expected to be called up and eventually tables were given in the newspapers showing what different categories and age groups could expect regarding call up dates. Working as I was in the printing trade, which can almost be done without during war, my prospective call

up date would be a short one. I did not want the PBI [Poor Bloody Infantry] so when I spotted a notice saying PRINTERS WANTED BY Royal Engineers – apply within – I did just that. If there is one thing a recruit would want above everything else it would be to serve in his own trade or craft within the army. It seemed too good and it was. I had to have a medical and some sugar was found in a urine test, necessitating further tests which, although passing me A1 medically, held up my attestation and when I got back to the recruiting office there was a notice saying that recruitment was discontinued for that particular arm. They offered me alternatives and, to cut a long story short, I signed up to join the RASC (Clerical duties). It was second best but I had already given my notice and I did not wish to cancel it.

Not all were so willing to accept second best. Although Forbes accepted change in his preferred regiment, many others in the same boat were not so quick to accept suggested alternatives. The whole point of volunteering rather than waiting to be conscripted was about expanding individual choice, not limiting opportunities. Some, like Ian Cameron, failed to get into their preferred choice. However, rather than take second best they chose to return home and wait until their call-up papers arrived. Refusing to accept second best did not mean young men did not recognise that they had a level of responsibility for the defence of their country. Ian Cameron chose to spend this 'waiting time' by joining the Local Defence Volunteers, the precursor to the Home Guard. He was scathing about the RAF selection process:

When the war started I was teaching at Lawside Academy, St John's as it was at that time. My brother was a regular Airman. Anyway, when the war started a couple of us wrote of to be aircrew, we got the forms back to fill up, didn't ask you what you did just which public school did you attend? Do you have any private means? Well I had no private means. So we were all in the huff. After Dunkirk we all rushed to join the LDV. We had a parade at Rockwell – no rifles, nothing. Somebody came out and said in future we would have to address all the officers as Sir. Of course all the LDV were from the First World War, sergeants etc. then they produced Draffen, the drapers son, he was to be the boss. I thought, fuck this, I'm not going to address him as Sir – a lot of folk walked off the parade. It's the sort of thing you never get – it's all patriotism. That was really funny. I refused a commission – we were bolshie. So we waited and got called up eventually. Called up in September 1940. They just registered us then we came back home, then they called you up.

What got me was the officers class. Course all of my generation were a bit anarchist in the thirties, a lot of them were teachers. When the war started I was teaching in St John's. I left school early because parents were unemployed, there were five kids under me – we were all bursaries at the High School.

Norman Campbell took a similar pragmatic attitude when unable to obtain his preference in service branch. He chose to wait until called up by the War Department:

Following an unsuccessful bid to join the RAF Air Crew in early 1942, I was called up into the Army on 17 September 1942. I was 19 years and 3 months old. I was sent to Gordon Barracks, Aberdeen.

As in the First World War, those who were already serving in the Territorial Army were among the first to be mobilised and dispersed to their pre-planned war stations. However, as Norman Patterson found out, there was as much confusion and corresponding lack of preparation in 1939 as there had been in 1914:

I was in the territorials, joined when I was sixteen. The 76th Highland Field Regiment which was down at the Lochee Road. 76th Highland Field regiment, 303 Battery. I was born in 21. There was forty of us too young to go to France, thank goodness. They pushed us up to Forfar, to the Reid Halls in Forfar, took us out of one battery and put us in 304. The regiment was formed from a battery in Dundee and a battery in Aberdeen and I can't remember where the third one came from. But it was a farce really, it shows you how inept things were.

When war was declared I was working quite nearby, my nephew was in the same battery, we went in to see how things were, nothing was happening then, and the RSM, who was a regular, said, 'just the two guys I'm looking for'. 'Course, I was a signaller. He said, 'go home, pack your gear and come here' I said 'we can't, we're working'. He said 'not now you aint'. He had us manning the switchboard. Two of us for twenty-four hours and he said 'at night time you've got a camp bed and you sleep and put a buzzer on and all this rubbish. However, that's what happened, but the whole gang, the whole regiment was put together and told to come down at a certain time and the women came down and, well we were going away to war. This is true, we all got on the buses and tears you know and waving goodbye, and the busses drove off, and we said 'where are we going'? So we headed down towards the first station which wasn't the west station but it ran across the west coast. Shit, we weren't going down to London we were going north, but we went up to the next station and passed it. We're going over by ship, we must be going abroad – where did we end up – Sandimans sweetie factory, Carolina Port. We had nothing, no cooking equipment, nowt. A van came down from Wallace's with pie's and bridies, nae bad. I always remember it was Saturday, the only reason I remember cause we were told 'now you'll have to come to church parade, you have to be here at nine o clock tomorrow morning, Sunday'. I, that'll be right. He said 'right, fall out, dismiss, you can all go home'. So we went out, I can't remember where we went that night, pictures probably.

Jimmy MacKenzie had joined the pre-war Lovat Scouts as a Territorial:

I joined the Scouts, the Lovat Scouts, and it wasn't for any desire I had to defend my King and Country, I just wanted to go on a holiday. [At that time Territorials spent a fortnight at annual camp]

The next step for me when war broke out was into the Royal Marines, I was in the police at the time and we didn't have much option, the Marines or the Airforce, I didn't fancy the Airforce and I went into the Marines. At that time we were a reserved occupation

and you couldn't join if you wanted to but for some reason they de-
regulated it and four of us joined right away. Its amazing how people
reacted in those days, I don't think you'd get four people today, and
out of a small force of 30, four is a big proportion. It was a different
atmosphere towards the forces, towards the army, towards war then.
The previous war ended in 1919, this was 1939, it was just a short gap.
It was expected, it was a part of life.

The dramatic change from civilian life to the discipline of military service came as a shock to many young men. However, for
some young men, like John Forfar, social position and service in
the Officers Training Corps prior to the outbreak of war meant
that the transition to military service didn't come as such a great
culture shock:

> I'd actually been in the university O.T.C. so I wasn't unfamiliar with
> the… I was prepared for it because I'd been in the O.T.C. before the
> war actually started. Then you train for a bit, then you get allocated to
> a unit. I was first of all allocated to Field Ambulance and then I was
> the medical officer of the 13/18th Hussars, but I'd put my name down
> early on for going overseas and I got this rather unique posting to the
> Royal Marines. Because I was an army officer, not a Royal Marine
> Officer nor a naval officer… the naval officers weren't too keen on
> joining the Commandos and they called on the army to do so. So the
> army provided doctors who were willing to do that kind of thing.

For others, impending service with the army came as something of a
surprise. Returning home from work one day, Ian Rintoul was surprised to find a letter from the War Department waiting for him:

> My joining of the A&SH was never in my thoughts – until I returned
> home from work, with my mother meeting me at the door and said,
> 'Ian, there's a message from the War Department'. I was stunned to put
> it mildly. It said, 'report to Stirling Castle for infantry training as you
> are now 21 years old and in the first batch to be trained there'.

Roddy MacLeod also found himself subjected to a call-up and quick turnaround:

> You were called up different according to your age group. It was 1941,
> I was about 18 and a half. I did nine weeks training then I was on the
> ship round the Cape to Africa, I had one weeks embarkation leave.

However, conscription did not mean that there was no choice at all. Even when drafted there was still the opportunity to choose a particular branch of service, although this was not always easy, as James Hogg discovered:

> I was called up, I wanted to get into the RAF, I volunteered because
> I knew, instead of going in the army, but saying that I wanted to get
> flying, because I was good at morse code and all the rest of it and I
> thought that would be half the battle. When I went in for the medical,
> I failed with my eyes and I discovered I was colour blind as well. They
> gave you a ball and the ball was like spaghetti, was full of lines and it
> was all colours and the boy says, 'now, I want you to follow that colour
> there and come out the other side'. I didn't even get a quarter of an
> inch away and I thought, 'I've lost it, I dinn'a ken where it is.'

Douglas Kerr also recalls that he was offered a choice of service branch when his call-up papers arrived:

> I waited until I was called up, I can't remember now whether I chose
> the RAF, whether you got the choice or not. My call up papers say
> the RAF so maybe I didn't get a choice. But I remember going to
> the Marryat Hall in Dundee, I've an idea that there I was given the
> choice of army, navy or airforce. I got the call up papers quite some
> time afterwards, this was April 1941, I was actually called up in June,
> I remember it was June when I was sent to Blackpool.

Not all were as lucky as Douglas Kerr and James Hogg. For others, conscription offered no opportunity for choice. Such decisions had already been taken for them. As we have seen, when Ian Rintoul was called up it was for service in the Argyll and Sutherland Highlanders. Ernest Jamieson similarly received specific call-up instructions:

'Call Up' papers arrived to report for service at DTC RASC 183 Company, Squad 3, Chesterfield. A special troop train was leaving Edinburgh Waverley Station direct to Chesterfield. The station was full of chaps from all parts of Scotland heading for Chesterfield.

Charlie Smith remembers his arrival at Perth barracks and the news that war had been declared:

In 1939 the Government brought out the Militia Act. Any youth who had attained the age of twenty by June 1939 was to be called up for six months in the regular army and four years in the reserve. Me being twenty in August 1939 I was caught. I had to go to the Queens Barracks, Perth on the 15th of July. They gave me a travel warrant. There were quite a few hundred guys being put into different platoons. There were sergeant majors in charge of us. The day war was declared with Germany we were all gathered together and the head lads came out telling us war had been declared and, if necessary, we had to lay down our life. And in September we went down to Aldershot and I was attached to the 51st Highland Division. I was in Perth right through from July until September. War was declared on the Sunday and we all gathered together to hear what had happened.

When Murdo MacLeod joined the Royal Navy he soon found himself transferred:

When I first joined it was the Royal Navy proper, General Service. I went to Chatham and they took me out of general service and put me into Combined Operations which was really landing craft and special services.

Choice depended on need, and when the military had need for men to fill a specific roll, choice became second to expediency.

BEF

We cam' frae oot the city, and frae ilka hielan' glen
Frae oot the ha' an' mansion, an' frae the but-an-ben
They pit us a' thegither, the beat o' Scottish bane
Ay! The 51ˢᵗ Division tak's second place tae nane

Ye canna mak' a sojer wi' braid an' trappin's braw
Nor gie him fightin' spirit when his back's ag'in the wa'
It's the breedin' in the callan's that winna let them whine
The bluid o' generations frae lang lang syne

We hae shivered in the cauld at times, we hae swe'tt in Desert Sun
We hae striv' for King and Country just tae gain some desert grun'
But we sure are makin' history for our Scots bit weans tae learn
That the 51st Division, it aye stands firm

As in 1914, once war had been declared, a British Expeditionary
Force (BEF) was dispatched to Europe, ill-equipped, ill-trained, ill-
prepared and destined to suffer the same ignominy as in the opening
months of the Great War.

Deployed to France in 1939, the British Expeditionary Force, commanded by Lord Gort, was stationed from Bailleul to Maulde and
on the eve of the German attack comprised nine infantry divisions.
One other division, the 51st Highland Division, was stationed on
the French Maginot Line in the Saar region on the French/German
border. The BEF found itself with the impossible task of patrolling
and protecting over 200 miles of the French frontier.

When the long-awaited attack came, the BEF was unable to
withstand the onslaught of the German forces and, along with remnants of the retreating French army, withdrew to the Channel ports.
Dunkirk was the intended evacuation port but British troops found
themselves scattered across a number of other French ports awaiting
an evacuation that never came. Not all of the British forces were
able to withdraw, and for many the sacrifice of the 51st Highland
Division was seen as a cold, calculated betrayal.

Fresh from his call-up and after a short spell of training in the Argyll and Sutherland Highlanders, Ian Rintoul was one of those who were sent to Europe as part of the British Expeditionary Force:

> One morning we were told we were moving to England to a town called Borden. After a few days there we moved to Aldershot and did some field tactics. We weren't there long enough to learn very much, war had already been declared. We were told we were going to France via Southampton to Le Havre.

Ian recalls his first few weeks in France; for the local population a mixture of joy and fear:

> The boat was loaded, we moved out to deeper water until morning then we were on our way. On arrival there, we were transported to a village in the north where we were fixed up with accommodation. We were given a fine welcome; perhaps because they thought we were their saviours. We were in this village for weeks and we got on well with the locals and the weather was lovely. It was a village of tears when they were informed we were moving on. Next morning we moved out of the village and on to the French/German border.

Arriving at the French/German border, Ian and his comrades found themselves taking up a position facing the enemy and digging in:

> On arrival (Franleu) on the edge of a wood, it was an outpost with sandbags built up round about us. We split up into sections of six and taking turns of lookout. The Black Watch was in the post previously and they said before they left, 'you might be hearing from Jerry soon, as we were out on patrol last night and disturbed them'. Sure enough, later, when the Black Watch had gone, Jerry fired a shell which landed short of the post but shrapnel hit a tree next to us and took a piece of the tree out. Not much happened with the enemy, they came out with a football and had a kick about. I don't remember how long we were at the post before being told we were going back down the line.

When posted to the BEF in France, Ernest Lovett found himself caught up in the confusion and complacency of the 'phoney war':

> We parade for our medical examination and receive countless jabs in the arms against all kinds of diseases and sent off home on one week's embarkation leave. One week later report to barracks. Our kit checked, issued with one blanket and a Lee Enfield rifle, but no ammunition. We travel by train to Portsmouth, where we board a ship for France. We land at Le Havre, and the envelope package containing our movement orders is handed over to the R.T.O. there. He is of the opinion that we were supposed to be at 2nd Echelon in Brighton. We are put into a cold concourse hall and wait for instructions. By overlapping our blankets we managed to sleep on the terrazzo. After 4 or 5 days we were told to leave for Paris, where 2nd Echelon is situated. We travel by train and eventually arrive in Arras, where we are told that 2nd Echelon is really situated. We are picked up by an officer who asks us where the hell we have been for the last 6 days. We are in a large house on the outskirts of Arras – an Intelligence Section training officers and men on aerial photographic interpretation. We are shown how they string aerial photographs together and with magnifying glasses, decide what pill boxes, barbed wire, machine gins and A.A. guns look like from the air. The section is making maps of the armaments in the Siegfried Line.

Ian Rintoul recalled the lack of material with the BEF as the 51st Highland Division prepared to stand against the expected German advance:

> As you are aware, Dunkirk was the evacuation port to get as many men as possible off the beaches and home. When all this was going on the 51st Highland Division was sent up to the French border to attempt to hold back the German armoured division under General Rommell. We had no armour, just a few Bren Guns to a company and a rifle each, this was all we had against Tanks, etc.

For many, like Ian Rintoul, the end result of the futile defence of the BEF was capture and internment. Many were bitter, not at the capture and sacrifice, but at not being given the opportunity to fight to their capabilities:

> Unfortunately, on the march our Commanding Officer, Captain Glenn Handley, was shot by a sniper, we couldn't have had a worse start. A Manchester Machine Gunner, attached to the Argylls, was also shot and had the top of his head removed.
>
> After being put into a defenceless position a despatch rider arrived with battle orders from Whitehall, London, and by Churchill. Our officer read out: 'You will hold this position, you will either be killed, wounded or made Prisoner of War'. We were expected to hold back the might of the German Armoured Division. We only had rifles, what good was that fighting against tanks.
>
> The British General before the attack happened, got in touch with Whitehall and Churchill pointing out to them that the 51st Highland Division should not be sacrificed but the reply – 'Get on with the orders given'. What chance did we have against the German Army, full of armour against us. We had no tanks or planes to support us. I ask you, what use is a rifle in a position like that? Churchill took all the hatred from all the Highlanders to his grave for being responsible for this 'Murder of Gallant Men'.
>
> The plan was to hold the Germans back to allow thousands of the British troops to escape by boats from Dunkirk. We had no chance of winning and were eventually overrun and taken prisoners. We were later taken prisoners, losing 500 killed and as many wounded.

In May 1940 Charlie Smith found himself right in the thick of the action:

> January 1940 I went over to France, to Lille with the 51st. We started to go up the line, we went up north. The further north we went the nearer we were getting to the Germans. On the 28th of May 1940, we were right in the midst of it.
>
> We were in Belgium, it was the 4th Battalion, Black Watch at this time, in Belgium. The Germans were just waiting on us. They let us come within distance and just let us have it. The Germans were right over us.

We were sacrificed, we were up against ten divisions of Germans. We only had about three thousand men. We had English officers with us and they said 'tonight we're going to make the final stand. Don't be afraid'. I was only a laddie of twenty.

As the BEF fell back towards the Channel, Dunkirk was not the only evacuation port. John Bell found himself trapped in Dieppe in May 1940 and was able to describe events there:

Dieppe was a hospital base. Hospital Carriers plied between there and Newhaven, fully illuminated at night, before the attack. The docks were attacked daily, the only defence being rifle fire, the area supposedly being protected by the Geneva Convention agreement.

Some 14 ships were sunk in the harbour, including our Hospital ships, Maid of Kent and Brighton; the Paris was also hit. I was on the quay when the Maid of Kent was hit and was blown of my feet by the blast. She was loading wounded at the time. Refugees had also been arriving from Belgium by fishing boats, many of these being sunk in the harbour.

Towards the end (which was well after the Dunkirk evacuation), there was considerable panic in the town. No evacuation by sea was possible, the Luftwaffe having blocked the harbour had also sealed off the sea area with electrical mines. One refugee boat was sunk in attempting to get away.

We the defenders were a mixed bag of small units. Because I could speak French (well, not perfectly), my skipper, Captain James, got me to join him checking refugees over the river bridge into the town, on account of the fifth columnists who were trickling through with them. We were in an area controlled (supposedly), by the French, and the last patrol I did in front of our perimeter was led by a French officer. We packed it up when our own trigger happy and scared defenders opened up on us – a real shambles.

When units of the 51st Highland Division moved back across France to the port of St Valery, Arthur Whitcomb was with them:

A wireless message was received at noon to say the bridge had been
blown up in front by the French. They were ordered back to a line
from the Seine to Fecamp, while a detachment of RE and Lothians
was ordered to block the road to Yvetet and to endeavour to delay
the northward move of the Germans for 48 hours to let the rest of
the Division with the French 31 and 44 Div's get back and embark at
Havre. We spent the night of the 9/10 at Bois Huwn and moved easily
on the 10th to Ouvillers. The day was dull and thundery but the rain
we'd longed for would not come. Everything pointed to the Germans
being behind us, and the Generals plan, which at the time had been
to move direct to Havre, had to be modified, when it was reported
that St Valery which was on our direct route westwards was held by
German armoured units. The Lothians were sent of to investigate and
drive them out. The plan was not to hold the line of the Durdent river
west of St Valery and try and force a passage to Havre and the same
time hold a line from St Valery facing the opposite way. The latter was
subsequently changed and the line facing east was to be about three
miles east of St Valery, leaving St Valery about the centre. Div HQ were
ordered to St Riqyie which was clearly rather far west.

The Lothians action at St Valery was successful and the Germans
were driven back to the river Dundent. Orders were now issued for
all surplus kit, personal or otherwise, to be jettisoned and destroyed.
We were to move with only what was essential for fighting plus a pack
and what we carried on our person. All surplus vehicles were handed
over for carrying the marching infantry. The move was to start about
10pm. By 9pm Ouillers was getting full of transport and I feared for
an air attack but luckily it never came. By the time of start, traffic
was packed in two lines on the road, and was made worse by the fact
that the French used our roads quite against any orders and made the
confusion worse. I stayed with Harry Eden till about 11.30pm then
he decided he'd go. This was easier said than done, but we eventually
got on the road, which was a solid stream of traffic two deep, rather
reminiscent of the end of an international rugby match. We had about
ten miles to go altogether and I thought we should never make it.
Div HQ had been changed to Cailleville but all the transport was
still directed on St Riquier and no plans had apparently been made

for distribution and our other party did not know of the change. At
3.30am on 11 June we were still packed on the road: messages kept
coming back that the Germans were here, there and everywhere. I
kept imagining dawn breaking and finding us strung out for miles,
a solid block on the road and air action turning the move into a
complete shambles.

By 4am we reached St Valery where we stopped to see the column
come through. It was really moving now and was clear by about 5am
or soon after. Harry Eden took half an hour sleep in the car and I
walked down to the front to smell the sea. You can imagine how I felt,
as you know I love the sea, and when I saw the navy off the shore I
was really cheered and thought we had a chance. They were taking
off wounded and the NO on the small jetty was fussing because dawn
was there and he was afraid of the destroyers being bombed. I talked
to him about our being taken off and he said they had heard about
that and asked how many we were. I was concerned though that if we
were to be taken off at all, it should start at once with full naval and
air support as the position was obviously becoming critical.

We met French soldiers coming back. They were poor soldiers and
did not want to fight.

Like Ian Rintoul, Arthur Whitcomb also railed against the sacrifice
and lack of support:

There was little to be done now. At 11am we got the order that all
efforts would be made to take us off that night and that all vehicles
and equipment would be rendered useless before leaving. German
reconnaissance planes were over constantly spying on our position.
Our air as usual, NIL. It maddened me the lack of help we were given
from home, they could easily have got us away, but they preferred to
sacrifice us. Why? Someone must answer it one day.

There was a stream of people moving along the beach, some were
trying to launch a small boat, which was clearly suicide.

It is clear from the recollections of both Ian Rintoul and Arthur
Whitcomb that troops felt abandoned by the lack of effort, not from

those on the ground but by those dictating strategy on the British side of the Channel. Many felt that not enough effort was put into evacuating ports other than Dunkirk. John Bell has poignant memories of the chaos of evacuation, and in particular his own participation and the unexpected outcome of his detraction from duty:

One of those fine but desperate days late in spring 1940 seems forever welded to my memory. It was the day I became a British soldier; during the previous nine months I had been just another civilian in uniform, a volunteer, in for the duration. I was serving with the BEF, in a small detachment on special duties; a veteran, I suppose, compared with the boys just attached to the unit. Their average age was 18, they had been called up less than three months and sent to France, supposedly to complete their training in the rear areas.

When they arrived the rear areas were in flames; they ran straight into a punishing dive-bombing attack, and scattering in small groups without any officers, had been living off the countryside, until found and brought in by patrol. They wanted to stay and fight together, and half a dozen of them were manning a small post on our river bank perimeter, complete with rifles and one inadequate Boyes Anti-tank Rifle.

I had been ordered to collect my full kit from my billet in the town and return to the post as soon as possible, ready to move at a moments notice. The raised tree-lined road leading to the town was crowded with refugees; they had been coming along the road for three weeks and more. They were the latecomers, the very old and the very young, hoping to get away to the South before the enemy cut the roads to Rouen.

An hour before, the column had been hit by the 'afternoon special', the daily raid by the Luftwaffe, the gradual softening up before the final coup de grace. The road was littered with a miscellaneous assortment of broken possessions; bicycles, handcarts, wheelbarrows, mattresses and ruptured remains of ancient motor cars.

A group of weary nuns sat dejectedly by the roadside, with heads bowed, some fingering their beads in prayer. A woman in pains of labour shuffled along supported by two others, muttering, 'l' (h)opital, l' (h)opital'. The dead, bearing the defeaturing impact of high explosive, lay, grotesquely shaped, by the roadside. It was the body of a child which affected me most of all; there it lay on top of a load of cabbages, on a broken down old camion, arms outstretched to the sky, in mute unseeing appeal. I'd seen the child alive and active earlier in the day as I checked the camion over the river bridge.

I was angry. As a boy I read deeply of army tradition; in vivid imagination I stood with that 'thin red line' of Argyle and Sutherland before Sevastopol. That was war; soldier fought soldier as long as the pipes played, the drums beat or the standard flew. But this was sheer bloody murder and any doubts I had about being able to kill were gone for ever; for the death of this one child alone, I knew I could kill.

My angry thoughts were interrupted by the sight of a girl ahead, sitting dejectedly on a large bundle tied in a white sheet and an old man standing listlessly by, surrounded by several shabby cases, whilst on the road, two bodies lay in the wreckage of an old car.

As I approached, the girl looked up, then ran towards me calling, 'Please help me, please help me', then half in French and half in English, she poured out her story.

She was from Metz, on the German frontier; this was her grandfather, her mother and father lay dead in the wrecked car. She was going to some friends who lived in a little house somewhere off the road on the way to Arques.

'You will help me', she said, 'you will help me, because you are a British soldier, you are not a French soldier, you are not a Belgian soldier, you are a British soldier, un soldat Anglais'.

I told her I was on duty but would help her to the road junction, where she would turn left for Arques and I must turn right for the town. As we talked a number of children gathered round us. I lifted the bundle on my shoulders and picked up one of the cases, the girl took a case in each hand, but the old man was past carrying anything.

A boy of about 13 stood with the group of children; he had a grubby freckled face, with a long fringe of sun bleached hair and was wearing rather long, short trousers. I looked at him and he picked up the remaining case and fell in at my side. Arriving at the road junction, I put my burdens down and pointing in the direction of the town, said to the girl, 'My duty is that way, je vais la, I can take you no further'. I felt bad about it but I had to get to the town, and quickly.

The girl was distressed but still persistent; once again she said, 'You must help me, you will help me, because you are British soldier'. 'Someone', she said, 'will be waiting for me by the road.'

The whole town seemed to be emptying itself down the Arques road. An army truck was coming towards me, threading itself through the straggle of refugees. Here was a chance to shed my load. I jumped on the running board and asked, 'Can you give the old man and the girl a lift to Arques'?

'Sorry old chap, not a hope', it was an infantry major who spoke and the truck was crammed with khaki-clad figures. I was too occupied at the time to wonder why they were leaving.

As we stood at the road junction more children gathered round, seeking company of their own kind. I wondered what to do; should I, or shouldn't I; it wasn't my problem, I had problems of my own.

Looking in the direction of Arques, I saw something which probably changed the course of my life; it could have been the answer to a prayer – if I'd been praying – and in terms of Army Ordinance, I spoke these words aloud to myself, 'Wheelbarrow one, French, Soldier for the use of'. So that was it; and there I was wheeling the barrow, loaded with the bundle and some of the cases along the road to Arques, the girl on one side, the boy on the other, and the old man, with bended head trotting along in front, and all around the children, like a trail of lost ducklings following a foster mother. I stopped for a rest, looking back at the receding town; I was, worried, my shoulders aching, and I was going away from my line of duty. I wondered about the girl; was she stringing me along; was there a little house just off the road, and would anyone be waiting for her?

I asked her about the children. She told me they had been bombed out of several refugee camps; their parents were either dead or lost and they followed me because the Tommies had been kind to them, on the way, giving them chocolate. My shiralee was growing: there was assuredly far more to the British soldier's reputation than Sir Colin Campbell's 'thin red line tipped with steel'. It was the children who now took possession of me; when I stopped to rest, they all stopped and quietly hung around, they never spoke and from their unwashed serious faces their eyes sought mine in silent quest.

I stopped again, looked at my watch, more than an hour had passed, by now I should be back at the river bank post. I must go back; I must tell the girl, but she was no longer by my side, she was running up the road ahead to where a group of peasant women stood. A woman detached herself from the group and in a moment the girl was in her arms, sobbing out her tragic story. So it was all true, there was someone waiting by the road and somewhere there would be a little house.

I walked back along the road with mixed feelings and looking back saw only the figure of the boy with long short trousers, watching me out of sight.

Turning right at the road junction, I walked back towards the town, passing the now dwindling column of refugees. From an army truck in the column a voice hailed me, 'You're going the wrong way mate, we're pulling out, jump on'. I hesitated for a minute, then called out. 'Got to get back to my unit'.

The day had resumed its own tranquillity, and for a moment, just a moment, it seemed that nothing had happened, nothing had changed. Only the dead remained where they had fallen and the body of the child lay on the heap of cabbages, arms outstretched to the sky, with one knee bent up.

No, things were not the same and for me I knew they would never be quite the same again.

I turned off the road near the bridge and walked along the river bank towards the post. All was quiet, too quiet, no one challenged my approach. A disturbed feeling of shocked expectancy rose from my solar plexus: things were not right, they didn't look right. A large uprooted tree lay across the track; there were two large craters on either side of the post, and a great hole had been torn out of the river bank. The atmosphere was rank with the acrid smell of burnt cordite.

And all around the young dead soldiers lay.

Stationed at Arras, Ernest Lovett was engaged in photographic recognition, building up the picture of German intention. His diary details the German attack on Arras and his subsequent involved in the evacuation from Boulogne:

> On Friday 10th May at 4.30 a.m. German aircraft drop bombs on Arras and the surrounding aerodromes. We hear that the Germans have attacked Belgium and Holland. A very ominous atmosphere. Some light French tanks move through Arras. Several French aircraft fight German aircraft over Arras. We are plotting aerial photographs taken by Blenheim aircraft attached to G.H.Q. They are supposed to demolish a number of important bridges. No success. All the Blenheims are shot down.
>
> Tuesday 14th May. German aircraft bomb Arras. On the telephone exchange: make a hash of it. Several Generals in the War Office threaten to have my guts for garters if I don't re-connect them properly. Put on sentry duty at the main entrance – find it very tough to remain perfectly still with bombs falling all around. Rumours that German parachutists are everywhere. The office is bombed during the night: not a lot of damage, but officers realise that things are becoming a little unsafe. We are ordered to dig trenches for protection. We unearth a bully-beef tin from World War One. A bayonet is stuck into the lid and a jet of foul gas shoots up into the air.

For the first time since he entered military service, Lovett was introduced to the workings of his rifle. A case of better late than never:

> Wednesday 5th – Welsh Guards train us in the use of our rifles – we are issued with ammunition. Arras bombed again. Unnerving to see bodies hanging on telephone lines after a bomb dropped in a nearby street.

His photographic unit was evacuated from Arras as the French army fell back before the advancing German army:

> The French line has been broken. Our officers know that communications with forward troops have broken down. Our French liaison officers are in tears – they know that their army is defeated. We have to move out of Arras in the dark. Coaches take our equipment to

the railway station. G.H.Q. is being evacuated; the train is bombed
when we are on the move. The train hides in a tunnel, and comes out
backwards, successfully avoiding the German aircraft. Lorries arrive
and take us and the equipment to a cliff top overlooking the sea at
Wimereux, about 4 miles north of Boulogne. There are other units
scattered about. We lay in the fields waiting for instructions. JU 87
dive bombers bomb and strafe us. All the troops fire at them but with
no success.

By Sunday 19 May it was clear that evacuation or capture was imminent:

Sunday 19th – in the morning we are given axes and told to destroy
all our expensive technical equipment and throw the debris into the
sea. In the afternoon we march under a sergeant towards Boulogne
– we lose our way several times. Men from the Royal Corps of Signals
up on telephone poles dismantling military lines give us directions.
we hear rumours that German tanks are everywhere.

Monday 20th – we are called to the docks and instructed to destroy
thousands of tins of condensed milk. We stick bayonets in a few and
drink – but soon feel sick and throw all the remaining tins in the
harbour. We are told there is a merchant ship in the harbour and that
it will be the last ship out. We are ordered to embark. Very cramped
on deck. We lie down near the stern

About half-way across the channel we sight a mass of bombers
flying from Britain towards France. The ship alarm sounds. Machine
guns and rifles are loaded. They get nearer and we realise they are
British flying to France to bomb the German advance. Everyone
cheers. We sight the white cliffs of Dover – a lovely sight.

Running, Jumping and Standing Still

Once enlisted, whether volunteer or conscript, personnel were introduced to the dubious 'pleasures' of military training. When they left
the comforts of home for the rigours of military service, they faced
endless training to prepare them for the years ahead. The military

had limited time to turn a collection of individuals into a cohesive fighting unit.

Ernest Lovett arrived as an innocent and was quickly 'educated' in the time-honoured fashion:

> Arrive at barracks at 7 p.m. – report to a sergeant who asks if I have got my 'biscuits'. I tell him I am not hungry. He blows his top and tells me that biscuits are mattresses for your bed. Spend a miserable night in barracks. Have to mop the floors in the morning. Issued with army kit. I am given a greatcoat – the sight of it sickens me – it only comes down to my knees. Spend the day being drilled, marching up and down the parade ground. Exhausted with the heavy clothing and the boots.
>
> Following day spend drilling in the morning. In the afternoon put on police duty at the gates, directing traffic in and out of the barracks.

For Charles Devlin, his early introduction to naval training took place in a more congenial environment as the armed services, faced with the demand to house ever-increasing numbers, commandeered a variety of types of property which were suited to receiving and holding large numbers of men:

> We did our training at Butlins camp, the navy confiscated the whole lot of them, and they were training establishments – they were ready made, weren't they? It was pretty cushy, you had a bed or a bunk. We didn't sleep in hammocks all the time we were there. We reported to Skegness, which was called HMS Royal Arbour, but there was bombing round about and you couldn't get a nights sleep. They sent us over to HMS Glendour.

For others, the shock was not so much the environment as those they were forced to share the experience with. The close proximity of large numbers of cultural strangers, coupled with the move to an alien environment, proved to be a shock for many. Norman Patterson discovered that even within the confines of Britain there were language barriers to overcome:

When they formed the British Expeditionary Force, forty of us were too young to go to. We went to Forfar – we were transferred to 304 battery, then when 304 battery went with the regiment over to France we were transferred to the Leeds Rifles in Leeds. It was absolutely, I mean, the guys we were stationed with were contract miners, broad Yorkshire guys and they said 'cant bloody well understand you', we said, 'the same goes for us', because they were speaking broad Yorkshire you see. To give you an example, I was going out this hut and this guy lying at the end, a chap called Jack Rearer shouted something at me and I came back and says 'what did you say?' he says 'put wood in t'ol'. I says 'what does that mean? He says 'shut bloody door'.

Douglas Kerr also discovered that sharing a barrack room with a large number of strangers had its moments:

In these days if someone could get hold of any chocolate that was something special, or cigarettes of course. Well I never smoked but chocolate I did like. And if I could get any chocolate in the NAAFI, they got it in occasionally. One night I was wakened up in the middle of the night by the fellow in the bed next to me. He was a bit merry and he said 'want some chocolate'? I would never say no to that, so I got some chocolate from him and I put it in my bag on my shelf and went back to sleep again. Next day when I woke up he wasn't there. I said 'where's what's his name'? 'What happened to him'? and someone said 'Oh, they came and arrested him, he broke into the NAAFI and stole all sorts of things'. I was always a good sleeper in those days and I didn't hear them come in and arrest him. The first thing I did with that chocolate was to get rid of it, I made up a bundle, I wrapped this lot up and sent it of to my parents.

When Ernest Jamieson arrived at his first posting he found the army had commandeered the local hall:

Arrived at Chesterfield to be greeted on the platform by officers and NCVOs; then marched into town where we were divided up and taken to various billets. I ended up in St James Hall with about fifty others. Some lads were on the stage and others in rows down the hall. After giving our names and showing our call up papers we were told we could go into town and be back at 11.00pm. most of us headed for the nearest pub (our last night of freedom). Went into Billy's Bar which belonged to a former British Lightweight Champion boxer. When asking a local if Billy was present he pointed to a man at the end of the bar. He must have weighed 20 stone!

As Jamieson quickly discovered, training was not all pubs and drill halls:

Paraded each morning and marched to Queens Park where we were drilled by two Scots Guards Corporals and a CSM from the Royal Scots Fusiliers and all this in our civilian clothes as they had no uniform to give us. Finally after two weeks we get our uniforms. Its just as well we got them as my weight dropped from 13st 7lbs to 11stone with all the drilling and lousy grub.

For others, the training accommodation was more historic. After receiving his call-up papers, Ian Rintoul reported to Stirling Castle to commence his basic training:

On arrival, someone in the guardroom told me to keep walking up that hill, and then someone up there where I was to report for service signing. He directed me to the room where I was enlisted, then taken to our accommodation on the ground floor. Next was kit collection from the Company Stores. When they finished the issue of kit and a rifle it would be very difficult to recognise me under that mountain of kit. After some time our billet gradually filled up and I learned later that we were now in A Company and a nicer sergeant you could wish to meet. He showed us how to arrange the blankets and utensils etc on the bed. The chap next to me said, 'how long is the sergeant going to continue being nice to us'? Well he kept it going and it paid dividends. He was delighted with us, and we replied by doing everything he asked of us. A contrast to some of the other sergeants bawling and swearing for the least mistake made on the square, with English holidaymakers shaking their heads at this sergeant who was white in the face with rage. All this was taking place on our first few days, marching up and down, with him making such a noise it was difficult hearing our own sergeant giving the command, 'about turn'.

The sergeant came in our billet and said, 'tomorrow am after washing, shaving and breakfast, get your P.T. kit out and an instructor will take you for a few miles jogging along the road at the foot of the castle. As we were running along the road next to a field with a herd of cows in it, they started running too; perhaps they thought we were also cows, quite a laugh it was. We made our way back to the castle and showers. Some of the lads were out of breath, others of us played football for local teams at home and it helped us quite a bit.

Orders for tomorrow: Marching with your rifles after being shown how to handle it first of all. Next morning washing, shaving, off for breakfast, which was enjoyed by most. When I saw some of them turn up their noses at it, it made me wonder if they had been dining too long at the Golden Lion. As time goes bye they will look back when things get tough and say to themselves, 'Oh for the meals at the castle again'. Well breakfast over and out on parade to be taught sloping arms etc. we really got quite accomplished at the exercise, we then moved down to the parade ground to do some marching with our rifles, this time without background noise from other Companies, and no trouble here this time hearing the commands from our own sergeant.

We were taken to the Miniature Range to try and put up a good show. Well it wasn't, I'm afraid; we will need lots more practice. We were getting quite a kickback when we fired. We were told to hold the butt firmly against our shoulder next time; we were told we must have a few more sessions in a day or two. It was getting close to our lunch by this time at the range, so we were dismissed and of we went to wash hands etc, then over to the dining hall.

Following lunch we were given instructions on bed making and after use in the morning were shown how to fold the blankets, put them on the bed again and no other way would be acceptable, so pay attention and do it right. The room will be inspected later, so tidy up your kit and anything lying about under your bed, put them in the wardrobe tidily not just flung in. your sergeant and an officer will be coming round to inspect your room, your bed made up, and if your blankets aren't folded correctly, as you have been instructed, you will be told to practice and get it right for the next inspection in a day or two.

Well, in a week or two all the things we were taught and didn't do so well then were beginning to fall into place. After a few weeks of doing all the things we were taught we were getting most things right and our sergeant was very pleased with what we had achieved so far in such a short time.

We clubbed together hurriedly and bought a little gift for our sergeant, which he received with tears in his eyes. Our time at the castle was coming to an abrupt end, as there were rumours of war. Sure enough, after breakfast we were told to get our kit ready, we were going to Tillicoultry and billeted in the Old Oak Mill down the Burnside. No transport, we were told we were marching with the pipe-band out in front, of course. On arrival everything was very basic and a change from the castle. No running hot water for washing and shaving in the morning. I think this was intentional, hardening us up for life in the very near future. After a short time there in Tillicoultry once again orders, prepare to move out, we were sent to an area near Dumbarton to guard oil installations, then back to the castle for overnight stop.

There were not enough suitable buildings to house troops in areas of high military concentration and, as in the First World War, soldiers were billeted in civilian households. In coastal holiday resorts boarding houses were a godsend for the military, with landladies used to dealing with diverse groups of lodgers. Ian Cameron found himself in civilian billets which were less than welcoming:

We did our training in Morecombe promenade on November and over Christmas. No greatcoats, on the front, eight hours a day. What stuck in my mind were the stupid things, this charging about. Charging over this field and there was a fence round this beautiful green patch, this chap leapt the fence and landed up to here in the cesspool, middle

of winter, the stench, nobody would go near him. Then they went
to the sports pavilion and they hosed him down, the poor soul, the
water was freezing. Kept his clothes on and hosed him down. Then
there was an argument, he had to pay for his uniform, his new one.
Stayed in the guest houses on the front at Morecombe, the old lodg-
ing houses – nine of us. There was a lot of trouble, the Airforce gave
them money to feed us but they just didn't feed you properly. When
you were out in the open, seven in the morning to six at night, always
outside, never inside, at night when you went home the place was
plastered with notices – don't do this, don't do that. For tea she put
out two or three thin slices of bread and margarine, all the boys could
have eaten a loaf each. Anyway, there were Welshmen in my lot, they
were no say bad, they all went to chapel, and got locals to feed them.
So one of them said they would get a turkey for Christmas, a country
boy, so we got the turkey all right, she cooked it and everything, then
he asked her to pay for it.

Went down to Merksholme, and that was funny there too. The
camp had been for about 500 people and we were about, god knows
how many thousand. The sewage packed in, we were all sitting in the
cookhouse and the MO came round and said that 'nobody was to
drink any water unless it had been passed by him'. Anyway, all they
did was just throw out passes to everybody – of course the poor
Scots boys couldn't go home – it was too bloody far. So, we were
left, supposed to be emptying toilets. Of course, I was twenty-seven,
I was an old man by this time. Another northern bloke and myself
persuaded the Padre that we would fix his organ so we hid in the
chapel while they were scouring the camp for blokes to empty toilets.
We were supposed to be doing these courses, did the course all right,
it was a farce actually because the stuff you had to practice on was
all broken and rubbish.

When James Hogg was stationed at Whitley Bay he found training
to be a bit hectic:

We did our rifle shooting at Whitley Bay and we were trained on the
camp you were on, now and again you went on assault courses, you

were away for a month under the supervision of The Green Howards instructors. This guy, he used to put us through the mill all right. From one point to another, getting on a rope and going across it, firing underneath you, getting you acclimatised to it. You were on parade every day and you were doing route marches and you were doing 15 mile with small kit, just train you up. You did all your hard training then. Just did the normal training at Catterick, York and did some at Whitley Bay. Did all the rifle shooting at Whitley Bay. We did all our training as far as fire is concerned in Whitley Bay.

Soldiers had to be nineteen years of age before they could be posted overseas. Joining as a young lad of eighteen, Bill Cochran discovered that for those who were under age the Training Battalions awaited:

In those days you joined the army then a few weeks later I got the train fare to go to Berwick upon Tweed. That was where they trained us and when I did go there most of the guys were volunteers. The were mostly young people, when I say young I mean about 18 or 19. this was so many months before they started calling up people. Everybody was just termed then the 'young soldiers regiment'. A training regiment. I had joined the Royal Scots and when everybody went there, in this amount that arrived there there was about 80 or 90 of us, and each and every one came from all different Scots mobs. But once we had done all this preliminary training for about eight weeks then we got distributed around to different places. I went from Berwick to what they called 'the barracks' in Edinburgh, Redford Barracks. In them days they couldn't send you overseas until you were eighteen. So I finished up, after Edinburgh we went to Inverness, to the Cameron barracks and then I went from there down to London. We got transferred down to London. Even though I was in Inverness I was still in the Royal Scots. When we went down to London we went to Essex and we were there, still being trained at different things, general training as an infantry mob. When we were in Essex we were in a place called Upminster, very close to Hornchurch fighter aerodrome and they used us while we were training to guard the perimeter of Hornchurch airfield. Then I went from there to Barrow in Furness and when we went there, for miles around there were all different mobs, all young men. Then the next thing we were on the boat to where we were going to go.

Stanley Rothney was another young man enlisting under the age for foreign service, who also found himself initially in the same Training Battalions:

I did my training at Berwick on Tweed, number 10 ITC, Magdalene Fields. We were there for twelve weeks basic training and then to Dumfries for further training where we joined the battalion. 'D' Company was where I learnt to drive Bren gun carriers. That took me to Newbattle and places like that. We moved from there to Redford cavalry barracks and other encampments round about Edinburgh and finished up at a place called Dudingston. From Dudingston we went down to England to a place called Upminster. When we got there I was a dispatch rider covering the whole area of Essex up as far as Colchester.

Once he reached the age of nineteen, Ian Niven was transferred from the training battalions to his regiment of choice, the Royal Scots:

From Inverness (after 12 weeks intensive training) we moved to North Walsham in the Norwich area. After a further, even more intensive training of a 12 week duration, we were granted a short leave of 10 days, following which we embarked at Liverpool for Bombay, although at the time we did not have a clue where we were destined.

After having failed his test for aircrew, James Hogg was detailed for general service in the RAF:

After I was refused for the RAF I transferred just into the Airforce itself. I started general duties in York. They decided they would train us into being gunners and put us on gun posts for the protection of the aircraft. I would be about 19. That would be 40/41. When we were on the gun posts the bombers, Whitley bombers, called the flying coffins, the crews used to come over and they used to test them say about between two and four o' clock, used to take them up and test them, before they went on a raid that night. Well we got two or three trips up in the bombers you see. And one of the pilots, on this bomber was the boy that was the observer on the American bomber that dropped the atomic bomb on Hiroshima, I didn't even know who the guy was. It was him that was flying the Whitley bomber that I was in.

He was part of an RAF recognisance unit equipped with armoured cars. Training wasn't all work and no play. When James was sent to pick up an American-made armoured car in Pompie he decided to make the most of the opportunity and dropped in to visit his girlfriend, who was stationed at a camp at Farnborough.

I got out of this armoured car, machine gun on top, white star on the side. I went in to the camp, told the boy in the guardhouse, I says, 'my girlfriends in here, I wouldn't mind kipping up for the night here'. 'Nae bother', he says, 'nae bother'. He says, 'park your armoured car over there'. The boy gave me a blanket and he put me into this nissen hut, I says, 'that's great'. He says, 'now, drink your tea and then you can go over and see your girl friend'. I says, 'I will do'.

It came as a surprise to his girlfriend when she discovered he was in the camp:

So in I go she says 'what, are you in the camp?' I says, 'aye, I'm in the camp'. We went awa' to the pictures and I came back and I said I'll have to be on the road first thing in the morning 'cause they'll be wondering where I am, especially with an armoured car. In the morning, I got my breakfast and that and I said to the boy, 'thanks very much'. Got in the armoured car and away. She told her sergeant and he snapped. It was a secret camp. Working on jet engines. I had never heard anything about that before, it was all props. I thought, never heard of them. She says, 'there's no propellers on them'. I thought, 'that's a funny bloody aeroplane'.

A.L. Forbes enjoyed his period of basic training at Aldershot:

> So, off I went with my rail voucher to Aldershot. I picked up with
> others on the way, some of whom had been in the territorials and
> were old soldiers compared to me. This would be about the last week
> in September 1939. I enjoyed the training, especially the route marches
> around the country lanes.

While Forbes enjoyed his basic training, many, like William Marks,
found it a bit tedious and monotonous:

> I went to Lancashire, to a place called Clithero and we were quartered
> in this big mill for our basic training. We were there a day or two,
> learning all the steps and that and getting our battledress. We were
> there for just a matter of months. We were up and doon tha'e stairs
> a dozen times a day, up and doon – put your best battledress on, put
> your second best on, things like that, just to keep you moving.

It wasn't only the training regime that came as a culture shock.
Douglas Kerr suffered the initial shock of a medical examination
with a lack of privacy:

> For the initial uniform, getting kitted out and so forth we went to
> Blackpool, I think it was the Winter Gardens in fact. Then you were
> given your physical examination, these women were all walking about,
> we were young lads and we were never in public like that before,
> anyway, then you got your uniform and your inoculation and all that
> sort of thing.

Being stationed in a holiday resort had its benefits. Douglas Kerr's
family were able to visit him during basic training:

> Then we went for our physical training to Morecombe, so that's
> where we went for that, Morecombe, on the seafront. My folks came
> down and saw us all, came down in the car, I had to get some petrol
> from somewhere. We were doing our square bashing along the prom.

We did other things like weapon handling, firing a gun on the range and all that. That was about a month. No matter what trade you were going to be in that was to see you were fit enough to get some basic training. You were taken onto the range and shown something about firing guns.

After leaving a good job in the police, Jimmy MacKenzie joined the Royal Marines:

So, I went into the Marines and was trained at Chatham and I quite enjoyed it, I enjoyed the barrack life, the square bashing, being in a team, everybody knowing what the other fellow was going to do. See they were all working together and it was everybody's job to make sure they kept up with the rest. I got on quite well there. During our training there were aptitude tests, we didn't know it but situations were created and we were there to see how we got out of that particular situation and we were assessed accordingly. One of them was digging a trench between – Chatham was also a naval dockyard and there were guns and things around to protect it and ammunition to the guns was done rather like pass the parcel at the time so they decided to put a little track with a buggy and we were sent up to dig the trench for it. We were marched up there and the sergeant pointed to a heap of shovels, said 'we want a trench from there to there, three feet wide and a foot deep, now get on with it'. We were standing there and I'm pretty certain that I was the only man there that ever saw a pick and shovel. So I just naturally – I didn't take charge but I advised what to do – one man take a pick one man take a shovel split up into pairs and spread out. And this was observed and I was promptly put down as a 'war leader' and two or three days after that I got my first Lance Corporals stripe.

If nothing else, the army encouraged training. After basic training there was always the opportunity to apply for further courses and postings. However, as Charles Devlin discovered, things were not always that simple:

There were a lot of unusual things happening round about that period, soldiers turning to sailors, sailors turning to soldiers. When I was in training you were always full of your own thoughts about what you want to be, and gunnery, I didn't like the idea of being on a warship. I thought the Merchant Navy had naval ratings manning guns, so I actually volunteered for that. They were called DEMs gunners, Defence Emergency, and I got to see the commander or somebody, well a high up naval officer, and he says 'I've let you come to see me because I always encourage people that volunteer, but unfortunately the navy has handed that job over to the army, Mercantile Ack Ack they call them'. He said 'while you're still in a voluntary mood why not submarines' I said 'oh no, here's mines again'. Submarines were a voluntary service, you didn't get posted to submarines. You got extra money but I hadn't even been on any ships at that time.

When undertaking specialist training, or more precisely, when he finished his specialist training, Norman Campbell fell victim to army organisation:

> Completing my initial 6 weeks square bashing, I was posted to The Cameronians, put on a 16 week specialist course and trained as a Bren Carrier Driver and 3" Mortar Gunner. Course complete, I went to Dalton-in-Furness for further carrier driving and gunnery practice. Typical of the army, after all my training I never drove a carrier or fired a 3" mortar again.

Ian Cameron remembers his experience of specialist courses in the RAF:

> We slept in a hanger in the middle of winter – that was where you got the classes – every half an hour they got you up and ran you round the hanger to get the blood moving. I didn't get on very well because they put us on machines to do things you couldn't possibly do – the machines were useless. I complained – I couldn't possibly do it. You weren't supposed to complain. Anyway, I went on another course, it was all right, a lot of Scots boys were there, they were quite

intellectual type of chaps, chemist, newspaper bloke. On the Sunday you got the day off and we would go up to the canals – Chambers, he worked with Youngers in Edinburgh and he got a bottle of whisky sent down, I had white puddings and some cigarettes and somebody else had some cigars. On the Sunday we walked the canals – go in the pub in England they wouldn't give you any beer unless you were a regular – so we managed to get glasses and were sitting drinking the whisky. We were quite posh – having a picnic with a bottle of whisky. One of our boys was Northern Irish, he was an art teacher. He just cheeked all the officers. It wasn't straight out or 'fuck you' or anything like that, there were other ways of doing it.

We went from there to Wigan, the station was overcrowded so you had to wait until somebody had left his bed before you could get into a bed. You were queuing up for beds. We went on to Stirlings – the first big bombers – I didn't know one end from the other, I'd been on a course for nearly a year, hardly been inside an aircraft, all they gave you was theory.

As Jimmy MacKenzie found out, a little knowledge got you a long way in the military:

There was another thing too, about the [Lovat] Scouts, I was well ahead of the rest of them because I'd learnt all the arms drill in the Scouts, sloping arms, presenting arms and that sort of thing, I never had the real touch but I was just that little bit ahead of the rest. I just had to be shown something once and I had it.

When it came to securing a favourable duty, Norman Patterson found out that dropping out of a training course could be every bit as beneficial as passing:

I was sent for when I was there and the major in charge of the battery, he said, 'you're a signaller'. I said ' yes'. He said ' wireless operator?' I said 'yes'. He said, 'well, there's a secret course starting up, would you like to go on it?' I said 'well depending on what it was'. And it was Radar in its infancy, RDF. I agreed to go – I can't remember how many there were – this school in the middle of the Jewish quarter in Leeds, it was totally secret, nobody brought in supplies or whatever, some of the guys did the cooking, we all did our own fatigues, and we did studying all day, theory and so forth, and our fatigues like sweeping the floor and all that rubbish. After 6 weeks of this we went on to Ohms Law, problems in Ohms Law and I thought 'oh bugger this' I didn't mind going to France with the rest, I wasn't racking my brains with Ohms Law. So I stuck it out for a couple of weeks then went. You could be returned to your unit, no problem. So I went back and the battery commander, he sent for me. He said 'what happened'? I said 'ach, just not my scene'. He said 'ok, how would you like to be headquarters store man'? I said 'that sounds a good number', so I became headquarters store man. There was a number of aircraft batteries round Leeds so I was based at Carton Barracks, right in the middle of Leeds. Career progressed from there up to Newcastle, which was hellish really. Ah heck, Newcastle and that area, because you were on the Humber, got a right pasting and it was the first time we had seen, Jerries used to come over and drop mines in the Humber. We were overlooking the yard where they were building the KG5, King George 5th, which was a very huge modern battleship. And then, I can't remember how long but we were transferred up to the Orkneys. On South Ronesay, overlooking Staffa, and we formed part of the barrage for the Jerries coming over Staffa Floe – a box barrage and theoretically nothing could go through it but practically, it was nae bother, they just sailed through. Was up there for a while and being headquarters staff it was good because you got a rum ration. And then went from there down to Southend for mobilising.

Charles Devlin also underwent a series of specific tests. He described the tests he received for night vision:

I trained at Skegness, Butlins, where we got kitted up and a few tests. There was a night vision test. You sat there just under red lights and then a nurse took you into another room which was pitch dark. 'Put your hand up' she says, then gave me a rod. 'I want you to aim along that' Aim along it! I almost put my eye out. I eventually got the general

direction and she said 'now just take it easy, there's no hurry. Can you
see anything, I'll give you a tip, if your looking in darkness like this
don't look straight, look slightly above and you will see better. I said 'I
think I see a round face'. She said 'now tell me the time'. I said 'you've
got to be joking' but she replied 'your half way there, you've seen the
clock'. It was more of a guess than anything else but I passed the test.
Another Dundonian failed and they re-enlisted him as a steward, the
bloke was broken hearted.

James Hogg recalls his increased training for D–Day:

Just before we went to Normandy we went to a place called Box
Grove Woods and it was all under camouflage all the way through,
and they used to get us up at six in the morning, get us out with
our big boots on, our shorts and our vests. We had to do this six mile
run round the camp. And this boy from Tunbridge Wells, I called him
Bluebeard, he had one of these beards, you shaved it and it was blue, I
called him Bluebeard and he always called me Mush. He says, 'I don't
like this, Mush', he says, 'six o' clock in the morning, I don't like this
at all'. I says, 'you've got to do your training, haven't you'? He gets at
the back and we started off and unknown to me he dives in, well in,
to a bush, and he sat there and waited for everybody to come back
to go in again. But unknown to him, the officer was at the very back
and the boy jumped out and joined me and he says, 'just you carry
on to the Guard Tent'. So the boy says, 'I know whose gonna get the
first bullet when we go ower there'.

  After that we went into the armoured side of it, light armoured, and
we got trained on that. So by the time the second front opened up
we were ready for to go out there, and we knew then that we were
supposed to be protecting the aircrews, if we captured any, things like
that, but we never even done that.

After an initial training period at Chatham, it was inevitable that
Jimmy MacKenzie volunteered for the Commandos and found himself training at Achnacarry:

Landed up at Achnacarry which was a training school for the
Commando not so much a training school more a sorting out school.
There was no training as such, two days after we were there we had a
seven mile an hour march, three and a half mile there and three and
a half back, with your equipment. That was done about twice a week,
then we did ten miles in two hours, five mile an hour. And it was strictly
adhered to. You were timed from the time the first man went out the
gate till the last man went back in. If one man didn't make it the whole
squad was sent back to do it the next day. So that gave everybody a
sense of purpose 'If I don't do it the whole side goes down'. If anybody
was lagging two fellows would catch him and drag him. That was part
of the training to make sure that we stuck together and helped each
other and get the whole unit through. There was no obligation on you
to see it through. If you didn't want to stick it you didn't have to. You
could say any time 'I'm finished with it', and you got sent back to the
unit you came from. But to admit that you couldn't take it?

I enjoyed it. We did one thirty miler at the end of the course, it took
us all day, and I remember that day – it poured rain the whole day – we
started off in the morning, it was late at night before we got home.
There were two or three of them that had to be carried back into
the gate. They made it, it didn't matter. If they were breathing regular
they passed. They were sorted out before they went there. Nobody
volunteered for the Commandos from scratch, you were in other
regiments before you went there. Your regiment would decide if you
were fit to go there. They were very realistic, it was all live ammunition
used. If you were told to crawl from A to B then you had to crawl. If
you put your head or your backside up you were in dead trouble. It
really toughened you and it gave you tremendous confidence. It was
a form of brainwashing, we thought we were the greatest, we didn't
think anybody would have been fit to beat us.

After volunteering for foreign service, John Forfar got his wish and
was posted as a medical officer to the Commandos:

I don't know if you've heard of Achnacarry, which is the home of
Cameron of Lochiel, the main Commando Training Centre was there

– and it was very rigorous training, there's no question about that, it was made hard to really test people out. To push them, or push them to the limit. And of course, there was a very high drop-out rate. Anybody who dropped out just went back to his unit, there was no shame or disgrace in dropping out because it was a pretty rigorous programme of training.

But that wasn't all. That was the main training centre. There were other long periods of training: in Ardnamurchan for instance, there was a training centre there which was related to actual landings on the beaches at Kentra Bay. We were also on the Isle of Wight for a while training there, so there was quite a lot of training. We were formed in 1943, the autumn of 1943, so that was what, six, seven, eight, nine months before we actually did anything

As Jimmy MacKenzie recalls, there was reasoning behind the tough training regime:

We never trained as a unit, we trained as troops, and each troop was trained individually. You had a thing called 'me and my pal'. When we were on route marches the officer in charge would often stop for a breather, you would always get two pairing off together, and if you left the camp you always left the same two together. This was 'me and my pal'. So that when two men were needed they always picked a pair. So there was 'me and my pal', the sub-section, section and then the troop. So when the troop broke down the section took over, if the section broke down the sub-section took over. There was a command you see. There was the sergeant in charge of the section, a corporal in charge of the sub-section and then there was 'me and my pal'. So if the Captain had got killed the operation would keep going. The idea was since there was not many of us the last two would finish the job.

As Roddy MacLeod was to discover, it was not only the Commandos who had a tough training period:

Tough training, most of it in the bombed out Limehouse area of London, five stories in the shell of a building and then you crossed on a single rope to these buildings on the opposite side of the street, they allowed for 25% casualties. They had other heights but that was the main one, five stories, if you came down on a cobbled street from that!

One of the problems envisaged for D-Day was getting off the beaches and through the German minefields. Flail tanks were one of the many designs intended to clear a path through the mines. Thomas Yates trained in the new 'flail' tanks for D-Day:

I along with others was transferred to the Lothians and Borders Yeomanry, who at that time were just a normal tank regiment, just moving up from the inferior small tanks to the bigger cruiser tanks on which we trained in various parts of the country.

About August 1943 at Warminster, Salisbury Plain, we were to become the 30th Armoured Brigade and were nominated to be trained on specialist equipment. Our C.O at the time, Lt Col Crabbe, informed us at a meeting that he had volunteered us for Flail Tanks. At the time it was so secret that none of us had any idea what a Flail Tank looked like. We were soon to find out when we were sent out to Wickham Market in Suffolk and introduced to our tanks, and commenced training out at Oxford which had become the large training area for several branches of the now new assault division, the 79th. Secrecy was paramount, and at the sound of the Air Raid Siren we would have to dismount immediately and sheet up the extended jib which was the revolving drum with chains attached to 'Flail' the ground as the tank advanced. That flail cleared the whole width of the tank, leaving about 6 feet of ground on which to advance.

Yates described his progression through his training in the tank regiment:

When I first went into the tank regiment, my previous training as a signaller came in very useful. The 'trades' in the tanks were driver/operator, gunner/operator, gunner/mechanic, and driver/mechanic. The word 'operator' meant Wireless Operator. Having already

mastered the morse code and the radio set and receiver, I had only
to do my tank and wheeled training, and in due course took the
standard tests and passed out as driver/operator. A further 1 shilling
and sixpence on the weekly pay. After that I took further training on
gunnery and mechanics, going through the whole book so to speak.
I was made L/Cpl and got my own tank and crew which comprised
of driver, co-driver, gunner and radio operator, five of us in total. This
was on the Sherman tank of course. Previously the regiment had
several different makes and models of tanks. Matildas when I joined,
then Covenanters, Crusaders, Centaurs and then ordinary Shermans
before getting the ones which were modified into flails.

Douglas Kerr discovered that home postings could be as dangerous
as going overseas:

I was woken up in the middle of the night, one of our aircraft had
exploded after landing. It landed with bombs stuck in the bomb bay
doors. After the crew got out this bomb went off. I had some apples
sitting on my shelf above my bed and that's what wakened me up,
I slept through the explosion and what woke me up was the apples
hitting me on the head.

When he was stationed in Italy, Ernest Lovett found that keeping
men motivated was a common problem. He decided to initiate his
own training regime for his men in order to relieve boredom:

In 1944 when I was leaving Scotland for an unknown destination
abroad I bought some more officers clothing at a Military Outfitters
in Edinburgh. Just before I left the shop the manager said 'Would you
like to buy one of our surplus commando knives'. I had a look at one
and bought it. I kept the knife with my personal equipment. Then,
one day in Perugia, my men had no work to do so I decided with
my sergeant Cameron that we would take the platoon to a secluded
grassed area. The platoon formed a ring and Sergeant Cameron and
I tried to demonstrate some of the moves in Fairburn's book. The
men enjoyed this and one man who I considered a bolshie seemed

interested. So Sergeant Cameron and I took it in turns to stand in the ring blindfolded to act as a German sentry. I handed my commando knife in its sheath to my other sergeant. He went round the ring and handed the knife to a man at random who would then get up and stealthily approach the sentry, the men showed their skills. Then the bolshie was handed the knife and came up behind me, tipped my helmet forward, put a lock on my throat and jabbed the sheathed knife in my back. I collapsed on the ground half conscious. He thought this was great fun and this seemed to break the ice. From then on I could get some reaction from him when I spoke to him.

At his first posting A.L. Forbes was able to witness first hand the confusion of large-scale conscription:

We were eventually fitted out with uniforms and moved to London to work in Thomas House, Embankment, in the department which dealt with the call up of the Army Officers Emergency Reserve. Things were in a confused state because many reservists had joined one or other of the armed forces without informing the Reserve. Their wives would return their call up papers saying their husbands had already joined the RAF, Navy, etc.

When Ernest Jamieson was posted to the 7th Armoured Division in North Africa he thought his training days were behind him; unfortunately they were just beginning:

Paraded after breakfast next morning in front of our drill sergeant Sgt Benny who pointed across to the parade ground and said it had just been tarmaced, but they were not using a roller to flatten it; our feet were to do the job. He certainly kept his word, but he was a good instructor and after a few weeks we became quite a good squad.

After six weeks we were taken to Moascar Ismalia onto the firing ranges. Apart from rifle shooting we also had a course on Bren Guns, firing, stripping and reassembling them. We even fired an Boyes anti-tank gun, quite a kick. The supervising officer from the SO staff highly recommended us on our performance. When our three months were up we had our passing out parade with a high ranking officer taking the salute. Everything went well and he was well pleased.

After his basic training Douglas Kerr was posted for further training as a fitter/armourer:

After about a month we went then for technical training, to see how good you were with your hands and making things, benches and metal and all sorts of things. That was at Weath. They were desperate for technical people then so we worked shifts from 7 in the morning till 1 o'clock. You had the afternoon off, supposed to be. At 1 o' clock the new lot, the other shift came on, doing the same thing again, continual training. By then we were training to be Armourers, but you were also given, in amongst that training, you were also given things to sniff in case the Germans used poison gas, this is the smell of Chlorine gas and that sort of thing. You had to be careful how you handled them.

The school must have been transferred 'cause we went to Hereford for a while and from there back up to Kirkholme, the 10th School of Technical Training, and there they must have decided some people were better with their hands than others. All sorts of people were there, we were getting office workers and everything who knew nothing about handling a file or even a gun of course. I was always pretty technical minded anyway, the aim was to make things from a chunk of metal and one of the things I remember having to make was an adjustable spanner, I had to make one from scratch. I must have been pretty good so I was made a fitter/armourer. These were all armourers to begin with you see and the better ones, the ones who were handier with their hands were made fitter/armourers which is another grade up, another penny or two a week kind of thing. So eventually then we passed out as ready for action.

I was then posted to Waterbeach, near Cambridge, that's where I was sent as my first place away from training. It turned out to be a conversion unit. Some of the aircraft were being changed, for instance, where I eventually went to became a Halifax bomber station, well there was Halifax Mark I and Halifax Mark II, that sort of thing and the pilots had to go on a conversion course themselves. On this conversion course I noticed that they had Stirlings there. What you do when you arrive there at these places, they give you a chit and you've got to sign in to various places, to get some bedding out. You're going to go into a hut eventually but you've got to go and pick up bedding and pick up all sorts of things, and sign in various places. You go round with your chit and I went round one corner and I just caught my first glimpse of the runway and here was a Mosquito coming in and there was only one of the undercarriage down and it landed, it was fantastic, he must have been a great pilot. He came in with one undercarriage down, and run along keeping it level but eventually when the speed went down sufficiently it went over onto the other wing and did a little half turn, perfect. I wasn't there very long. When I reported to the armoury there, right away they said 'you're getting posted'. They didn't want the new man, so they posted the new guy and kept their own.

Pal MacLeod was able to take advantage of the widespread shortage of skilled personnel and the demands of the military:

> I volunteered at the end of 1939, about the end of the year. Got my basic training with the Gordons in Aberdeen then went to an RASC depot in Peabrouse. We were hanging about there, things weren't so well organised then, we were waiting there to be sent abroad when they found that they were short of electricians and they wanted volunteers. So, fed up hanging around, quite a few of us volunteered. We went to Birmingham and had a crash course on electricity there. A six months course you had to do in three weeks. If you didn't you were just sent back but if you did they were so desperate for electricians. I got through that and I was classified as an electrician.

Douglas Kerr also evidenced the reality of aircrew training and the reality of the first 1000 bomber raid on Germany:

> Where I arrived next was Drifield in Yorkshire. What they had there was old Whitleys, which were bombers, dead slow things, they

had about six of them and Defiant night fighters, twin cockpits. What they were used for, the Whitley and the Defiants, they were used for training for air gunners. The Defiant night fighter had a power operated gun turret, the same as the bombers, so they got trained on that and the Whitley's being so slow were used for towing the target drogues. About then I came home on leave and while I was home, on the radio it was announced that the first thousand bomber raid had taken place. But when I got back from leave I couldn't see any Whitley's, I think they sent all these old ones out to make up the numbers. That was a suicide mission because they were so slow.

Douglas discovered the hard way that promotion in the services was dependent on 'not' making mistakes:

This particular Defiant, we had to load the four guns in the gun turret. So, I was inside the gun turret and the other guy outside on a ladder feeding in the new ammunition belt through a little hatch there. What you had to do then, you cock the gun which draws the next round into the breech and then you press the firing button, and there was a 'firing safe' button on it, with it on safe you pressed the fire button and it pushed that round inside the breech, but it doesn't fire because you've got it on safe. And then you cock it again and it withdraws the whole thing. Well we did three like that and I came to the fourth one and I was up inside and the guns were about level. I couldn't see, the 'firing safe' was underneath this one, the switch was underneath. I couldn't see it but I could feel it with my hand, but I knew it wasn't right, it wasn't safe. I said to this fellow 'that's not right, have a look, check it, that's not safe'. He could see it 'cause he was outside. I got him to check it three times. Three times I said to him 'check it, it's not right, that's just gonna go through those windows over there'. We were facing a hanger you see. He says 'that's ok'. I pressed the button and it fired. Of course, the Brownings, they fire very fast, 1200 rounds per minute or something like that. So, that one had fired and I was panicking, there was a jingling of glass, the burst went through to where the air gunners were getting trained. When I think on it, I could have killed all these people. I was just lucky it didn't because of the elevation. It went through their window, none of them were hit, they thought it was an air raid or something. That was my fault and I was confined to camp. I never became a corporal because of that, I think it was. It didn't bother me too much.

T'was in the middle of September 1941 at Dunfermline to assemble we began;
our military career stretched before us our future known to not a single man.
Fate threw us all together willy-nilly, the noisy, quiet, shy and simple man, but under
canvas we caught to one another as at night we shared our lives, our loves, our plans.

A month in Fife, upon my soul, they nearly had us up the pole.
Turning left and turning right, we dream about it through the night.
About turn, stand at ease, they nearly had us on our knees.

The whole day long we march about, then the bread and cheese, the N.C.O.s,
to the front salute, turn out those toes;
stand still, fall out, fall in again, it really did become a pain.
It looked so daft I'll no deny to have seen us at first would have made you cry.

Dunfermline done we went away and landed in Leeds one October day.
The folks down here they sure are swell as most of us lads are sure to tell.
To the cricket ground we went to train they nearly had us all insane.
Detachments rear the whole long day, you got to know it like a song.

On Friday nights we ran a dance, our boys did make it 'Hum'.
The 'Q' one night he got us wrong he nearly went right through the drum.
In the bar we went our mile, the lassies too did it in style.

Three months in Leeds we'll no forget we parted heavy with regret.
I'll no deny though many a lass with a broken heart did watch us pass.

Then away to Wales, to Aberporth, they took us there for our firing course.
Four days we tramped through all the muck,
wee Somerville got pegged for not getting our 'chuck'.
At night in the hut we dried our socks and rattled Grady's music box.
An argument or two we had many a true word spoke or said.
'What's up the noo'? somebody said, 'T'is Leslie fallen out o' bed'.

We packed again and away did go, to where nobody seemed to know.
Manchester. Oh boy what a place! Our luck's in again lads we've backed an ace.

We roamed the town and found it swell, the 'Dog and Eagle' and the 'Star' as well,
this gives us such a tale to tell.
Our lads the fairly went their mile, could'na blame them you had to smile.

Four months the lads had the time of their lives;
you could hardly believe some had hames and wives.
But no harms done I'm led to believe though I'll bet many a lass our lads did deceive.
To this day, and I believe it's true, to their Lancashire sweethearts the mail gets through.
Then came the news, we're away overseas.
Embarkation leave. At the time you felt kind of pleased.

When we got home, our news to unfold, the folk's there were sad, but they tried to be bold.
Four glorious days, then we had to part, sweethearts, wives, mothers with pain in their hearts.
You try to keep smiling, bluffing it out, no crying, no weeping as the train pulls out.
To Manchester again for a few weeks to stay, then off to the coast on the 19th of May,
we boarded the ship on this fateful day.

Then from 'Bonnie Scotland' we sailed away on Thursday the 22nd of May.
Our shores left behind us, Scotland no more, in our throats came a lump, it was sore, it was raw.
Sweethearts, wives, mothers foremost in our minds,
when we sailed from our homeland our heart stayed behind.

Six long weeks we sailed o'er the seas then landed at Durban and did as we pleased.
The folk's here they gave us a rousing good cheer,
and of course here we sampled South African beer.
Port Tewfik in Egypt, we landed at last, our long voyage was over and past.

We thought this land of Egypt would be all right, that we were in clover, no pain and no fight.
We soon found out this was not true, oh 'Bonnie Scotland' how I love you!
So cheer up lads, be brave, no fear, we'll forget it all with three 'Acker' beer.
We'll do our best, we will not fail, you should see us when we get some mail.
Sweethearts, wives and mothers too. O speed the day we return to you.

William H. Clark

Posted

The first overseas posting was a time of anticipation and dread as the recruits' future was decided by faceless bureaucracy. Charles Devlin was stationed at HMS Collingwood and recalls when he received the news of his overseas posting:

> At HMS Collingwood we loaded ammunition barges for the guns on the ships that were bombarding at Normandy and then in July the chief came in and announced 'right you lucky lads, you're going on leave'. He said 'I've got good news and bad news. We said 'what's the good news'? 'Your going on leave'. What's the bad news'? 'It's embarkation leave'.

Willie Morrison's first 'overseas' posting was not quite the journey to distant parts that he was expecting:

> I was ground staff. You need some on the ground to keep them flying. The squadron was posted to Borgangrove in Northern Ireland. That was a smashing station. We could get into Belfast. They had troubles of a sort, I mean, the Falls Road was out of bounds to us even then but we never saw anything like that.

After having been sent down to Southend for mobilisation, Norman Patterson was once again on the move:

> Sailed from the Clyde – why go to Southend to mobilise you then put you up to the Clyde? It was called the Orion, we went on the Orion, twenty-odd thousand tonner. In Southend a month or so – less than that – no specific training for going abroad – it was just in the boozer every night. You got issued with your tropical gear when you were there, (you knew whereby you were going) we were told, well we weren't told until we were on the ship. We were going to Port Tewfik, which is at the top of the canal, when we were on the high seas. We were the first major convoy from the UK going out that way, and when we were on the high seas the Japs of course had advanced towards Burma and through Burma on towards India and we were diverted to stop them.

I know it sounds a hotch potch now but just when we're going on about it that was the sequence of events. Went into Cape town – the route of the vessel, well the convoy, went from Greenock right across the Atlantic towards America, down there and turned to go round the Cape. You'll never guess, in the Bay of Biscay we got PT on the deck, in forty foot waves, sounds ludicrous, doesn't it? Sailed into Cape town, splendid sailing into it, we were told we were disembarking everybody cause they wanted the ship to go back to Britain so we stayed at a place called Retreat Camp. That was quite an experience – there was slabs of butter and cases of apples and all the rest in food tins – we hadn't seen this in yonks. Then we were put on the ship – she wasn't converted for trooping – it was a big luxury vessel, when you went down for your meals, I was a sergeant at the time, dining room was absolutely fantastic, lined with glass and so forth. We had no escort 'cause this ship, she could outstrip submarines. We were up every night because going round that way, you know, it was a submarine trap. I had a cabin which I shared with another guy and the bells would go to get you out your bed and up to your muster point. Not once did I ever reach it because everybody was jammed and eventually we said, ach to hell with this, what's the point, so we just stayed in our kip.

We landed at Bombay and we were taken of and put on the train which turned out it was coolie carriages – we didn't know this, we were green as grass, and we were eaten alive with the bugs on the seats – we were three days on the seats On the train they used to draw into a siding to use the hot steam to make the tea. Don't suppose you'd get away with it nowadays, but needs must.

After his embarkation leave Charles Devlin returned to HMS Collingwood:

We had our leave, came back and a couple of days later we were on a trooper at Liverpool. The set up with the navy was you do two years abroad on a ship. The Hunts [Hunt Class destroyers] had been out there from the North African campaign and the crew was due to be relieved, so we were actually sent out as relief's. They didn't change a whole crew at once, we went in batches. and were absorbed into the work of the ship. We went out to Naples, that's where we landed, we just got off with all our gear, cause everywhere you went in the navy you carried your kitbag and your hammock. We marched along the dock onto a French liner which took us down to Malta – the French liner was filthy. It had Kapok lifebelts and when you touched them the lice were jumping all over the place.

In Malta I was placed on HMS Vindictive which was a First World War cruiser once upon a time but meanwhile it was a depot ship. I was on the Bosun's party making up ropes and splicing. I was only on it a month.

Ernest Jamieson recalls the long journey from Liverpool to Egypt:

At the end of July we knew it was 'Goodbye Blighty' as we were issued with tropical kit and a weekend leave pass. On returning to Chesterfield after saying goodbye to our loved ones we were issued with rifles, many of them thick with oil, salvaged from Dunkirk I think.

Goodbye Chesterfield. We march down to the station and board a train for Liverpool. It's dark when we arrive in Liverpool and as we march down to the docks crowds of civilians walk alongside us handing out cigarettes and bottles of beer.

Boarded the liner 'Empress of Britain' but alas we were billeted in the bowels of the ship with hammocks slung all over the place. There were a few of us who never slept below after the ship sailed. We took our bedding and slept on deck.

August Bank Holiday and from the deck we could see the people on the beach at Southport. Sailed out of Liverpool and up the west coast of Scotland, where Sam Hardie who was to be a great mate of mine threw a letter sealed in a bottle to his wife in Fairlie, Ayrshire. We heard later it was picked up on the beach by a gentleman who posted it on to his wife. We were part of a very large convoy with destroyers on patrol on both sides. One night we were all ordered below decks and the sound of depth charges could be heard. Life jackets were to be worn. A ships officer came down and we asked him what happens if a torpedo hits below where we were. 'Oh, he said this area is sealed off with these water tight doors'. Very reassuring! Every morning the ships news was put up on a notice board and this morning the captain announced that we were now travelling on a ghost ship as according to 'Lord Haw Haw' we were sunk last night, but sad to say it was another liner carrying evacuees to Canada, many of whom were children. We were now heading for Trinidad and then changed course for West Africa.

We were now travelling with a Polish cruiser as escort. She had a seaplane on board that would take off and circle round the convoy out on the horizon. Refuelled at Freetown, West Africa, then headed for Capetown. We knew we were nearing Capetown when planes of the SAAF flew over us. Land ahoy! and there is Table Mountain. Good to be in port again and get your feet on Terra Firma. As we came off the ship for a few days leave, people were waiting in lines of cars to pick us up and entertain us for a day. Sid Abel and myself were picked up by an elderly couple by the name of Sneddon, who had a house on Table Mountain overlooking the bay – wonderful time. Sailed from Capetown and this time we were given a transfer to cabins for the last part of the journey, which took us by the Red Sea to the port of Suez, Egypt.

Roddy MacLeod also wound up by the Suez Canal. He and his colleagues had a distinctly dangerous method of dealing with the troublesome native hawkers:

We landed at Port Tewfik on the Suez Canal and went by train so far up towards El Alamein, there was as many blooming wogs on the roofs of the carriages trying to sell watches and God knows what, but the boys were having fun shooting at them, they didn't stay on top of the carriages very long.

For Pal MacLeod it was a long twelve-week convoy voyage to Capetown:

On the first of January 1941 we were embarked from Gourock. We took nine weeks to go from Gourock to Serice. The convoy of course had to go according to the slowest ship, but there was no escort, there were about 50 ships and they one or two destroyers. They went straight out from here to the coast of America, keeping out of the normal shipping routes. Three weeks after leaving Gourock we reached the American coast, went down the American coast and back across to Freetown, West Africa. A long journey and you can imagine what it was like with three thousand troops packed on that ship. We didn't get ashore at all in Freetown. We were there for a very short time. We left there and went down to Capetown, another three weeks.

After my training I went to an outfit, I'm not very sure what they called it but it was connected to the 3rd Division in a way. I was in the engineers. We were attached to the 3rd Division. That was our job, building bridges and lifting mines and things like that.

As Ernest Lovett discovered, the army makes no allowances for family, or in his case impending family:

My movement orders arrived. Helen was expecting a baby in a nursing home. I managed to see the baby for about an hour and had to move of to Barton Stacey to wait for other officers. We then moved to Longmore, the R.E. Railway Centre and then by train on a mystery journey. The officer in charge of the draft ordered us to keep the blinds down in our compartment. For hours and hours the train travelled all night and then it stopped. One of the officers pulled up one corner of the blind and looked out. It was daylight I took a peep and said 'I know where we are, we are in Liverpool, the building over there is the famous Liver Building'.

The train moved alongside a ship and we all got out. We marched into a warehouse where we were all handed a pith-helmet. We went up the gangway on to the ship and went below deck where we handed the pith-helmets back to a member of the crew. Some hours later large bundles were lowered over the side of the ship and taken into the warehouse. I presumed that this was a ruse to deceive spies. The ship moved out of the river and joined a convoy. When the convoy neared Gibraltar, it split in two. Half went south round Africa. Our half went to Naples. From Naples we went by goods train to Capua, the R.E. Reception and Training Centre.

After his period of office work A.L. Forbes was posted closer to home, at Gibraltar:

> About January 1940 I and five others were told that we were to be posted to Gibraltar. No code name was given to hide the identity of our destination; I expect peace time practice still prevailed. We had a few days leave and after much checking and verifying of names and numbers we, along with other contingents, marched to a band playing from W square in Aldershot.
>
> Our route to Gibraltar was a circuitous one. We were ferried to Cherbourg, entrained for Marseilles, embarked for Malta, Alexandria, Malta again and finally Gibraltar. During this very pleasant voyage we got to know each other.

Keith Hodgkin was at sea in the Mediterranean:

> While passing through the channel near Pantellaria, we came close alongside one of the troopers and had a ribald conversation by means of semaphore and loudhailer. The trooper started with 'How do you like our WRNS?' then we followed with 'Fine thanks, how about sending a few over'.
>
> 'What for?'
>
> 'Well, I was told I was sent to sea to get experience'.
>
> This reply was from our captain through our loudhailer.

The 'hardening up' process began en route to the Far East, as Norman Campbell discovered:

> We called at Freetown and Capetown but did not go ashore, then on to Durban where we had a very pleasant six weeks stay, sleeping on concrete floors in brick built barrack rooms – the hardening up process had begun. Travelling on to Bombay on the Stirling Castle and after a short sojourn in Deolali we joined the 1st battalion, The Cameronians (Scottish Rifles) at Dukwan Dam, somewhere near the confluence of the Betwa and Jumni rivers in Central provinces. Here we enjoyed jungle training and several exercises, putting it all into

practice. When we got into Burma we discovered how much they had missed in training and became very quick learners.

Stanley Rothney recalled leaving the training battalions and journeying to the Far East:

> Come the day when I was 19, there was my name up on orders for embarkation. I was joining the King's Own Scottish Borderers. I was posted directly overseas, travelling on a troop ship from the Union Castle Line, round by the Cape of Good Hope, stopped at Capetown for three days, and then went on to Bombay. The journey took about three months. We landed at Bombay then went on to Deolali. There were thousands of us and from there you went wherever they put you which in my case was the 1st Battalion, The Cameronians.

The crowded conditions on board the troopship came as a shock to Norman Campbell:

> After embarkation leave in July 1942 I departed for India on the SS Rangitata, a ship of about 17,000 tons, packed to the gunwales with troops and no single cabins.

Bill Cochran found out that the age-old game of guessing the destination was not a precise science:

> We got the boat from Liverpool. Went up between Ireland and Scotland and waited up there for maybe about four or five days. And in them days when we went up there you were in a convoy and then we went out into the Atlantic and we finished up in the Middle East, down at the bottom of the Suez Canal at a place called Aden.
>
> They were all talking about how the war was going – they were talking about a force was going to be collected and we were going to go up to the Caucuses. Next thing we're on a boat and we finishes in India. Bombay.

Arriving in India, Willie Morrison eventually discovered that first impressions do not always last:

> Eventually the day came when I had to report down in Lancashire somewhere for overseas posting. Not knowing where you were going except you got some idea from the kit you were issued. We eventually boarded a boat in Liverpool, The Britannic, a huge ship. And I remember being down on the pier and thinking 'my God, its going to take something to move that'. Two or three days later we went round the north of Ireland and the damn thing was bobbing around like a cork in the storm, you just wouldn't believe it. On to Capetown and we were put into a transit camp. From there we went overland to Durban by train and that took two days and we went into another transit camp there. We boarded a ship again which landed us in Bombay. That wasn't so nice. Different culture and they chewed beetle nut and spat it out – the pavements in Bombay were red with this. It was the filthiest place I'd ever seen in my life, Bombay. We crossed over to Bengal and the climate didn't agree with me. Eventually I got posted up to Peshawar in the North West Frontier. That was marvellous – I could see snow on the hills. From there I had to come back eventually to Bombay to make my way home. In contrast to what I'd first thought – I had seen so much worse in the meantime – I was quite taken with Bombay on the way back.

Murdo MacLeod found himself posted to an LCF (Landing Craft Flack), flack ships which were used inshore as convoy escorts:

> Before Normandy we were escorts in the North Sea escorting merchant ships. The North Sea, the Channel and the Western Approaches.
> We were escorts for convoys but we weren't big enough to go right to Russia. We took them up the north of Scotland where they would join a convoy going to Russia. The north sea was a dangerous place with E Boats and acoustic and magnetic mines.
> Ordinary tank landing craft were hollow where they could fill them up with tanks or troops and the bows dropped to let them get

ashore. We didn't have that dropped bow, we had a steel deck which
was Tar Macadamed. No wonder we were forever wet, damp with
condensation. When you slung you hammock at night your blankets
were damp and you always slept fully clothed at sea with your lifebelt
on. It was a sausage like tube that you inflated with your mouth. We
were down the Wash, the Wash was full of ships that had been sunk,
it was shallow there, you could see all the masts sticking up. German
E Boats, something like out MTBs, but they were far superior to
ours. German warships were far superior to anything we had as far
as armaments were concerned. When you were at sea the crew had
to be well knitted together. One man could sink a ship, and we were
all interchangeable. There was only 20 of us. The telegraphist up on
the bridge and engine room men and seamen, Abs. most of the ships
company were marines, you carried about 120 marines, all armed
ready to go ashore if you sent them into shore. It was cramped. We
had a couple of hooks and you slung a hammock and in the morning
when you got up you had to lash it up and clear it because the mess
deck where you ate your meals was underneath. The navy men were
at the stern and there was a big Kedge anchor and in rough weather
it would crash against the stern.

Part Two

Far East

Arrival

By the time he reached Burma, Bill Cochran had the distinction of serving in three Scottish regiments

Straight away we went to what they called 'jungle training' in a place called Mysore. And then we went, and this training only took about four or five weeks, and this was the early part of 44, and then the next thing (when we were on the boat we had been transferred out of the Royal Scots and we were supposed to be Cameronians) we went to a place in India, in the Mysore area, Bhopal or something, and we did four or five weeks running about in the bushes and the trees and all that gubbins – just to get used to the jungle. And of course there's blokes telling us all the fighting stories. It finished up then the next thing we were in the Black Watch as we were to be used as reinforcements. We went to Rangie which the Black Watch had just left, and by this time we were down to about 30 blokes. We went from there to catch up with the 2nd Battalion, The Black Watch, and of course they were being primed, they were getting all trained for the jungle and they were up in the north part of Assam, Burma. And then we went from there looking for them. Eventually we did join them up in the north. We joined them at the beginning of March. Sometime around the 20th of March we flew into Burma. We went in as part of, at that time they weren't called the Chindits, we were called a LRP, Long Range Penetration. When I met up with the 2nd battalion we were not living in any barracks or anything, we were just living in the fields, just to get us used to it. We did fly in, the battalion was broken in two, we were in the 17th Indian Division, the 2nd battalion was in 14 Brigade, and we flew into Burma. We were supposed to be flown in there to do things and then flown out and another lot would go in.

When Norman Campbell arrived in the Far East he had the good luck to be selected for the job of Column Clerk:

I had been a clerk in civvy street and almost as soon as I arrived at Dukwan Dam I was invited by the Sergeant Major, in that quietly persuasive manner that all Sergeant Majors seem to have, to fill a vacancy for a clerk in 90 column office. Without too much argument (none in fact) I accepted the post and soon found that not only was I Column Clerk, but would also be a cipher operator and be second man to the Cipher Corporal, Eddie Walsh. So Cipher Clerk was added to my impressive list of Army Qualifications. Unfortunately Eddie went missing, I think during the evacuation of 'Blackpool', as, so I heard, did the Cipher Sergeant with our sister column, 26 column. While at Dukwan Dam I went down with enteritis – it must have been due to a change of water or something, and spent ten days in Jhansi Hospital.

After Christmas 1943 we entrained to travel by rail, Burma bound. I seem to remember that the journey took ten days, with day-long stops at various places. Hopefully, Indian trains have improved from the long open coaches with a wooden bench along each side, in which we travelled – I can assure anyone that ten days in one of those coaches is enough too last a lifetime. We arrived at the railhead in India and crossed the Brahmaputra on a ferry boat at a place which I recall as Jaganathgangi, then onward to Sylhet and then to Silchar over a jeep track built by American Engineers. Each day we climbed up to 6,000 feet and then descended to the valley, and after six days of up and down, arrived at Bishenpur. I do not know which was the worse, climbing up to the top of the hill or marching downhill for five or six miles on leaden legs. The first few paces on level ground felt very strange, rather I should think, like a sailor stepping ashore for the first time after a long voyage. Fortunately, I never had any problems with my feet or legs, they served me nobly over the five months we were in Burma and all the marches before.

When Stanley Rothney arrived in the Far East he was sent straight into a period of intense jungle training:

We went to Jabolpour, and from there right into the heart of the central provinces and from then on we slept out in the open under intensive training on what was known as Long Range Penetration, this was a technique dreamt up by General Wingate and as such from then on we were known as Wingate's Chindits.

Landing in Bombay, Ian Niven and his comrades in the Royal Scots received a shock:

From Bombay we went to Deolali transit camp and to my surprise our contingent were transferred to the 1st Battalion, The Lancashire Fusiliers, some use my volunteering for the Royal Scots! Thus a large contingent of Scots found themselves Lancashire Fusiliers! We were quickly dispatched to Jhansi Jungle Training Camp after agreeing to 'volunteer' for General Wingate's Chindit force – then known as the Long Range Penetration Group. However, following 12 weeks jungle training in Jhansi we were moved near to the Burmese border and joined the American 1st Air Commando Group. All was extremely secret. Apparently Churchill, Roosevelt and Stalin agreed at Stalin's request that the British become more active in the Far East. Consequently Churchill agreed to a glider force commanded by General Wingate being trained, with the 1st American Air Commando carrying out the very difficult air operation of flying gliders into north Burma. Our brigade was under Brigadier Mike Calvert (Mad Mike). You had to be daft, eccentric or mad to consider the operation – Wingate was eccentric and Calvert was mad. On 5 March 1944 we flew into North Burma, 180 miles behind the front line. I understand two other brigades followed us. We split into columns of approximately 350 men and mules and the Japs did not know what had hit them. Imagine 24 desperate bands of Chindits popping up here, there and every bloody where, 180 miles deep in North Burma, an area they considered as their territory.

Stanley Rothney gives a description of a column on the move:

> Overhead, a solitary reconnaissance plane quartered the sky, its observers peering down on an inky backcloth which was etched only with the converging silvery lines of the Chindwin and Irrawaddy rivers as they flowed ever westward towards the Bay of Bengal. Up on the Indo/Burma border, near a place called Imphal, long lines of men and animals were approaching from all points of the compass. Men, armed to the teeth with heavy weapons and wireless equipment on the animals, moved silently through the night conscious that numerous Japanese eyes were fixed on them from the surrounding jungle. The only occasional sound came from the jangling bit of a mule as it padded close behind its handler.

Columns of men were inserted into the jungle by air, by Dakota transport plane or by towed glider. Bill Cochran flew into a temporary jungle airstrip carved out of the undergrowth by American combat engineers:

> The column, each unit had two columns, our unit, the Black Watch, the column I was in was the 73rd and the other half of the battalion was in the 42nd column. Then we just started, when we flew in it was not a recognised strip, just one of those places that was created by American engineers that went in there and dropped small bulldozers. From there we marched all over, done a few flipping ambushes, was ambushed, and the plans really going not so well. Gone all to cock, when Wingate got killed things went all to cock.
> Always marching, looking for things to do…

Stanley Rothney retains a clear recollection of the condition of the jungle strips and his journey by glider:

The immediate destination of this huge force was an airstrip which had been hurriedly bulldozed by Army engineers on what had been open paddy fields. It had no tarmac surface, only roughly smoothed-down dirt. Here drawn in long lines were the many Dakota transport planes, all showing the insignia of Uncle Sam. Strung out from the rear of each were two long tow ropes, for these machines were ready for the 'off' with two gliders following on behind. Anyone examining the latter would have been horrified at the flimsy construction. These, like the planes, came from America and had the dubious name of 'Waco' and were designed for one-way use, i.e. expendable. Not the sort of thing to instil confidence in anyone boarding one. It is unbelievable, but one of the glider pilots was none other than the former child film star, Jackie Coogan: we had adored him on the silver screen back home.

Not all the columns were intended to enter the jungle by air. Norman Campbell recalls how, initially, he and his colleagues were to be inserted by boat, in the process crossing the Chindwin river:

It was during this march that we heard we would be going into Burma by gliders, instead of crossing the Chindwin by boat, raft or holding onto a mule's tail. Mules are very strong swimmers and when swimming kick their legs to the right, so it is important to keep on their left hand side if you don't want to suffer severe damage below the belt. For the river crossing we has been supplied with a lifebelt, a heavy rubber article which must have weighed about three pounds, like a car inner tube. How the hell we were supposed to blow the thing up, I never did discover. However, on hearing our mode of transport had been changed, there was a mass 'pegdoing' (disposal) of the rubber goods down the hillside, and we went on our way with a lighter load. Strangely, the lifebelts were never mentioned again – probably the officers had done the same as the squaddies and lightened their loads also. What we would have done, or had done to us, had the information proved wrong, I dread to think.

To the relief of many, the planned river crossing was cancelled and Norman and his comrades were inserted into the jungle by air – accompanied by 'flying mules':

I think it was on 10th March 1944 that we marched to the airstrip at Imphal and boarded our Dakota. This was the first time I had flown and was accompanied by 29 other soldiers and three mules. They, the mules, were tethered at the front, each tended by a Muleteer, the humans sat on the floor, there being no seats. Nor was there cabin service, so I passed the time by sleeping during the flight.

I was alerted to the fact that we were about to land when I half woke-up and bleary-eyed saw the moon pass the aircraft window, then pass again. Realising that there was only one moon over Burma, same as everywhere else, I knew we were circling for landing and became instantly wide awake. On landing I was greeted by my two 'muckers' Bill Stanton and Fred Tatham, who had arrived earlier and they led the way to our column area.

We had arrived in 'Broadway', the codename of an airstrip about 150 miles behind enemy lines in Northern Burma. The serious business of sorting out the Japs was about to begin and the thought that I might be wounded, get killed or worse, get captured, never entered my mind. We had confidence in ourselves, in our officers and in our boss, Wingate.

With his jungle training completed, Stanley Rothney was flown straight into the defensive roadblock codenamed 'Broadway':

The 5th of March 1944, on that particular day, after doing all the training, coming up into Assam, up to the frontier between India and Burma, from there we went by air, flown by Dakota or by gliders into a jungle clearing. In my case I flew by Dakota into 'Broadway', a Chinese, American, British effort.

The insertion of men and animals was not the only use for transport aircraft – they were used extensively to keep the Chindit columns re-supplied. Bill Cochran describes such an air drop:

We were supplied by air, the old Dakotas used to come in, about every five or six weeks, the different parts of the brigade would collect at a certain place for a number of days and we would get a brigade drop.

There were other times when there would be a small drop when we had run out of grub and they would have to get on the wireless and a couple of Dakotas would come and we would have a night drop. Not all drops were at night. During the day there would be 'free drops' from low flying aircraft. But at night time, not everybody would be in the pick-up area. The night I was on a free drop, obviously we must have been in a dodgy area because it was only a small unit. We couldn't wait a day or two there because the Japs might come along. We had to stay within the drop area and you got behind plenty trees when there were free drops. One of our boys got hit with a free drop piece. Generally the free drops were just certain things – bags of animal food for the mules. But then we were organised to pick up things like ammunition. They had different coloured parachutes for different things. Red for danger, other colours depending on the cargo. Blokes used to find out, wonder what the, there would be one or two pack with stuff for the officers and of course the blokes that were collecting the drop, as soon as they found a yellow and red one, 'that's the one we want'.

Norman Campbell recalled the pleasure of sending those radio messages calling for an airdrop:

The messages we liked best to send were those requesting airdrops, particularly a drop with a luxury content. It was in the lap of the gods if we got the full drop, but whether or not, we would not get another for five days and two days rations had to be stretched to 5 days on more than one occasion. Sometimes a parachute would be stuck up a tall tree and this was soon brought crashing down with a slab of 808 (explosive) fastened to the trunk.

As Bill Cochran discovered, the Chindit columns were intended to operate as part of a long-term campaign:

We were supposed to be there about six months but I think we were only there for five and a half months. And by this time we were just walking here, there, anywhere and every now and again one of the columns would be in action.

Stanley Rothney was also conscious of time:

> I went in in March and I was there until August of that year and we
> lived on American rations, known as K rations, there was a box for
> breakfast, dinner and tea and there was a selection of things in them.
> These were emergency rations designed by American experts to be
> used for six days only and we existed on them for six months, we all
> lost stones and stones in weight. We finished up like survivors from
> Belsen. The K rations were augmented with a little bit of rice. On
> one occasion we were so hungry that we resorted to dispatching one
> of our mules that was badly injured. The animal was one of our great
> friends called Albert, and Albert must have been the toughest – I think
> my boots would have been easier to chew than he. And when I was
> masticating this mess in my mouth I was thinking about Albert up
> in his equine heaven looking down and having the last laugh. They
> could never have fought that campaign, the way they carried all the
> heavy equipment, the three inch mortars, the Vickers machine guns
> and the wireless equipment, which was big and bulky.

For Stanley the role of the Chindit columns was clear:

> The overall role of the unit was to go right into the heart, the soft
> underbelly of the enemy and cut his lines of communication and then
> run as fast as you could before he could mount any sizeable attack.
> You would regroup and come back and attack or place another road
> block. Virtually a case of hide and seek, but very, very effective.

The men who formed the Chindits came from all branches of the
service and from all nationalities. Stanley Rothney explains:

> And what about the foot soldiers? Any observer would have been
> struck that no-one had any badges of rank, divisional identification
> or any means to show which regiment they were from. They were
> a motley crew and came from many countries. There were those
> sun-tanned figures from the English counties and the Highlands and
> Lowlands of Scotland. With them were their comrades of many battles,

the hardy hill men of Nepal, better known as the Ghurkhas. From the continent of Africa came men from Nigeria who stood out from the rest by electing to carry their kit on their heads. Here and there you would see an ebony figure marching along quite unperturbed with the spare barrel of a bren gun on top of his bush hat. All had been welded together on very special training which had taken place in the depths of the forest in India during the previous twelve months. The whole scene seemed surreal. All sorts of topics crossed the minds of the participants. 'Where are we going?' 'What will the morrow bring?' 'Will there be a tomorrow?' Others thought of home and Sunday school and sought consolation in a silent prayer. Even the moon above had a beckoning look. Soon Zero Hour was nigh. For Wingate's Chindits, this was kick-off time on Operation Thursday, a title picked by the great leader from the nursery rhyme 'Thursday's Child has far to go'. The force's destination was a jungle clearing in the enemy's soft under-belly and miles behind their front line. Their purpose was commando-like but had the specialist title of long-range penetration with the principal aim of cutting the Japanese lines of communication.

James Tulloch recalls one unfortunate incident:

Then there was the incident of Buck Taylor – one battery captain – a gentleman who had an inexhaustible supply of stories. He was holding court one particularly quiet day with about a dozen men and two NCOs sitting on boxes of cordite about ten yards away and listening to the tales, when suddenly, from the most unexpected direction, a shell whistled overhead and dropped about 300 yards away. We dismissed it as a dud from one of the guns on the other side of the box but two minutes later another shell whistled over and dropped 100 yards away. I just said to my two NCO friends, boys I'm off to a slit trench and they followed my example. The next shell landed on the cordite boxes which we had just vacated and Buck Taylor was killed and Bombardier R Key, one of our Bengal Artillery members was seriously wounded.

Counter-Battery Troop

With clothes to mend, and washing too
A stove prepares a welcome brew
As dark and angry on the hill
A purple cloud now hovers, still
With savage force, the lethal blast
Sends jagged splinters scything past

Once more speaks that distant gun
To each of us it speaks as one
Two seconds to get underground
Before we hear that rushing sound
The bursting shell blocks out the sun
May God preserve us, everyone

'Take post' the order echoes round
we race across the open ground
no time to heed the horrid din
each to his place, we scramble in
four muzzles quartering the sky
all eager, now to make reply

The fire controller, posted near
Relays his orders – loud and clear
Four sergeants arms are raised as one
Reporting ready on each gun
With flash above and dust below
They hurl defiance at the foe

'Cease firing' now the order comes
and silent fall the waiting guns
the sweat grimed faces swap a grin
'I think we've done the bugger in'
Too late – the cookhouse has been hit
And just when we have need of it

The sergeant cook is filled with ire
To see his stove of fat on fire
And if that was not quite enough
He spies his shrapnel riddled duff
So cock an ear and listen still
Next time a shell may burst to kill.

Pat McEvoy

The Columns

Orde Wingate liked to visit his men and check on their training and welfare. Norman Campbell describes the meeting between Wingate and one rifleman, 'Cooky':

> Moving on from Bishenpur, we came to rest at Imphal, a mile or two from the airstrip. There was nothing provided, no tents, no charpoys – nothing. We merely had the light-weight American blanket which was part of our Burma kit. We bedded down on the bare ground and were there for several days. Even the food was appalling, both in quantity and quality. A day or so after wed arrived we had a visit from Orde Wingate, during which he asked one of our lads (one rifleman Cooke) what the food was like. Most squaddies talking to a General for the first time in his life would probably have said, 'Not bad Sir', or 'alright Sir'. But not Cooky. He told Wingate in no uncertain terms that the food was not fit for pigs. In a very short space of time the food improved beyond recognition in both quality and quantity. Well done Cooky!

However, while Orde Wingate was liked and respected by his men, not all VIP visitors left the same impression:

> Just before we went into Burma, we had a visit from Mountbatten. Looking very handsome and in naval whites, which were so startlingly vividly white, they had no place where we were. Clearly he had not spent the night sleeping on the ground. It would have been better if he had turned up in jungle greens. He stood on a box, called the troops around him, and delivered a pep-talk. We did not rate Lord Louis as highly as Orde Wingate.

Stanley Rothney recalls a visit by General Wingate:

> Wingate came and visited us quite frequently. There was no difficulty identifying him because despite the fact that we were in jungle green he persisted in wearing a topee.

Chindit columns were expected to be self-sufficient in the jungle. Men were expected to carry supplies and equipment for an extended period. Norman Campbell details the kit men were expected to carry in the jungle:

We were equipped with field service marching order (FSMO) and my personal load consisted of (a) small pack on the left hip containing two mess tins; mug; knife, fork and spoon; towel; soap; razor; shaving soap; shaving brush; toothbrush and toothpaste; code books (2); message pads; pencils; rubber; housewife, etc, etc. (b) on right hip, filled water bottle (c) on belt, 2 hand grenades primed and ready, 2 pouches each containing 1 filled Bren Gun magazine, bayonet and scabbard, 24" Dah (machete) (d) over shoulder one bandolier containing 50 rounds .303 rifle ammunition in clips (e) in large pack (valise) 15 packets American K rations, plus as many packets as I could legitimately get my hands on, lightweight American blanket, groundsheet and carried 1 Short Lee Enfield rifle (9 pounds weight). After this obligatory load, you were free to take anything you wanted, subject to security and carrying ability. In all, a load or 50/55 pounds. Later on in 'Blackpool' block, I exchanged my rifle for an American .300 semi-automatic carbine with a magazine capacity of 16 rounds, and weighing only 3 pounds. It made a welcome lightening of the load apart from being easier to carry and quicker to use. It had a range of about 300 yards, which was really as close to the Japs as I wanted to get. We were also issued with 20 or 30 silver Indian Rupees, with which we were to buy, rather than liberate, food from the local Burmese, and I came out with about 150 rupees from subsequent issues, which I spent quickly in Tinsukia after we came out, and before we were told to hand it in.

At this distance in time it is not possible to remember how long we remained at Broadway, but it could only have been a matter of hours or a day at most. Because of all the aerial activity, the Japs who were all around us and not very many miles away, would have realised that there was something unusual going on and would be coming along to investigate. We formed up in our columns, ours was 90 column under the command of Lt Col W J Henning, our sister column, 26 column was under the command of Lt Col B J (Breezy) Brennan, and set off.

As Norman explains, the Chindit columns had one specific purpose:

> Our brief was to harass and destroy the Japs and anything Japanese, to create the maximum damage without getting involved in pitched battles, for which we were not equipped. The two Cameronian columns did not always travel together or operate together but were never too far apart.
>
> During my sojourn in Burma, I did not keep a diary, did not possess a calendar or even a watch, so it is difficult to associate events with dates and places. But for several weeks, until we entered 'Blackpool Block' we floated about in the area of Katha, Wuntho, Pinblebu and Banmauk, on a more or less free ranging role and generally leading for 111 Brigade in a northerly direction. A number of confrontations with the Japs took place in which we gave infinitely far better than we got. In one little 'duffy' we caught a number of Japs at a small depot making breakfast. They were dealt with, their breakfast consumed and spare supplies of rice taken away. Anything we couldn't carry was destroyed.

Like others, Norman Campbell collected his 'good luck charm' on the way, although it hadn't brought much in the way of good luck for its previous owner:

> I remember the first Jap I saw in Burma. Fed on the myth that all Japs were short sighted and universally wore round, metal rimmed glasses, this one was a bit of a culture shock. He was over six feet tall if he was an inch and seemed a very well proportioned individual, able to look after himself. Fortunately for us he was flat on his back, unfortunately for him he was dead – someone had given him a third eye. This was the first job for Intelligence Sergeant Bill Pullen, and he buzzed around happy as a dog with two tails, frisking the body and collecting anything which might carry some information. On Japanese soldiers caps they wore a metal five pointed star and I think it was here that I picked one up and wore it on the pugree of my bush hat as a lucky charm. Had I been captured I might have been

asked some awkward questions – or something. It was also about this time that we captured our first Samurai sword and later sent it back to base via a light plane. The intention was to hang it on the wall of the officers mess, whether it arrived or not I do not know, but I have my doubts.

Pat McEvoy discovered how tenacious the Japanese soldiers were, even when wounded and cut off:

The Japanese put in a battalion to cut of our line of command, which it did for a few days before being practically annihilated. A party of survivors, the battalion commander, a warrant officer and twelve men all wounded, one on a stretcher, sodden and exhausted, made their way south loaded with explosives – apparently a 'gun bursting' party aimed at our own 'box'. About half past three in the morning their sentry saw a figure approaching him, he challenged three times then saw the glint of a sword, fired and missed – he got in his second shot just in time – the falling sword wounded him in the arm. The warrant officer died on the edge of the gun pit. I saw the remains polished off in the morning, we even brought up a medium tank to blast the survivors out of a bunker they had occupied – when the last man, unarmed, broke cover, it was just like a rat hunt

Norman Campbell discovered that in the jungle eccentric behaviour was considered the 'norm':

When we were nearing the end of a day's march, Colonel Henning and his batman would go on ahead to seek a safe and suitable place to harbour for the night. We always knew when we were there because Bill Henning would come striding down the track just wearing his boots and bush hat, with his rifle draped across both shoulders. His shirt and trousers which were saturated with sweat he had left out to dry.

Colonel Henning knew me by name, and one day he asked me to cut his hair. Despite my protestations that I had never cut hair in my life and could not be held responsible for the result, he insisted that

I do it. I thought the result was not too bad for a first time, a step or three at the back perhaps, and I left him with both ears. Strangely, I was not asked again by him or any other officer.

Through these weeks Eddie Walsh and I had been kept busy with our cipher work, deciphering messages sent to us and enciphering messages to be sent out. It was not so bad during daylight hours, as we could work in the open, even though it took up most of our lunch break (if we had one) and we worked with our meal in one hand and a pencil in the other. But it was less easy at night when we lost many hours of well earned sleep, working away with a torch and a blanket over our heads to hide the light. Often the dawn arrived, when we had a quick drum up (make a cup of tea), on with packs and off we set having had only one or two hours sleep.

We worked closely with the two radio teams. The Royal Corps of Signals lads, led by Corporal Needham, who grew the most magnificent black beard I think I have ever seen. Their radio had a shorter range than the RAF set, and if a patrol went out with a radio and operator, a cipher operator went also and it was usually me. The RAF radio team, led by a Canadian, Flt Lt McDonald, with a Sergeant and a Corporal, who was wounded, had a more powerful set, which could reach base back in Assam or other units anywhere in Burma.

On one patrol we encountered a Burmese, who after questioning by one of the Burrifs (Burma Rifles), was confirmed as 'loyal'. He gave information about a large number of Japs who had detrained and were then encamped at the edge of the jungle near the rail track. I was given a message calling for an air strike which I encoded and the signals boys sent off. We heard later that there had been a strike causing many casualties, but I cannot validate the result.

In a letter home to his parents Pat McEvoy describes the efforts to keep the Tiddim Road open through the Chin Hills in Burma:

The cutting is about sixteen feet deep and was the last length to be completed, so we had to work four hour shifts, night and day to get it done and the road open. We watched the first trucks come down into a valley where the wheel was unknown and the white man still an object of wonder. The Chin hunter with his leopard skin trappings and flintlock rifle was still not an uncommon sight. I mention all this as it is ancient history now – and in any case, as you can see from the papers, that part of the world is now in the hands of the Japanese.

James Tulloch recalls one story about Japanese treatment of wounded prisoners:

The casualty clearing station was taken over by the Jap and there is the story of one of our gunners, an Anglo-Indian, who was seriously wounded when our gun had a direct hit. This gunner who was badly wounded asked for water and was refused, but there was a bucket quite close to where he was lying and he made a move to get it but was killed instantly by a burst of machine gun fire from the guard. This story is second hand but I believe it to be authentic because a gunner in the casualty station at the time told the story.

While in a defensive position for the night, Pat McEvoy found himself subjected to improvised Japanese psychological warfare:

During the retreat from Tiddling while still cut off, went into 'box' for the night at the bottom of deep valley, with the Japs in the hills. Pitch black – no sleep the night before, just crawling into bed when the most fiendish yell (real red indian style) and all hell let loose – running feet, shouts of 'stand to', bren guns, rifles, automatics, medium machine guns, grenades, quick firing dual purpose guns, and possibly 2 pounders and mortars, not to mention 'the fireworks' all opened up at once. Was I terrified, bullets whizzing about, tracer everywhere at every lull I expected them to come in with the bayonet and imagine the confusion (pitch black). Nothing developed – after four or five hours I got bored and went to bed but the firing continued all night. My first introduction to the now familiar 'Jitter Party' very effective against inexperienced troops, as here (mostly Indian Service Corps) the result, numbers of our own men shot by our own men and thousands of rounds wasted. The Japs – no trace. This cannot happen among experienced troops, and I think everyone learnt their lesson – it certainly put the fear of God into me.

Norman Campbell also had a brush with the Japanese:

Another brush we had with the Japs resulted in a few dead Japs and one badly wounded. Judging by his uniform he was either a senior NCO or a junior officer. As we approached him he appeared to be reaching for his pistol, a course of action from which he was quickly dissuaded by the sharp end of a bayonet. It was during this encounter that I had one of my near squeaks, when a burst from a Jap machine gun hit the tree that I was standing against, about a foot above my head. I guess he had his sights set a bit too high.

Even the simple act of crossing the road was fraught with danger in the jungle, as Norman Campbell describes:

Normally on the march, the column would travel in single file which stretched back for 300 yards or more. On occasions when a road had to be crossed, clearly we could not have a procession of that length crossing, so the procedure was changed. We would line up in rows parallel to the road and back under cover. On a signal, the first row would surge forward and be across the road into the jungle on the other side in seconds. Then the second row would move until the whole column was across. On one such operation the first row was about to cross when several Jap trucks came along. We could easily have sorted them out and would have loved to have done so, but it was required not to give away our presence in the area. So, frustrated, we remained crouched down and watched them drive away.

In a letter home in May/June 1945, Pat McEvoy described his time with the Chindits:

Dear Mary Ross
Since I wrote my last rather 'browned off' letter, the monsoon has broken and though rather deep it is decidedly cooler. Also the

censorship blackout on this front has been lifted – I sent mum a brief summary of my activities here during the last three years (2 years, 11 months to be exact) but in case you have not heard – spring of 43 working on the Tidding Road (Chin hills) with pick and shovel and a pair of feet, not to mention full arms and equipment; winter 43/44 in fairly static action around Tidding and on Kennedy Peak; 44 up to end of Monsoon, bombardment of Kennedy Peak, cut off, 3 week fight out of Chin hills 200 miles back to Imphal, ten week battle of Bisherpana (static). 1945 long road journey from Brahinaputra down to Irrawaddy over tracks eight inches deep in dust, 16 day, 80 mile trek through to Meektila, four weeks defence of Meiktila, four week 300 mile advance to forty miles short of Rangoon. I am now aprox 100 miles back up the road to prevent the Japs escaping across the Sittang river into Siam.

Norman Campbell and his colleagues discovered that not all 'natives' were friendly:

On one occasion we stopped for the night near a village still occupied by the Burmese, the villagers known to be loyal. The signal boys decided to set up their radio underneath one of the huts which were built on stilts and normally housed cattle, so Eddie Walsh and I joined them. There were only a few chickens in residence, which we evicted and got down to work. It was not very long before we were scratching ourselves like mad. The place was infested with chicken fleas, who seemed to enjoy a European meal for a change, and we beat a very hasty retreat. It was preferable to risk the rain than be eaten alive.

Soon after we went into 'Aberdeen', code name for a stronghold and safe harbour, where we could eat, sleep and relax. Our next task was to be the setting up of a road/rail block codenamed 'Blackpool', at a position about 100 miles north of Aberdeen. Although at this stage we had not been told about it.

Stanley Rothney also took part in the 'Blackpool' roadblock:

We set up another road block called 'Blackpool' and the force had to virtually sit and duck there and the Japs brought up heavy artillery

and forced us off and there were high casualties for the Cameronians.
The badly wounded were evacuated by the Royal Airforce using
Sunderland flying boats which were brought up from Ceylon and
landed on the lake and then took the casualties from there up to the
Bhrama Pootra river.

Norman Campbell gives a detailed description of life in 'Blackpool',
along with the evacuation:

After several days march we had arrived at the site which was to
become 'Blackpool'. We had been marching all day, from early morning with only short halts and a lunch break. It was well dark and we
were knackered. We walked up a stream which was to be our water
supply, up a hill and at the top were told, 'this is it, dig in'. without
taking of my pack, I sat down on the hillside, and leaned back to rest
my pack on the slope. The next thing I knew it was almost daylight
and I had slept for about five hours – the longest sleep in a long time.
Why no-one wakened me, I never knew, perhaps like me they too
were asleep. I went in search of Eddie Walsh and together we decided
where our trench would be.

The topography of Blackpool, or so I heard, was like a left hand,
palm down with the fingers extended. On this hypothesis, our trench
was sited on top of the little finger about halfway along. Each 'finger'
was a hill. I must admit that I did not go 'walkabout' to confirm the
geographical features, but I did see enough to suggest that it was
correct.

Down the hill behind our position, perhaps a quarter of a mile
away, was the stream we had walked up when we arrived at Blackpool.
Twice I went down for water, until I realised that going alone was
a bit foolhardy. The possibility of a Jap or two sneaking in was very
real, so having spotted a large basketful of small potatoes on my first
visit, I took them with me on my second (and last) visit. Boiled in
their skins they made a welcome addition to K rations. I should have
left a rupee or two in payment but I am afraid I didn't. If the former
owner is still around, and can prove ownership, I shall be pleased to
send him a cheque. Later on the Japs did attack up the Chaung (river

bed) where I had been drawing water. Eddie and I dug an 'L' shaped trench about four feet deep, both arms long enough for us each to have our own bedroom, with a ramp at one end to run down rather than jump in and risk injury. After all, the odds for 'copping something' were already high enough without adding to them and as the jap shelling got heavier, we thought it prudent to get a little closer to Mother Earth and increased the depth to about five feet. This was to be our home for the next 18 days.

Looking out from the corner of our trench we were looking almost straight up the Mogaung Valley. At about two o'clock was Namkwin Railway Station and behind it ran the road to Mogaung. This was why we were here, to block the road and railway and prevent the Japs moving men and supplies up the valley against Stilwell and the XIV Army on the Arakan.

Stilwell was not at all well disposed to the British and he was instrumental in keeping the Chindits in Burma long after they should have been withdrawn, and long after they had outlived their usefulness because of the depletion in strength due to casualties, sickness and sheer exhaustion.

As the Japs knew we were there, there was no restriction on lighting fires during daylight, and in a way, to send up smoke was like putting up two fingers to them, so a mug of tea was available when wanted. No fires were allowed after dark, so we had our supper before darkness fell. Almost everyday, just as we were about to eat our meal, the wind direction changed and blew from the north, bringing with it the smell of the rotting bodies of Japs who had tried to join us on previous days. Rotting human flesh has an unmistakable sickly sweet smell, once smelled never forgotten and in imagination, I can smell it yet. However, nothing should put one off a good meal and it didn't. during the days and at night Eddie and I would be working away on messages, but at least we did not have to don a pack and march, so we managed to get some sleep.

One of the officers had the bright idea of starting a Block newsletter and being the guy with the paper and pencils, I was nominated as scribe. We managed to get some sort of a handwritten newsletter out, how far round the block it went I never knew. How far round the block it went I never knew. I can well imagine it being waylaid for some other purpose! As an item for the intended second newsletter, I wrote a skit on the Bob Hope song 'Thanks for the Memory', but as there was no second edition, it did not get published. It went something like this;-

Thanks for the memory
Of slogging over hills
Taking Mepacrine pills
Of road blocks, ambushes
And other little thrills
How lovely it was.

Thanks for the memory
Of eating rations K
Three square meals a day
Of LP ones
And whizz bang guns
They livened up our day
Oh, thank you so much.

Few were the times that we feasted
But many the times that we fasted
Still it was fun while it lasted
The aches and the pain
I'll never do it again.

So thanks for the memory
And if I make it back
I'll refuse to touch a pack
I'll be a gentleman of leisure
Lead a life of wanton pleasure
A soldiers farewell to all that
So thank you so much.

On our sector we had a couple of days of relative quiet before the Japs really got started, a few shells lobbed over, probes at the perimeter wire at night, leaving behind a few bodies which caused the smell later on. The thing which really annoyed us was a 'Whizz-bang' gun which the Japs had and seemed to be on the isolated hill, 12 o' clock from our trench, about half a mile away. You heard the bang as it was fired, the whizz of the shell and the bang as it exploded. The bang-whizz-bang seemed to take place simultaneously. It fired at anything that moved and to make matters worse, we could not pinpoint it. Patrols were sent out to destroy it, but they did not find it. One day I was sent with a message to an isolated trench 30 yards or so down the hillside facing the isolated hill and I knew the damn gun would fire. I did the run down and the run back, quicker than Linford Christie would have done the same distance on the flat. If the gun fired – I didn't hear it.

This problem with Japanese artillery was not a one-off, as James Tulloch discovered:

The Japs had a small gun just behind the crest of the hill about 500 yards in front of us which he used to let loose periodically but he could not get a large enough angle of depression to get at us and likewise we could not get at him. Apart from that he was doing damage in other parts of the box. Then our C.P.O. had what he thought was a brainwave, he took one troop back about ½ a mile to get at this Jap gun but when the guns were just moving into this position the Japs let loose and one of the gun towers got a direct hit but luckily the gun team had just dismounted but the driver was killed and our guns were withdrawn without a shot being fired.

The Gun

Monster crouching in its pit
Muzzle pointing to the sky
Gunners nearly worship it
For it are prepared to die
Squat and deadly on its bed
Ever hungry to be fed

Watchful guards await its will
Keeping vigil night and day
Fiery breath intent to kill
Scorches all that come its way
Bursting forth a fearsome roar
It is the very God of war

Leaping o'er the rutted ground
Bounding up to drop its trail
Gunners, running, turn it round
Infantry, we must not fail
How to get three ton of steel
Get your shoulder to the wheel

Gunfire orders from the rear
Layer's hands the dial sight reach
Ammo numbers crouching near
Rammer kneels beside the breech
Sergeant bawls out 'ready one'
Back recoils the smoking gun

Infantry must face the foe
They're the ones that win the wars
To support them we must go
Never for an instant pause
Forward into action, we
Dashing Field Artillery

Pat McEvoy

Blackpool

When supporting the troops defending 'Blackpool', Norman Campbell discovered that the RAF could be devious when required:

> One day we heard the roar of approaching aircraft and hoped it was the airdrop we badly needed. As the aircraft flew overhead we saw parachutes dropping and knew instantly they would land on Jap territory. We stood there, cursing the stupidity and inefficiency of the fliers and mourning the loss of our supplies, as the parachutes drifted onto the isolated hill and seemed to arrive on the ground at the same time. As they hit the ground there was an almighty explosion and clouds of black smoke and dust. When the smoke cleared, the top of the hill was transmogrified, almost as flat as Table Mountain. I don't remember hearing the whizz-bang again and it was one airdrop we were glad to have missed.
>
> Daily the Japs shelled different sectors and at night they would attack, sometimes at the same spot, and they suffered heavily for it. What a blessing barbed wire is, provided you are not the party trying to get through it, and they tried hard, repeatedly.
>
> Using the 'hand' metaphor, between the little finger on which we were dug in and the ring finger, was a battery of 25-pounder guns, manned by the Royal Artillery lads. They were ranged on where the road and railway bridge crossed. The bridge had been blown up on our first night in 'Blackpool' and for a while the artillery stopped the Japs mending it. But the guns were in a very exposed position and I heard that the Gunners were killed to a man. I would think that their position relative to ours meant that we received a few stray shells intended for them.

It was always a good thing to be able to recognise friend from foe:

> I remember one night when I nearly shot one of our own. There was a heavy attack going on and I saw this shadowy crouching figure approaching. The imagination plays tricks when you are keyed up and

I thought I saw the round helmet and small pack on his back, which the Japs usually carried. I had him in my rifle sights with the first pressure on the trigger when he spoke. No Jap could have imitated that broad Scottish accent. If he is still alive, he will never know how close he came to being dead. Who he was, I know not.

The monsoon was fast approaching, we had already had some rain, and we had hoped to be out of Burma before it got much worse. We had no wet weather gear whatever, but it soon became clear that our departure date was not imminent. Light showers soon turned into heavy showers, then into torrential rain and the ground soon got muddy. One day during a particularly heavy attack along the wire, I was sent to Brigade HQ with a message. Expecting to return to our position, I took just my carbine and four filled magazines in my pockets. Message delivered, I was told not to return to our position as it had been evacuated and Blackpool was also being evacuated. I was detailed to help carry a wounded man on a stretcher. I took the front end of the stretcher and we set off down the track which ran along the hillside behind Brigade HQ. The rain had made the track wet and muddy and we slithered along rather than walked. Some distance along I saw what I thought was a West African soldier, who was taking a breather from carrying a Vickers machine gun, which was on the track beside him. With all the slithering and sliding and wet hands, I began to lose my grip on the stretcher handles and called for a halt. As we crouched to lower the stretcher, I heard a bang up ahead and felt something hit my face. I wiped my hand across my face and it came away bloody and I thought I had been hit. I looked down the track and the soldier was no longer there. I wiped my face again and there was no blood so I realised I was not hurt. We picked up the stretcher and carried on down the track. The Vickers was still there, so were the soldier's boots with his feet inside them, and his head lay on the track. He must have suffered a direct hit from a shell or mortar bomb. I picked my way through the human debris and remember thinking how big a human head looked when detached from the body. I soon put it out of my mind, so hardened had we become, the attitude being, 'poor sod. But I'm glad it was him and not me'. The blood on me had come from him, but it could well have been mine had I not crouched down when I did.

I carried the stretcher for what seemed hours until relieved and by now we had come down of the hill and onto the flat. In front of us lay a stretch of flat open ground, perhaps half a mile wide, hardly a tree, no cover whatsoever. Beyond the flat, the ground started to rise into hilly well-wooded ground and we had to go there for cover. There was no panic, we moved as quickly as we could, with an occasional 'splat' as a bullet hit the wet ground. That didn't worry us too much as we didn't think much of the Japs as marksmen, and it would be bloody bad luck if they hit one of us. Then they started shelling us and looking back, I saw the shells exploding some way behind, then the next one would be a bit nearer. We moved a bit quicker and by now we had reached the tree-line. We dived into our friend, the jungle, as if into the arms of a lover. We knew that they could shell us, but at least they could not see us.

On the forward slope of the hill, just I front of the tree-line, we came across a lot of trenches which had been occupied by the Japs. Why they had pulled out and why they had not re-occupied the trenches, when the big onslaught on Blackpool began, was a mystery. Had they done so, every Chindit on Blackpool would have been killed or captured. A dozen men and a few machine guns would have been the finish of us.

We moved up the hill, deeper into the jungle and somehow a small bunch of us got separated from the main body. I don't know where or how this happened, but for the next five days our small party struggled over the hills, through the jungle. All I had was my carbine and four filled magazines, not a crumb of food and the others were in much the same state.

I was not fond of cheese and most of the time we were in Blackpool, I had stored the tins of cheese from the K rations in a slot in the wall of the trench. There must have been 10 or 12 tins of cheese. I thought about those tins many times during the next five days. The more hungry I got, the more I thought about them. But there comes a time when you stop feeling hungry and start losing energy and power. After a night sitting with your back to a tree, trying to get as much shelter from the rain as the brim of your bush hat will give you, you would set off in the morning and gradually your energy ebbed away until you were dragging one foot after the other. The process was repeated every day, except that your strength ebbed away a little quicker. Continually soaked to the skin, how I wished that I had the cheese, and hoped if the Japs had eaten it, it had choked them or given them constipation forever. Then on the sixth day we found the main body of men.

Somehow, somebody had managed to light a fire from sodden bamboo. He was a hero, stark naked we stood and dried our clothes. Not that they would stay dry for long but it felt so good to be in warm dry kit again.

I found what was left of my battalion and reported in to Captain Neil Mclean, who was 90 column 2 i/c. when he learned I had nothing except my carbine etc, he cut his blanket into half and gave me a piece. He also gave me some of the very small amount of food he had.

When 'Blackpool' was eventually abandoned, the lack of food became a serious problem:

I am not sure how much longer our trek across the hills continued, it was for some days during which we arrived at the point where there was absolutely no food, and sadly one of the gallant mules paid the supreme price. My mucker Frank Hunt who was a butcher in civvy street got the job of skinning and cutting up the poor animal. I got some liver and an unidentified piece of meat. It helped to keep body and soul together but I never ate mule again.

We were greatly assisted over the final hill by a flight of steps cut into the hillside by West African troops and found ourselves at the south end of Indagwyi Lake, which must be the largest stretch of inland water in Northern Burma. We were at Indagwyi Lake for several days, resting up, getting re-equipped, watching the two Sunderland flying boats, Gert and Daisy, landing on the lake to ferry out the sick and wounded and probably some who were neither, and generally done nothing much. We felt safe there, we were pretty certain the Japs would not follow us as they had not been too anxious to follow us into the jungle in the past.

Stanley Rothney recognised the high price paid by those at 'Blackpool':

> After the 'Blackpool' road block was broken up, high casualties meant
> that we ceased to be a fighting unit.

Norman Campbell was offered the job of officer's batman:

> Captain McLean's batman had been flown out sick, and as I was no
> longer needed as a cipher operator, he asked me if I would do the
> job. It was not a job I would normally have wanted to do but as he
> had been so decent to me, I was happy to take it on. There was no
> valetting or boot polishing to do, mostly making tea, meals, tidying
> up etc. I remember buying a chicken from one of the Indawgyi Lake
> locals, chopping its head off and watching it run around in diminish-
> ing circles. Poor thing, it was either it or no supper for me, so it was
> really no contest and made a good meal for Captain Mac and me.
>
> We were on the march again. I remember we were in or passed
> through Mokso Sakhan, the name is very familiar, and on up the valley
> to Lakhren. It was either at Mokso or Lakhren that we were issued
> with American jungle hammocks. What a joy they were; it was sheer
> luxury to lie in your hammock with the rain pelting on the canopy,
> not a drop reaching you; the mosquito netting zipped up and listening
> to the frustrated mozzies trying unsuccessfully to get at you. I had a
> few good nights sleep.

There were times when food was not always so scarce:

> We spent a few days at Lakhren and it was here that I celebrated my
> 21st birthday, 13 July 1944 (I was a Friday the 13th Baby). I had manu-
> factured an oven from two large tins which had contained British
> Army biscuits. The bottom one, with lid removed was filled with soil
> and saturated with petrol. We had plenty of this to run the engine of
> the battery charger for the wireless, etc. The second tin, placed across
> the top of the lower tin, the lid acting as the over door. Hard tack
> biscuits, crushed to a flour in a piece of parachute cloth, mixed with

butter or margarine, made a not bad pastry. The larger half of a K ration tin (I was back in the cheese now), lined and lidded with the pastry, then filled with whatever meat was available, or apple from a luxury drop, baked in the oven was a gourmet meal.

On my birthday I made a pile of meat pies and apple pies and invited my muckers to dinner. The pies were washed down with rum and water, the rum having been 'liberated' from the officers stock. I went to bed in a very happy frame of mind, and slept exceedingly well in my hammock, having managed to get in it after a number of failed attempts. Captain Mac enjoyed a few pies but I did not push my luck by offering him a drink.

Justice in the jungle was often swift and final:

I remember one incident, apart from my birthday, which happened at Lakhren. A Burmese, claiming to be a loyal, came into our camp asking for weapons. These were sometimes given to known loyals and they made good use of them against the Japs. Unfortunately, for the gentleman concerned, already in the camp was a known Burmese loyal, who promptly denounced the new arrival as a Jap collaborator. He was questioned, the case considered proven and he was led away by a sergeant carrying a rifle. On the way, the two passed Captain ##### who handed his Thompson Sub-machine gun to the sergeant and said. 'try this, I've never used it'. A short time later there was a burst of fire and the sergeant returned alone. He handed the gun back to Captain ##### and said 'it works'. Summary justice indeed, and we lost no sleep over it.

Bill Cochran recalls the 'forgotten' feeling and the improvisation in the jungle:

There was not much action because by this time Impale had more or less finished. We were trying to stop Japanese supplies coming up to there. We had blockades on the railway line. As time went on, after D-day, we were beginning the think we had been forgotten, we were saying, 'how the hell are we going to get out of here'? We were in central Burma and stories were going round that we would have to walk out. Eventually in the end we marched up. What was coming down as the leading force into Burma was the 36th Division. We met these guys, they were asking us if we were there reinforcements, we had been in there for five and a half months. We marched up north and finished up in the hills at a railway line and we got onto some of these big flat wagons and the front of the train, where the engine should be, was a jeep with extra wheel rims on the tracks.

When the survivors returned from 'Blackpool' they came under the command of General Stilwell. Unfortunately Stilwell was not made aware they had been 'in country' for over five months and were suffering the effects of malnutrition and illness. He used the depleted columns in a normal infantry role – a task to which they were unsuited.

Norman Campbell recalls their first meeting with the Chinese troops under Stilwell's command:

We had now come under the command of General 'Vinegar' Joe Stilwell, who sought to change our role to that of ordinary infantry and we were ordered to assist the Chinese to take Myitkyina, the airstrip having been captured already. The monsoon rains were getting heavier, the mud deeper and to add to our joys, we picked up leeches as we went along. The little brutes seemed to smell us coming, dropped off the foliage and took up residence. The procedure when we halted was to light a cigarette, take off pack, shirt and drop trousers, and dab the horrible things with the glowing cigarette end. They soon dropped off, but come the next halt, there would be another bunch to deal with. Where they managed to get is quite unbelievable, and modesty forbids me from saying!! As we were always sweating, large yellow blisters formed under the arms, round the waist and in the groin, smelling horribly when they burst. All the medics had to treat them with was talcum powder – and not my favourite brand at that – Old Spice.

Our first contact with the Chinese was nearly a disaster. There was no instant recognition and a shoot out nearly started as they were taken for Japs, but luckily was averted. We went into the Chinese camp and were surprised how comfortable they were. They had built long bamboo bashas which were lined all over – floor, walls, ceiling in clean white parachute cloth and it looked as if they had been there for some time, having a more comfortable war than we were.

On we went over territory through which the Chinese had driven the Japs, and there was plenty of evidence of the fighting which had taken place. Trees and bashas blasted by shell and mortar fire, empty shell cases and other war debris and Japanese bodies by the dozen, many grossly swollen as they decomposed and filled with gas, many badly decomposed, some were skeletons in uniform.

90 and 26 columns had been combined and could just about produce a company between them. Men were still going down, totally worn out or sick and were being carried on the two elephants we had enlisted. Wonderful creatures, they kept going through the deepest mud, walking non-stop all day long in a seemingly imperturbable way, and must have saved a few lives. Personally I had been extremely lucky. Apart from the sweat rash, a couple of jungle sores on my left leg, two cuts on the same leg from my own Dah which skidded off a length of bamboo I was chopping, a burst from a Japanese machine gun which rattled into a tree a foot above my head (told you they were lousy shots), and having a load of rations nearly landing on my head during an airdrop, I emerged virtually unscathed. I fully intended to finish the march and go out on my own two feet so did one of the other lads, Dougie Walker, his name was. He had malaria and now had jaundice. We pleaded with him to go out by Sunderland, but he refused. Nor would he ride an elephant. He said he had walked in and he was going to walk out. And walk out he did, straight into hospital where he sadly died.

So it was with relief and delight that we received the news that we were to make for an American airbase at Warazup, to be flown out. The march to Warazup, however long it took was over the same kind of terrain we had been on for days, except the mud got thicker, the streams wider, the rain came down incessantly. But somehow it didn't seem to matter quite so much. We had food to eat, plenty of tea, a hammock to sleep in, we were safe in friendly territory and most importantly, this bit of the war was over for us – we would soon be leaving Burma. A prospect nobody regretted. We felt as if a load had been lifted and we could relax a little.

The morning of our last day's march arrived, tomorrow we would be at Warazup. I decided to take a liberty and stowed away the Captain's and my hammock on the elephants, one hammock on each elephant, a little less for us to carry. We marched all day, I hadn't seen the elephants since we set off in the morning and duly arrived at our final night harbour, but where were the elephants? Where was captain McLean's hammock? I looked for a 'phone to make a trunk call!!! If he did not have a hammock to sleep in he would have me shot – or worse. Then, as nonchalantly as ever, in strolled an elephant with Captain Mac's hammock on board. Saved by the bell – at least I wouldn't be shot. No sign of mine though, but I didn't care. I wouldn't want the hammock after tonight, I could find a dry spot somewhere. And then, with that measured gliding walk, in came the other elephant. Well done Jumbo, I would sleep of the ground after all!

We were in the American airbase next day where a friendly Yank took care of each of us, seeing we got fed and watered and fixed up with anything we wanted. Gave us cigarettes by the packet. If you had to go to war – do it American style. These lads had just about every comfort known to man, decent beds, water-proof tents, coke, ice cream, a PX, a canteen, radios and a mobile cinema. The only thing they were short of was socks. I had three or four pairs in my pack, which I gave to one Yank, along with my panic map and trouser buttons compass. I felt I no longer needed them, the pilot of the Dakota should know the way to Assam.

We boarded Dakotas a day or two later and were flown to Shadazup and by road to a reception camp at Tinsukia in Assam. We went through the door of a long hut, handed over weapons and equipment and stripped off. We were given a large towel apiece and went into a hot shower. This was the first time I had had hot water on my torso for about seven months. It felt marvellous, I could have stayed there for hours. The hot water released all the accumulated muck in my pores and it ran down me in grimy rivulets. Then came a cursory medical examination, a trip through a clothing store to be issued with some new clothing. Tents and beds followed.

As Campbell discovered, the condition of the men coming out of the jungle was a cause for concern to many:

> I have one abiding memory of Tinsukia. After showering and getting dressed in baggy shorts and singlet, no shirt and still sweating profusely, we were offered 'Char and Wads' at what was probably an Indian WI tea wagon, manned by two ladies who were chatting to each other and having a laugh. As I approached the counter one lady turned to serve me and I saw the smile leave her face and she looked at me with disbelief, sympathy and pity written on her face. I had lost a lot of weight, all my ribs were showing, gaunt in the face and all over yellow as a canary through taking Mepacrine anti-malaria pills. Maybe she was thinking of her son or husband, perhaps still in Burma. Maybe she felt sorry just for me and the state I was in. I don't know but I remember that look.

It seems that even out of the jungle and removed from the danger of combat, lives were still at risk:

> We travelled to the railhead, driven by Kamikaze Indian drivers who seemed more intent on doing what the Japs had failed to do, i.e. bump us all off. I think they must have been given driving instruction on dodge 'em cars at a local fairground, then on by rail to Dehra Dun, a pleasant place in the foothills of the Himalayas. While we were there it snowed for the first time in living memory. (Norman Campbell)

Norman discovered that jungle service brought with it the constant threat of long-term illness:

> The battalion was sent on leave company by company to places in the hills, to Mussoorie, Naini Tal, Simla, etc. We had stopped taking anti-malaria pills when we came out of Burma in August 1944 and towards the end of September, I came down with Malaria. I had the original illness followed by six relapses, in hospital for ten days or so, out for three weeks, then in again and again and again… My trips to hospital caused me to miss my leave but after the third or fourth bout

I was sent on two weeks convalescent leave to Chakrata up in the hills. Of course, while I was there I went down again and finished up in the RAF hospital. I remember it was very pleasant up there, warm by day and cool by night. The air was constantly perfumed by the pine trees which covered the whole area and surrounded the hospital. Back to Dehra Dun and to two more spells in hospital in February and March 1945. Eventually I was cured.

Many men, like Pat McEvoy, took a self-effacing and philosophical attitude to their involvement in the Burmese campaign:

As a gunner I am merely a spectator of a war which the tanks and especially the infantry fight. My primary weapons are a pencil and a book of tables – there was a little story in our paper recently – one of our patrols ambushed an enemy tank out of which tumbled an immaculately dressed Japanese officer 'Excuse please, don't shoot, I am not a fighting man, I am an artillery officer'.

Norman Patterson took the opportunity to apply for a commission and recalls the interview process and subsequent training:

I can't remember where I was, somewhere along the line, the troop commander, a lot of the guys were going getting commissions, he said why don't you go Norman, I said ach, I'm happy where I am. Eventually I seen some of the numpties that were getting commissioned. You had to go down to a war office selection board in Calcutta and the Japs had cut the railway – it was a nightmare going down. You were on tenterhooks whether you were going to be attacked or what. Lying asleep with a revolver in your hand. I had three or five days in Calcutta doing the war office selection board and it was a morning to night business, up early in the morning, start, doing interviews and all the rest of it and doing problems. I always remember one problem they set up was the sergeant major set up word association, and he said there'll be 96 words and one will be displayed for five seconds and fifteen seconds to write down you immediate reaction.

We're going to Dhelli – oh great. So the Welsh were kicked out
of Dhelli to Singapore, so we went down to Dhelli – we all had our
own private villas. Its also who you know. John Stuart, a teacher from
Glasgow, became intelligence officer, I was a platoon commander in
Burma but I became assistant adjutant and Frank Martin – Frank
had a terrible impediment – phut, phut, phut. They ran day after day
patrol. Because I'd been out all day on patrol they left me to guard the
supplies, cause you'd mules and so forth. All hell let loose, everything
blasting and stuff flying over your head. I said Christ, what's going
on? And then a runner came round, he says, you've got to come up
sir. I said what's wrong. Ha said there's only Mister Martin left. What?
Everybody else had been wounded. There was only Frank Martin and
me. I couldn't believe this you know. One of those situations you're
horrified to find yourself in.

Used to have to speak Urdu. We used to have a Munchie, which
is Urdu for teacher and this guy, Tony Evans, a boy from Cardiff,
used to take it very lightly and this guy trying to teach us Urdu
from seven in the morning till eight, then we got wir breakfast. But
about 6 weeks before I was commissioned – he said 'How can I
teach you my language when you don't even know your own? Tony
was good at it, I was passable. You got a written and oral and not a
word of English was said. You were paired off with a British officer
and an Indian soldier and he spoke to you for about fifteen, twenty
minutes in Urdu, telling you about his life and all the rest of it and
then you had to question him in Urdu. I was really struggling when
half way through the British officer, he pulled a cigarette case open
and it was empty. I smoked socially then and they had sent me fags
from blighty and I had a tin so I spoke to him in Urdu and I said
take a cigarette so he took one cigarette and I said no, no, no, fill
your case, so he filled his case, so of course I passed. After the test we
were all gathering and Tony says 'how did you get on? You passed!!
How did you get on and he says 'I failed'. Because he never had any
cigarettes with him. I lied through my teeth on the application to
get to officers training school but I was horrified to find that one of
the senior officers in charge, he was from Dundee. I had put all the
crap of the day in my form.

I left the Leeds Rifles in Burma to go to officers training school. Saw them again, that's really amazing. At one stage, on the Burma road, was ##### who was a Padre, I think he was Padre with the battalion, and he came past and said 'your old regiment is further down the Burma Road. I said 'what are they doing away down there', you see. How am I going to get back to their camp, plenty transport on the Burma Road. So anyway, I went down, of course, I hadn't seen them since I'd been commissioned so it was the officers who entertained me and that was some night. So I thought 'stay overnight' so I did. When I went back the next morning to where I was based, I was waiting to go further up the line when some of the guys said 'you're in the shit'. Why's that? He said 'the adjutants been looking for you' 'Oh, what for?' he said 'to take the men on PT or something, I said 'oh Jesus'. I was up in front of the Brigadier. So he say's 'where were you last night?' and I telt him this story about being down and seeing the guys. He say's your lying through your teeth so I says 'with all respect I'm not' he said 'yes you are' he says 'you've been with a woman'. I'm saying 'I wish' you know. 'Ach well, it happened and that was it, part of your life'.

I was with the Leeds Rifles right through, until I was commissioned. I was with them quite a number of years, became a troop sergeant, senior sergeant. Well we went to Bombay, Bombay to Calcutta and we were under canvas on the racecourse there for a number of weeks. I went to Jabapour and collected the anti-aircraft guns. Then we went up to a place called Pourpour in Assam. It was fascinating because, where did they dig the gun pits to put the guns in – there was tea planters association, because the place was festooned with tea plantations, their committee came along, a number of people from their committee, and said, you can't do this – white people don't do this. The officers said but we have to do this. No, no, you tell us how many coolies you want and we'll do it. So we had to stand and watch them, aw, it was really hilarious. They took us up there on their broad gauge railway, to Gahattie, and then we went over by a ferry, like a Mississippi steamer, and then you went over, on to a narrow gauge railway which took you up to Inpour. And when we came of the boats coolies were there to carry the kitbags.

In India at the outbreak of war, working in the jute trade, James Tulloch was 'persuaded' to volunteer for the Bengal Artillery. The Bengal Artillery was then used as the core for the new 245 and 246 Medium Battery, Royal Artillery. James recalled his years serving in the Far East:

Sept 1940. 245 Med Battery formed, ex Bengal Artillery members. Almost immediately, infiltration of Anglo Indians.

Nov 1940. Proceeded to Barrachpore and became part of 6th Medium Regiment R.A.

Early 1941. 245 Battery was split and 246 Battery came into being. Members of Bengal Artillery in both Battery's. Major Corsar in command of 245 + Major Stevenson in command of 246. The batteries were issued with BL 6 inch Howitzers, relics of 1914–18 war. Ammunition was 100lb shell.

1941. The Batteries were transferred to Durtha where the 246 Battery was split and 247 battery was formed. Thus 8th Medium Regiment R.A. came into being comprising 246 and 247 Batteries. All batteries did normal training at Durtha.

The batteries were called upon to dig gun emplacements at Chaman on the Afghanistan border, these were never used. One morning at 8.am when 245 Battery was on its first parade of the day the big earthquake of 1941 took place and caused momentary confusion in the ranks. During the year drafts of men from home arrived to complete the batteries.

1942. 245 Battery was transferred to Ranchi prior to proceeding to Malaya but the Jap was to quick for us just running through Malaya and Burma result being, we were denied the chance of getting into action. After a short spell at Anchi the battery was transferred to Barasut a few miles east of Barrackpore. There we did some vigorous training during the monsoon. The battery was again transferred to Ranchi when we joined up with the other battery of the regiment namely 18th Medium Battery. About this time the number of our own battery was changed from 245 to 19 and for the first time in our career we were part of a full regiment under Lt. Col. Fox.

1943. The BL 6 inch Howitzers were then taken away and we were issued with the new 5.5 inch gun, 100 lb shells and maximum range of about 15.000 yards. Col. Fox then transferred half of the Bengal Artillery members to 18 Battery and replaced them with regular soldiers from 18 Battery. During the last 18 months many Bengal Artillery members left the battery to take commissions in other units of the British Army and Indian Army. About the end of 1943 came the time we had all been waiting for, going to Burma. The battery went by train to Madras where we embarked and sailed to Chittagong. During the short stay there we had quite a number of Jap bombing raids. Also at this time we lost a few senior NCOs and men, all Bengal Artillery members, to ordinance factories in India. From Chittagong we proceeded by road down the coast to the border of Burma where a number of troops were grouped prior to going into action. There, Lord Louis Mountbatten came and spoke to us. He said his two aces for the next push in Burma were ourselves and a regiment of tanks. The medium guns would be the heaviest that had ever been in Burma.

Jan 1944. We proceeded to our first gun positions, 18 Battery to the west of the Magu ridge and 19 battery to the east. To cross the ridge 19 Battery went over the Ngakyedanck Pass, a road of hair pin bends and 's' bends. negotiating one of the 's' bends one driver had to reverse and in doing so he lost control and the lorry went over the side down the hill, it went over so slowly that the gun team and driver had time to jump clear. The gun at the back was pushing the lorry and when the gun went over the side and the lot careered down the hillside until a tree stopped the lorry and the gun went through the lorry. Two days later that gun was in position alongside the others. For the first three weeks most of our targets were map reference harassing. During this time the gun that went down the hillside had a premature and one of the gun team was killed. The piece was blown to smithereens and I think we were very lucky to get off with one casualty. We were bombed once by Zeros and after the bombs were dropped these planes rose to about 10.000 feet and waited above us for half an hour, then they were chased by Spitfires. At the end of three weeks our O.P. called for fire and for a whole forenoon we were in action. The men were glad of a rest but it was not to be, a Jap 150 millimetre gun dropped 16 rounds on Dog Troop, 4 rounds within yards of each gun with the exception of No 4 gun which got a direct hit. I think there were five killed there including Bombardier James Wark, a Bengal Artillery member. That night Dog Troop was withdrawn about 2 miles and everything was left in the old position except the guns, it rained that night and things were pretty miserable, and there was small arms fire going on all around us. We discovered in the morning that the Jap had attacked 9th Division H.Q. about a mile from our new position. All that morning we were under continuous shellfire but no casualties. Jap was all around but no one seemed to know what was going on. One message on the telephone that afternoon was, stay put and fight to the last man. About an hour later that order was cancelled and we were ordered to proceed to the front of the Ngakyidawk Pass with all possible speed. When we started to move the fun started, Jap could see us slipping away and he opened up with small arms and mortars. Two guns were limbered up and ready, the BSM sent them off, the other two guns were stuck in the mud. It was then our monsoon training came to our aid and in a short time the third gun was ready and the BSM sent him off. It was here that an accident happened, right or wrong I don't know, the G.P.O. stopped the third gun and made the detachment dismount and line up and gave them all a lecture on discipline and finished up by saying no guns would move until he gave the order, he then ordered them to mount and told the sergeant to get out as fast as he could. The B.S.M. then got a lecture on discipline and note that both lectures were given under fire. In the long run I got away with the clothes I stood in and nothing else.

The next position was 'The famous 'Ainzwenga' Box' at the east end of the Ngakyidawek Pass where about 10.000 British and Indian troops were surrounded by the Japs and completely cut off from the outside world for 18 days. Quite a number of the troops there were non-combatant. The first night was a nightmare of small arms fire with tracer bullets flying in every direction but the Japs did not attack, the reason for this being our defensive box was in open country and there was no cover for the enemy to take us by surprise. We were not

long in getting organised there and a barbed wire fence with pairs of
cartridge cases hanging was erected. The guns were taken outside this
fence during the day and brought in at night. Every night was a 'stand
to' from dusk till dawn and nobody was allowed to move. Standing
orders were 'shoot first and ask questions afterwards'. One of our
signallers made contact with our other battery on the other side of
the Magu Hills and we called them into action to help our defence.
Life settled down and despite the bombing, shelling and sniping it
was quite pleasant at times, with long spells of quietness. Nights were
really bad; Jap had spotted our ammunition dumps and every night he
would drop mortar bombs on a dump and for hours the shells would
be exploding and there was a continuous hail of shrapnel. We ran out
of shells for the guns and a volunteer party was made up under Lt
Anson to break out of the box and collect ammunition which was
kept at our previous position. The party consisted of our men in Bren
Gun Carriers with Ghurkhas and tanks. The mission was successful
and without casualties. For the first few days food was pretty rough,
biscuits and bully at all meals but later the R.A.F. got organised and
dropped us quite a selection of food by parachute. In the supplies
dropped were cigarettes and even toilet paper.

Relief came to the box and all the troops were re-deployed and
19 battery enjoyed a fairly quiet spell, one position after another was
relieved until one day we moved to a spot just north of Buthidaung.
The infantry were only yards in front of us and the smaller infantry
behind. There we settled down to three weeks peace and quiet, even
the 'bull' commenced and gun and kit inspections were ordered. At
the end of three weeks one day at lunch time everyone was sitting
enjoying lunch (we could call it lunch, the food was excellent) when
an enemy shell dropped during which time a compass bearing was
taken on the gun and six rounds gunfire was ordered, no more enemy
shells arrived after that. But the game was on, Jap had infiltrated behind
us again. Orders came out, withdraw to the box again and we had
to take with us in our lorries a battalion of Queens Infantry. The
Regiment moved out, 18 Battery, 19 Battery and R.H.A. I travelled
in 19 Battery's last truck, a Ford three tonner carrying 60 rounds of
ammo (6.000 lbs) cookhouse and staff and 9 infantrymen, grossly

overloaded. About halfway to the box we came across an 18 Battery gun with trailer ruined by a mine and from the side of the road appeared Sergeant White and asked me to help him out with his gun. A few hundred yards away Jap had let hell loose with machine guns and mortars. Notwithstanding the 6½ ton gun was hooked onto the Ford and the gun team also clambered on and away we went in second gear. We were now running toward the Jap and I must record how an M.P. dashed from cover and signalled us to turn about, this was done under a barrage of machine gun fire, the truck ultimately got quite a few bullet holes but nobody was hit. We proceeded to a small deserted village about 500 yards away and everybody dismounted and I posted them at vantage points. While doing this the colonel appeared and told our drivers to turn the gun around so that he could get it into action, during this one gun wheel went into a slit trench. No tools were available to free the gun from the truck and we were well and truly stuck. However, with the aid of a tank we were soon mobile and by this time the few hundred Japs had been cleaned up. Infantry remarked 'we always thought you gunners had the easy end of the stick but after today I'll take the infantry every time'.

This was the finish of the Jap in Burma as an attacking force and with the monsoon approaching we were withdrawn to Ranchi again. Five months were spent there during which time all troops had a months leave and training was rigorous. In November 1944 we were again embarked for Chittagong, this was 4 years after the battery was formed and as active service overseas had been reduced to 4 years all the original members were to go home. On the day the unit moved to Burma, 80 members returned to Calcutta. This left not more than half a dozen Bengal Artillery members in 19 Battery.

Part Three

Africa

After his long sea voyage from Liverpool Ernest Jamieson found himself disembarking in Egypt:

> Disembarked onto a train which took us to Geneifa Camp on the Bitter Lakes where we were met by two officers at the station and marched into camp. Given a very welcome cup of grape juice then billeted in large tents sleeping twelve. Paraded next morning in tropical kit which were Boer War style collarless shirts and shorts with turn-ups which you were supposed to turn down into your long stockings to protect you from mosquitoes.

Ernest wasn't too impressed by the appearance of himself and his colleagues in their newly issued tropical kit:

> We all looked like a Music hall joke, Fred Karnos army. Finally there was good news: we had to go to the QM stores and draw new shirts with collars and pants were to be shortened by the Dhobi tailors and the topee was to be taken off and replaced by forage caps. Surprised to learn we had to keep our battledress uniform and overcoat but

were told it became very cold at night and during some seasons up in the blue.

Ernest wrote of his experience in North Africa:

The day had come at the end of November to go our different ways, our postings had come through. We paraded in alphabetical order and it turned out 'H' to 'M' were directed to 5 Company RASC. Fortunately all my close mates were there, Hardie, Hutchieson, Liddell, Johnston, Moyes, myself and some others. Two 30cwt Chevrolet trucks picked us up and for the first time saw the 'Red Rat' of 7th Armoured Div' sign. Arrived in 5 Company lines and taken to HQ where we met our OC Ernie Marshall. Bob Liddell and myself had to report to a gun truck which we had to take over with a Lance Corporal. It was a 13cwt with a bucket seat that worked on a swivel with a single Bren gun. Just as well the Italian bombers worked at 30,000 ft as we only fired the gun once in anger when three fighters came in low.

Fort Capuzzion fell with white flags flying all over the place. When the prisoners came out you wondered how so many could crowd into one place. They were just told to march back on their own until picked up further down the line. Christmas dinner outside Bardia. Before we ate cook said it would be a fine hot meal. He had found some mustard to put on the 'Bully' slices!

Carried on to Tobruk and Benghazi till the last battle at Beda Fomm where the Italians were finished of (by this time I was driving 30cwt Chevrolet). The Brigade which was badly depleted by this time returned to Cairo arriving there on February 23rd 1941. Moved into Mean Camp where the train terminals stopped just beside the Sphinx. Day pass into Cairo where I had a marvellous shampoo and haircut, then onto the Tipperary Club and finally 'Jackies Bar' for egg and chips and Stella Beer. Refitted with new trucks, Bedfords. Quite liked them though very warm as the engine divided the driver and co-driver seat.

When I joined 5 Company in the desert all my illusions of Beau Geste and the Foreign Legion vanished.

It was mostly flat with scrub we called 'Camel Tufts', but inland you did come upon high escarpments with deep gullies which looked like dry river beds. I always appreciated being well away from the coastal area. I never liked being in the main coastal road or Div-Axis Tracks as there was more danger of air attacks. I remember on one occasion when quite a number of punctures happened on the Track due to a German plane flying along the Track in the night dropping three pronged spikes which became buried in the deep rutted sand. They also dropped what looked like fountain pens. If you took off the top it exploded in your hand. Company orders were issued to stay clear of them.

We were back out of the line and static our CO would take out parties of five men map reading and taking bearings. He had a bucket seat fixed above the driver and he had a sun compass in front of him. His feet were placed gently on the drivers shoulders and would press left or right for directions and both for straight ahead. He would start by laying a map on the ground to get references and compass bearing and take readings on the compass. He would then drive the truck directly behind us and when we took over the wheel he told us to pick out a landmark in the distance: a large scrub or some rocks then make straight for it and pick out another landmark and so on. I enjoyed it very much.

It's a very harsh existence in the desert. Flies, shortage of water, extreme heat and cold. I remember one morning rising up to find the top of my water can frozen. When I was driving in the petrol section I used to put my bed roll down and sleep at the rear wheel. I woke up one morning, rolled up my bed roll and under it was a scorpion. Not a very good sleeping partner! The desert had its own beauty, the sunrises, sunsets, the moon when it was full. The stillness at night got to you. You could hear a match drop. It was said that was the reason most fellows spoke just above a whisper, you didn't have to raise your voice to be heard. There was an unhealthy side to life in the desert: sand fly fever, dysentery. I was fortunate enough to escape both but I did have desert sores. You get them on your joints, knuckles, knees, elbows, even today I have the white marks where they were – souvenirs.

Rumour spread that we were going to Greece but I think the fact that the Germans were now in Libya stopped that. Returned to the desert driving in the petrol section which followed the officer with the blue flag on his truck (white for rations and red for ammunition). Met up with echelon trucks and while loading tailboard to tailboard a dog fight started above us. One of the planes was hit and was coming toward us and crashed about 200 yards away. The pilot was descending by parachute and on the way down one of his flying boots fell off. He landed about 100 yards away – he lay very still and as we approached him he said 'Pommies'? he was Australian and he wasn't sure if he was in our lines or the Germans. When an officer came to pick him up he asked us to help him fold his parachute as it had saved him once it may do so again.

This was the period when we were trying to relieve the garrison at Tobruk. Every time you replenished, you went back to DID, loaded up and returned to your camp. One night we set off to make up a new dump for the tanks to follow through the next morning. We broke the wire at Kilo 40 (which formed the border between Egypt and Libya) we went through the gap and travelled some miles and made the dump and returned to our own lines again.

Next morning the tanks, mostly Matildas, went through the gap refuelled at the dump and went into action. By coincidence on our last push to Tripoli after Alamein the CO sent our trucks to this dump and recovered hundreds of gallons still intact which we had to dig out of the sand.

Our brigade took a terrible beating before Rommell finally retook Tobruk; practically all the tanks were lost at a place named 'Knightsbridge' but our tankies called it 'The Cauldron'. The heat was terrific and they ran into 88mm guns. My wife must have been very worried as months later I received a Sunday newspaper saying that the 4th Armoured Brigade had been annihilated. A number of our chaps had been taken prisoner – Corporal Percy tried to escape but was shot in the leg; another, Taffy Jones did escape and was picked up by an armoured car and returned to the company.

What was left of the Brigade was pulled back into Egypt for a time before being sent to the rear for a refit. A new company from home was coming up to take over our trucks, I was on the detail which went to pick them up at the last railhead in Egypt. Lieutenant Rapier was in charge. The new company was 10 Company whose OC was Lord Beecham's son. We nicknamed them the 'Shiney ten' because of their appearance.

It was a very hot day and all we were wearing were shorts and socks pulled down over our boots. There was a long line of shrub growing alongside the track so we pulled our trucks in alongside to get some shade as we waited for 10 Company to arrive. I was in my cab eating biscuits and jam being pestered as usual by hoards of flies when I noticed a chameleon in the shrub alongside so I picked him up and placed him on the engine cover in the cab. He soon got to work flicking the flies with his tongue so we both enjoyed ourselves.

When 10 Company arrived they were lined up and inspected, divided up and put in our trucks. Our canopies were open back and front to let the air through. After a very dusty ride we reached camp and 10 Company again were lined up and a driver allocated to each truck and for the next few days broke them in before handling over our Bedfords and picking up our new 3 ton Chevrolets. The chap serving with me told me that when their Major inspected them he said no one serving under him would go about looking like scruffs.

I told the chap that with the heat and the sweat and only a pint of water a day it would soon change. They were attached to 1st Division and after we were back at base we heard that they took a severe mailing in a Rommel offensive. Poor old 'Shiney Ten'.

I had heard of 'Jock's Column', but never thought I'd go out with one. We were settled down in camp when one morning I was awakened and told to form behind officers truck. There were ten trucks loaded with petrol. We set off and after a few miles met up with a laager. Thought we were just there to replenish, but were told to form up in centre of the laager. We knew then we were part of column. There were armoured cars on both sides of the column with 25 pounders and Bofors guns and ourselves with other trucks and ambulances. Next morning before we broke up into desert formation saw Brigadier Jock Campbell's open staff car. His Adjutant, a Major of the KRRC gave us a pep talk telling us he didn't know how fast we were used to driving in the desert, but when following Jock you forgot about broken springs and just kept the boot down. He told us we would be going deep into the desert then swing north and disrupt the German supply lines and communications. Our windscreens had to be taken out to stop reflection from the sun and moon. We travelled many miles then stopped to brew up and eat our bully and biscuits. We had all drawn our rations for seven days. I was travelling just behind Jock's staff car along with another petrol truck from the company driven by 'Old Ridge'. I'll just call him that as he was over forty and had volunteered for service. When I asked him why, he told me he had been a PT instructor and Sports Master at a borstal for young offenders from the east end of London. He had them out for a game of cricket when they started to argue and fight so he stopped the game and told them to bring the equipment back to the store. When he got there he was attacked. He said he picked up a bat and hit a few of them for six! That's when he quit. I believed him. We paired of and brewed up.

Carried on travelling till almost sunset and formed into a laager again. One of the petrol trucks off-loaded, replenishing the column. Next morning we travelled on until we reached a trig point. These trig points were cairns of stone that were used as map references. All our maps had been charted over a number of years. It was said that Rommel would have loved to get his hands on them. The Germans never moved far into the desert.

As Jock was taking the next bearing we heard a plane, and flying low over us was a Messerschmitt 109. He circled round then flew off. Wider dispersion between vehicles was ordered and we moved off at good speed. Later in the afternoon the expected happened, the Luftwaffe had caught up with us. Fifteen Stukas with fighter escort. We were spread out, the rear of the group was about a mile from Jock. The Stukas came down with sirens wailing, quite terrifying, diving down the soaring up after dropping their bombs.

Our Bofors were pumping away as they came down and as the dust cleared we could see a couple of vehicles had been hit and were on fire. We found out later that a Bofors gun and all the crew had been wiped out by a direct hit. Luckily none of my mates or their trucks had been hit. Before we set off again I had to pick up a sapper from the RE as his truck had been knocked out and a couple of his mates wounded. He had his kit and rifle with him. I told them to put them at the back of the truck but instead he dumped them on the co-drivers seat. I asked where he was going to sit. 'Outside', he said. As I had a Maple Leaf Chevy' he put his feet on the step and sat on the mud wing and put his arms round where the windscreen used to be, facing me in the drivers seat. I knew then he was 'bomb happy' and before long he was getting on my nerves. When we bedded down that night he wouldn't get into his bedroll. He kept wandering up and down the Laager until the guard took him over. Next morning he was sent back down with two empty petrol trucks and an ambulance with three wounded chaps.

Came to a large gully with a large escarpment on one side and a smaller one on the other. Jock parked at the top where there was an outlet into flat desert again. That night something rare happened; it poured with rain. One of the most miserable nights I ever spent. Next day word came that a German column had been sighted. The bad news was that they were escorted by two Mark III tanks and a couple of half tracks. Our 25 pounders opened up and quite a battle started. I climbed up the side of the gully and in the distance saw flame and smoke rising. Shortly after the shells started coming over and explode on the escarpment on the other side. I got down sharply into the slit trench.

After the shelling stopped I was cried up to go out and pick up a 2 pounder anti-tank gun and crew whose truck had been put out of action. I found them some distance out. The sight of the 2 pounder was damaged. The corporal and crew hitched the gun on the rear of the truck, picked up their kit and made back. The corporal was one of those chaps you didn't forget. He was slim built, very blond hair and walked with a slight limp. The crew called him the 'limping terror' due to a previous wound and was the holder of the Military Medal. After he recovered from his wound he was asked to take a base job but he refused. A real dedicated soldier. The crew said he had the MM but wouldn't be satisfied until he won a VC. I don't suppose he did but I'm sure he had a try.

The next morning I was cried up to see Jock who was shaving at the time. He asked me how much petrol 'old ridge' and I had left. I told him about half a load each. He then ordered me to go round the vehicles as we were about to pull out. I topped up my own tanks and kept three cases under my camouflage net in the truck, (all for self preservation). Before we set off, the gun crew, 'Ridge' and myself made a biscuit duff by breaking up our biscuits, stirred up in water then adding sugar and tins of Carnation Cream. Very tasty and filling (and sweet).

Set off back with much depleted column. A lot had been sent back previously. Pulled up just before sunset when three ME 109s came strafing along the column. They only made one pass, possibly because the light was fading or they had been trying for some time to contact us. We had been expecting them all the next day but we learned later that a large Malta convoy had been attacked. Maybe they were occupied there. No real damage done. Two fellows wounded, one in the hand and the other in the head. Next morning they were sent on ahead by ambulance but unfortunately the fellow with the head wound died on the way back. At last we reached the Div Axis Track on the road to Fort Maddelena where we were to disband. After travelling for a while saw a column of trucks moving up, Good Old Five Company. When we reached Fort Maddelena I told the Major that our company was on the way up as we passed. He told us we could leave at any time, so we unhitched the anti-tank gun, said goodbye to the crew and the corporal. We drove until dusk then we bedded down and continued up the track next day until we came on DID. Spoke to a Staff Sergeant and asked where 5 Company were camped and he pointed to a large group of vehicles on the horizon. We told him that we had been on Column with Jock Campbell and that we were out of emergency rations. We ended up with a sandbag each filled with tea, sugar, tins of sausages, pilchards, cans of milk and a large tin of jam. A real gentleman. Arrived back at 5 Company and reported to the OC. I don't think we had even been missed! He told us to draw our cigarette and emergency rations from the Q bloke. Nice to be back home again.

During our retreat to Alamein we stopped to await further orders when a KRRC officer came through followed by Bren carriers. He told us to get the hell out of it as the Germans were right behind and to prove the point, shells started dropping in our rear so we set off and as far as you could see tanks, guns, trucks and men were heading for Alexandria. One 'tankie' truck stopped driven by a Post Corporal who asked us if we wanted to send telegrams as he was heading straight for Alexandria so most of us paid him. You picked out certain sentences, (so much a word) such as 'safe and sound, don't worry', which at that time was ludicrous. After they left most of us thought they were going to have a good time in Alex with our money, however I received a letter from my wife saying she received it.

When we reached Alamein we stopped just past the rail station mixed up with 1st Armoured Division. Suffered a great deal of air attacks. One morning we were just leaving the cookhouse when ME 110s came in bombing and strafing – luckily the bombs fell in deep soft sand and you could see the bullets causing spurts in the sand. Not much damage done – I saw one of the most amazing air battles I'd ever seen. Eight Stukas approached escorted by fighters. The fighters were engaged by Spitfires and as the Stukas carried on and came down in their dive, a squadron of Kitty hawks followed them down and as they dropped their bombs and peeled out they were caught in a burst of machine gun fire and down they came. What a sight! One Italian fighter which had been shot up was coming down fast. Its pilot bailed out but pulled his ripcord too soon and caught his parachute on the tail rudder, and there he was, legs kicking as the plane hit the deck and burst into flames. Happy landings!

After some time we linked up with our Brigade again who were just alongside the Qattara Depression overlooked by Mount Himeimat. There were three minefields along the line, January, February and March and one was a dummy. When Rommel made a push to the south to outflank the line I was attached to the RHA. We withdrew to a rear position which was highly defended with anti-tank guns and artillery. When the German tanks came through they were met with devastating fire and they withdrew leaving many burning tanks. At night Chandelier lights were dropped above them and planes from the Fleet Air Arm came in dropping bombs and eventually they withdrew completely.

On the morning of 23rd October woke up to find hundreds of dummy tanks behind us made of canvas to fool the German reconnaissance planes which came over regularly. The famous barrage opened up about midnight. You could see the flickering of the guns for as far as the eye could see and the earth trembled like an earthquake beneath your feet. I dropped a whole load of 25 pounders and cartridge before the barrage ceased. After the infantry broke through in the north we travelled at night through the minefields which had paths made of railway sleepers and at about a distance of 20 yards were lights which were shaded, only throwing a glimmer of light to keep you on the track. Arrived at the north sector where Australian gunners were firing away and in the distance hundreds of prisoners being marched back by a few infantrymen, then began the long chase. Our Brigade was linked up with the New Zealanders coming of the main road and circling to meet us. We cut off a large force of the enemy at a place called Nofilis and what was most satisfying is that they were mostly German. That was the 16th December. I was still attached to the RHA. We had 4.5 NZ guns behind us. Our KRRC went into action. The Germans tried to break out, I think some did but the gap was sealed. The most astonishing thing happened next morning. It was still dark when we were all wakened up and the order came to brew up. We couldn't believe it but our officer said it was alright as the German airforce is too far away. Fires were lit in this huge circle. Amazing sight. Maybe it was to scare them. Next day 17 December we kept up the shelling and about noon this airburst came just above us, a range finder. We prepared ourselves for a bit of dirt. When the shells came over they were not HE but armour piercing, one ricocheted and passed through a truck, another tore through the signal truck aerial then suddenly it died out. They must have run out of ammunition.

Two Bren Carriers came up to us escorting about 50 German Panzer Grenadiers and left them with us. That night we held the prisoners in a circle gave them a tin of bully, biscuits and water. They had a young officer and three NCOs. The officer looked like your typical Aryan – tall and blonde and spoke perfect English. I was on first guard that night with five others and an NCO. Our officer spoke to the German who then turned to his men and gave them an order then they all burst out laughing. Our officer asked him what the joke was and he said that if they had to go for a sit down they had to notify the guard, for if they didn't they would finish up with two… holes!

One of the Germans had a button accordion and started playing and the prisoners joined in. The officer told us most of the men were from the Rhine and the songs were sung at wine festivals. Obviously 'Lili Marlene' was sung and everybody joined in, but the biggest surprise came when they sang 'Roll Out the Barrel'. The German officer told us they learned it from our own prisoners of war as they were told to sing as they marched to their POW camps. Next day empty trucks took them down the line. Auf Wiedersen.

On the latter part of the drive toward Tripoli, I was attached to 4th RHA along with other company trucks. A German desert aerodrome had been captured and the position consolidated. It was sighted on a plateau and from the top you could see for miles around. The Germans knew it was strategic as they had tried to retake it. The trucks were parked down in the valley on each side and we got to work digging slit trenches. Just as well as Stukas and fighters came over next morning bombing and strafing. Among other units the Chief Surgeon Captain Bell's Field Hospital was positioned on the plateau where tents were marked with large red crosses. My mate Tom Donaldson from Fife was with me – we used to say Tom was the best air raid warning you could have, we all reckoned he could hear the German planes taking off. When we saw him grab his helmet and rifle and dive into the trench we all followed. He took a dive at mid-day and sure enough they were over again bombing and strafing. Later that afternoon they came again by which time we had loaded our rifles with every second bullet an incendiary. As the fighters came in strafing low we all started firing. You could see the bullet soaring up but unfortunately off target. Still it gave you a bit of confidence. Word was sent back to the RAF for support but they were almost seventy miles away at Sirte. They told us they could only give us cover for a limited period. However, next morning they sent over eight Spitfires but about half an hour after they left, over came the Germans. This happened several times. I think the Germans had ESP. word came down to us to stop firing at enemy planes as we were more of a menace than they were. Very funny!

Our Bofors guns had run out of ammunition and some of our trucks were sent back to pick up some more. The present Lord Halifax was an officer in the KRRC and he lost both his legs in one of the bombings. I don't know if it's true or not but one of the medics told us he and some of his men dived into a previous bomb crater and this bomb hit the same spot.

The last afternoon we spent there the RAF appeared and some dogfights occurred. We saw a Spitfire trapped by three ME 109s – one on either side and one above. He came in low to practically ground level to try and escape. Our Bofors couldn't fire in case they hit him. The fighter on top caught him, sending him down in flames. Early next morning we had our last raid – just fighter bombers. Instead of coming down the valley they shot across the sides. One of our trucks which was parked in a small gully leading into the valley was put out of action. The bomb fell in soft sand in front of the truck, blowing in the radiator and engine.

The driver was in the slit trench alongside face down. His battle-dress was blackened from the blast. Very lucky. So it ended with Jerry withdrawing and us following after him.

I must mention this young man because his story was quite remark-able. After Stuka valley, we kept on the same track, which in parts was very rocky. To our left was open desert with escarpments in the distance. We came to a halt when we caught up with the German rear-guard. Three ME s came in from our rear dropping bombs. We dived for cover among the rocks. An armoured car was struck and two of the crew killed. As we lay there, we saw three figures approaching from the desert – a man and two women, the two women were dressed in the usual black. The man wore a turban and cloak with socks and sandals. When he came up to us we could see his skin wasn't so dark, but he did have a wonderful Valentino moustache and spoke good English. He remarked how glad he was to see we were British. The sergeant beside us pulled out his revolver and asked who the hell he was. I could see the women were frightened as they stood back behind the man. He opened his cloak and underneath he was wearing British shorts and shirt, a pair of powerful binoculars and revolver with belt and holster. From his breast pocket he took out his ID card which showed he was an Army Intelligence Officer. He told us he watched the Germans pass through, then he saw us appear and it wasn't until he saw the German planes bomb us he knew we were British. He lived with this tribe in the desert. He had a radio set and at specific times a Wellington bomber would fly over to transfer intelligence and drop supplies. Apparently he made trips to Tripoli at night where he made for an Arab burial ground to meet with other agents who gave him information on shipping and troop movements. He was born in Alexandria and his father owned a restaurant. I hope he survived the war. It also says a lot for the people who supported him.

On to Tripoli where there was a large Victory Parade. We moved on to Tunisia and on February arrived at Medenine. An RAF aerodrome was in operation about a mile from our camp when one night German bombers came over dropping flares then the 'ack ack' and Bofors opened up from the airfield. Heard the bombs drop then they came over low on the way back with the gunners firing tracer bullets towards the ground. They flew over us onto the 51st Highland Division lines where a Bofors sent up a stream of shells – we watched as they struck the first plane bursting it into flames and everybody jumped and cheered. We got an encore as the second plane came over at the same altitude and the Bofors got him too. Great shooting. You could hear everybody cheering right along the line.

I was sent back from Medenine to pick up rations from a third line truck. Just before I turned off the tarmac road to wait for the truck I passed a blown up RASC truck with two graves alongside. I should have taken this as an omen. I stopped at a place which was marked off with tape and an RE sign saying 'Clear of Mine' so I drove of the road and onto the hard sand. I dropped the tail board and waited for the supply truck. With me were Joe Hardcastle and Ben McKenzie, both from Liverpool. The supply truck arrived so I started to make a brew of tea. As the truck was reversing on to mine its rear wheel stuck in a patch of soft sand. Ben and the co-driver of the truck went to give a push and as they told the driver to give it the gas there was a terrific explosion. I was kneeling down at the fire when I felt this terrific thud on my back and was thrown forward. When I stood up and looked round, Ben McKenzie was lying on the ground, his leg badly twisted and his right thumb hanging by a shred of skin and the other chap had blood coming from a wound in his thigh where a pellet had pierced an artery. We did what we could for them and gave them a cup of very sweet tea. An ambulance arrived with a doctor who gave them both a jab and bound Ben's leg together. He looked at my back and saw it was badly bruised then told me how fortunate I was. A pellet had severed the buckle on my web belt and caused an indentation on the belt itself. He told me to report sick and have a complete check up. Fortunately. Everything was OK. We received a letter from Ben a few months later from Britain saying his leg was now 2-3 inches shorter than the other.

After Medenine on to the Mareth Line. On one side of the main road was the Perth Track, where the Guards Division were. The Germans had a large gun we called 'Big Bertha' which fired periodically from the heights above. When the shell landed on the Perth track it was like a clap of thunder, not that it did much damage, but it was certainly a nuisance. Eventually some Ghurkhas, supported by machine gunners from the Cheshire Regiment, went up and silenced it and brought back the ears of the gunners. After the breakthrough at Mareth we went along with the New Zealanders, past a minefield where the place was strewn with dead guardsmen and as Ginger Rawlands, a five foot cockney said, 'There lies the flower of the nation, they should have kept them on guard at Buckingham Palace'. On through Tunisia, past the holy city of Kairoan (I believe they made flying carpets there). Met up with our first Americans at a large railhead with long lines of goods wagons. As usual we saw a Staff Sergeant who was in charge and we gave him a list of the number of men we were drawing for. He just tore it up and said, 'Help yourselves buddy'! we backed onto the wagons and loaded up with KP packs and cigarettes. Pity we never had to call there again, but we did live well. Linked up with the First Army at Medjez-el-Bab, on to Tunis then back to Homs in Libya to prepare for Sicily.

Went on parade for the inspection of the 7th Armoured Division in Tunis by his Majesty, King George VI. Picked for the 5 Company contingent as you had to be five foot ten or over. Camped overnight before inspection and each man got three bottles of beer and as there

were some non drinkers, quite a good night for the rest. We paraded
on one side of the road with 16 Company of the 22nd Brigade opposite. Heard all the Hip-Hips down the road until the King stopped
in the middle of us. We presented arms, hats off then three Hip-Hip
Hoorays. Thought the King looked tanned, but on closer inspection
it looked like powder. Back to Homs for numerous truck and tool
inspections and visits by the top brass.

One good break was a night at Leptis Magna, the old Roman theatre where the star was Vivien Leigh (Scarlet O' Hara). The best turn
was by the Black Cat Division concert party. One of their officers did
a very good Carmen Miranda act. An order came round that all pets
had to be destroyed or given away. We had three dogs all belonging
to the cookhouse. Sheba, a desert dog picked up as a pup with no
signs of her mother, Sheila, a German Daschund taken from an Italian
officer during Wavell's campaign, and Trixie, a little black and white
mongrel. Sheila and Trixie were handed over to units staying on but
poor Sheba was shot. I thought it might have been better to take her
into the desert and perhaps found a mate. The company moved onto
Tripoli to board an LST with tanks below and us above. We reversed
our trucks onto a lift which took you to the top deck where you
fastened your truck with chains attached to the deck.

Arriving fresh from Liverpool, Pal MacLeod was destined to spend
the next three years in the desert:

We were there till the desert campaign was over. We were a workshop section, recovery and repair of all machinery. Anything that
was knocked out on the battlefield you had to collect it and bring
it in for repair. Anything at all, lorries, tanks, guns, anything, gun
carriages, anything with an engine. Everything had to get shipped
across and if they could repair anything there it saved sending new
stuff out.

You were working in sandstorms, you couldn't keep out of it and
you couldn't keep anything out. The sand would be crunching in
your teeth as you ate the bread. I got lost in the desert once for
two or three days, absolutely lost, in a sandstorm after the siege

of Tobruk. We were supposed to go through the corridor. On the way out we ran into a sandstorm. The workshop section was the last section so that anybody that fell out or any vehicle that broke down you took it along. A sandstorm came down and we lost the convoy.

I've seen it in the desert when you couldn't find the cookhouse from the mess tents.

Water was more precious than gold. A water bottle full every morning, that was to last all day. You couldn't taste or smell anything. I once drank the best part of a mug of paraffin without being aware of it.

We went up and down the desert there for three years, back and forth, back and forth. One time you'd be advancing the next time you were retreating. Until Alamein, that was the finish of that campaign. Then we went across to Sicily for the invasion of Italy.

Roddy MacLeod recalls carrying one of his wounded companions to safety:

Johnny MacIntosh was shot through the thigh and that was in the mountains, the only mountain range in the desert really. He was lying there and he was buggered, he could only hop along on one leg. So I says 'come on I'll take you out of here'. And he says 'you look after yourself Roddy if I'm taken prisoner that's it' I says 'I'm not leaving you here' and I dropped him over that edge of rock. I'm sure it was about twelve foot high. There was sand below and I held on to him to try and get him as far down as I could then dropped him. Then after that I carried him. I'll never forget as long as I live, the gully that I carried him down I hardly put a foot on dry land it was all bodies of Italians and there were a few Germans and that, but most of them were Italians. Gurgled when you stepped on them. But anyway, I got him off of the mountain and on to the flat below and I took one or two breaks. By this time the German machine guns, I was getting out of range and a bullet went through the heel of my right boot. Too close to be healthy.

1 Stuka dive bombers bombarded the retreating British Expeditionary Force as it fell back across France and bombed both civilian refugees and soldiers as they waited for evacuation from the Channel ports.

2 German artist's impression of the Dunkirk evacuation.

Above left: 3 Not everyone managed to escape from Dunkirk. Thousands of British and French troops were taken prisoner after the evacuation.

Above right: 4 German soldiers take the opportunity to examine an abandoned French tank after the collapse of France and the evacuation from the Channel ports.

Below: 5 Japanese tankers take a rest at the side of the road in Burma.

Clockwise from top left:
6 Major-General Orde Wingate – the motivating force behind the Chindits.

7 Wingate briefing pilots of 1st Air Commando Group in India.

8 Men from the Royal Scots during a river crossing in Burma.

9 Norman Campbell, who fought at Blackpool with the 1st Battalion, the Cameronians.

Left: 10 Norman Patterson in India.

Above: 11 Footlights. The players in Oflag 7b. This photograph demonstrates their ingenuity in making costumes.

12 The Big Band Sound. The camp swing band in Oflag 7b. Note the matching music stands and band 'uniform'.

13 Every prison camp should have one. The pipe band from Oflag 7b.

14 The Pipes and Drums ready for action. Oflag 7b.

Left: 15 Prisoners were able to buy musical instruments, paying by instalments, to help pass the time. Here we see Ian Rintoul and his colleagues – four 'likely lads'.

Below: 16 British troops get ready for the off. Preparations for the big event.

17 Assault craft. Note the metal doors set well back from the bow ramp, giving added protection from rifle and machine gun fire.

18 Preparing for departure.

19 It wasn't only the beaches that were dangerous. This picture shows a gunboat sinking off the beachhead.

20 Tank landing craft heading for the shore.

21 One of 'Hobart's Funnies'. A British flail tank lands on the invasion beach from an LTC (Landing Craft Tank). The chains hanging from the drum on the front of the tank are used to 'flail' the ground in front of the vehicle and clear a path through the minefields.

22 'Hobart's Funnies'. As a flail tank lands on the beach, part of another device can be seen rising from the body of the landing craft. This was a tank with a section of bridge mounted on front for clearing obstacles – the bridge section can clearly be seen towering above the LCT as the 'jib' is transported in the upright position.

23 Caring for the wounded as they wait to be evacuated from the beachhead.

Right: 24 Washing day for RAF recon'. Gunner Wilfred Pickles doing the laundry.

Below: 25 RAF recognisance unit on the way to Denmark having a rest at the side of the road. Note the American star on the armoured car and the RAF roundels on the trucks.

26 James Hogg and his crew with their Humber Scout car.

27 Time for a beer: just how many men can you fit on an old car?

28 Cleanliness is next to godliness: washing day in the field.

Above left: 29 A Group pastime.

Above right: 30 Scottish pastime – tossing the caber.

Below: 31 A squadron of British Shermans moving up.

32 A Bailey bridge and the original, destroyed by the Germans as they withdrew.

33 British Sherman tanks about to cross a Bailey bridge. Note the second bridge in the background with oncoming traffic – a one-way system is in operation to speed up movement. Civilians also wait to cross.

34 Tank landing craft lie off the beach and disgorge 'Buffalos'.

35 Buffalos heading for the beach at the Scheldt during the operation to clear the approaches to the port of Antwerp.

36 Buffalo coming ashore and climbing up the beach.

37 As the tide goes out, a line of Buffalos come ashore. It was this ability to come ashore whatever the conditions that made the Buffalos so indispensable. Note the armoured bulldozer in the foreground, used to create a path across the beach and deal with any obstacles.

38 Troops wade ashore from landing craft while the Buffalo is already on the beach.

39 The assault craft are beached at low tide while the Buffalos can run up out of the water and onto dry land.

Above: 40 Assault craft on the beach at the Scheldt. Note the windmill in the background.

Left: 41 Assault craft on the beach.

42 Stuck in the mud: note the American star on the vehicle, although it was used by British troops.

Above: 43 The beach
– centre background – flail
tank bogged down in the
churned-up mud.

Left: 44 Line of Buffalos
offloading – the troops are
still wearing their life vests.

Below left: 45 Offloading the
landing craft.

46 Landing craft had to be offloaded at the water's edge, while the amphibious Buffalos took their load directly on shore to where it was most needed.

Right: 47 Buffalo-eye view of the beach as troops are landed.

Below: 48 German prisoners are herded into this Buffalo. Note the two MPs at the front with drawn pistols.

49 Tank landing craft discharges its cargo onto the beach.

50 German prisoners were quickly put to work. In the background trucks are brought over on a pontoon.

51 Street fighting – clearing up pockets of enemy resistance.

52 Moving forward street by street.

Above: 53 Moving forward amid the rubble.

Left: 54 Grub up!

55 Still wearing life vests, the men of the Royal Scots stop for a 'cuppa'.

56 Long lines of captured German prisoners. Note the American star on the British Bren Gun Carrier. A lot of allied equipment was transferred between units as need demanded.

57 Wounded being
evacuated.

58 Moving forward
at the double. Street
fighting in Belgium.

59 Captured
German seaplane at
Hamburg.

Bill Edgar took part in Operation Torch, the invasion of North Africa:

The last sight I had of Britain really was on the train coming through Port Glasgow, put on a lighter and went into the Clyde and put on a trooper. I think that was October 43. The name of the ship was the Cathay, a P&O boat. We didn't know where we were going.

We landed west of Algiers at a place called Sidi Peruge, the 11th Brigade landed and then we pulled out and went into Allergies, we pulled out of there and went hell for leather further east to a place called Buge and the German Fockerwolfe Condor, they spotted us and fetched all their mates. They hit the Cathay but the ship was all right and we were put on landing craft and then the timer on one of the unexploded bombs went off and blew the stern of the Cathay. Getting on to the landing craft was in a ten or twelve foot swell and you would stick your arms out and two sailors would get hold of you and swing you down onto the deck of the landing craft with full equipment on. You were glad when you hit that deck. My mate and I we were the two smallest in the unit and he had the anti-tank rifle and I had the ammunition – not the lightest of things. If you wanted to lose something you just dropped it over the side as you were getting on.

I started with the 78th Division, we never seemed to be out of action, after we landed we were formed into a force called 'Hart Force' and went hell for leather towards Tunis. We had nothing, we called it the First army. Whenever anybody mentions the First army I say, 'I was the First army'.

We got to a place called Tabatta, just over the border from Algeria into Tunisia, and He came with his friends again. Ambulance planes we used to call them, black crosses. And he knocked hell out of us again. We would drill holes in a bridge and fill it full of explosives ready to blow in case he broke through. What happened actually was the Stukas who dive bombed us set the charges off and blew two great holes. Then we had to look for stone and stuff to fill the holes in and went up the road to a place called Sabat el Subilaba where there was a quarry. Coming back with the stone they strafed us – our corporal got one right between the eyes, the driver got his eye knocked out another chap got two bullets in his back. We were real bomb happy then. It's a terrible feeling when it knocks the sap out of you. They came with tanks then, we had nothing. We got the two-pounder. The entire brigade came up, that was the tanks, the buffs and the Argylls and they had two-pounder anti-tank guns and when they fired at them they were so light the stuff just bounced off. What they did, they got the 25 pounders up in their place and knocked them out straight away, open sights they did. Straight away, bang. The Germans used to say that our 25 pounders were belt-fed.

Roddy MacLeod forgot the old adage 'never volunteer':

So then we eventually ended at the front line and from there we did patrols and so forth. Then they was looking for volunteers to go behind the German lines and me, not knowing what I was in for, volunteered. And there was this Maltese officer who spoke seven languages and German fluently, so we were a week behind the German lines, we even passed Germans going to the cookhouse at night for their grub and gave them the password. He was brilliant really. All of us got back. It was at night we worked, you would be spotted during the day. And trying to sleep through the day. One time there was a wrecked Canadian Chevy behind the German lines and we all got behind it out of sight and the Germans seemed to miss us but we could see them, they were only two hundred yards away but they never spotted us, they never expected us to be there. When we got back the C.O. said 'Right, the men that volunteered get 10 days leave in Cairo', that was a bonus.

They had 21 miles of the front line to find out where the defences were and the troops were and how many were there and all that bullshit.

For Roddy, on leave in Cairo, leisure seemed to be as adventurous as fighting the enemy:

We had leave in Cairo. Anyway, I seen Tony Begg and I gave him a shout and he says 'get that carriage' (four wheel carriages that they use for taxis). I caught this bloody wog and I threw him off the bloody carriage and off with the horse and Tony was across the road and said

'come on Roddy, we're off for a race'. So of we went and I slashed
with the reins and went galloping of down the streets. We came to a
junction and I thought Tony was going to turn at this junction but
he didn't and of course I was trying to turn my bloody horse round, I
was tugging on the reins and the wheels caught on the two carriages
and the bloody 'tams' were sticking to the horses going down the
road. Big Tony grinning from one ear to the other.

A graphic description of the attack at Alamein is given by Ewen
Frazer:

The attack on the enemy strongpoint code named BRAEMAR shown
on the map by air photographs as possible company strength was
planned as a Night Attack by 'A' and 'C' companies, 1st Gordons.

In the five months since our arrival in North Africa and Gen.
Montgomery's assumption of command we had been training for
this action and in the last month unbeknown to us specifically for
this night attack. The desert at Alamein is generally flat, the smallest
incline which gives cover to a crouched man or machine gun/anti
tank gun is an important feature and grandly called a ridge. Our final
objective for the attack [code named Aberdeen] which was called
Kidney Ridge became a vital feature in the battle. Its exact location
became an important item of dispute between tank, artillery and
infantry commanders for days to come. The night previous to our
attack we advanced without fuss to slit trenches specifically prepared
for us as part of the deception plan. There, we spent a long day of
silent introspection, isolated, immobile in our trenches before being
released at nightfall to enjoy the freedom of moving one's legs, a hot
meal and contemplate final orders for the night attack, 8 o' clock for
10.30pm.

Thus it was with considerable relief we mustered, again in silence
on our start line, set out on white tapes on the desert floor in charge
of our intelligence officers, Lt Miller and Tyler, who could navigate
us to our objectives, laying out tapes and signs behind them in a very
orderly manner. We were beginning to feel the night cold after the
heat of the day and becoming a prey on our thoughts. Our morale was

high. We were physically and mentally strong. The unknown factor was how we would stand up individually under fire. This is said to pervade the thoughts of soldiers on the eve of their first battle. Our accoutrements must be mentioned. The weight seemed excessive to us because apart from carrying a day's ration of food and water, the entrenching tool to dig our slit trenches (shared between two), ammo for one's personal weapon, a private soldier's rifle and bayonet (which I preferred to the officer's revolver). We shared carrying ammo and spares for the platoon Bren gun and anti-tank rifle (which I think we later discarded). In addition we carried a pick or shovel each and as many of the excellent Mills hand grenades as we could stuff into the pouches on our chests. Someone in our platoon of 25 soldiers carried the anti-tank sticky bomb which could blow a hole in the side of a tank. It was the size of a child's football and very awkward to carry, however I never heard of anyone heroically stupid enough to apply it to a tank in the desert, though no doubt it was used elsewhere, in close country perhaps.

Thus we were sat uncomfortably on the desert floor in extended order at four yard intervals, companies 'A' and 'C' covering a 100 yards with rear sections behind, awaiting the big event. The biggest artillery barrage since the 1914/18 war opened up on time to dramatic effect. We hoped it would soften up our enemy sufficiently to gain our objective – they being dug-in, we on top of the ground we had mixed feelings.

This first barrage was an anti-counter battery fire to take out the enemy's guns. The second barrage we were to follow was to be a creeping one at walking pace, (100 yards to the minute) pausing at intervals on known enemy positions to enable us to overcome them before they had recovered. We duly advanced for an hour behind the 5th Black Watch to our start line proper without incident. There we found a wall of shell fire and our Bn. Cmdr. Nap Murray, held us up for ten minutes suspecting our own artillery falling short, which of course we knew nothing of at the time, thankfully. Our further advance has not been chronicled but was described as confusing, that is until 10 o' clock the next morning when our CSM got back to Battalion Headquarters from our objective on Braemar. Our strength was then reported as down to three officers and 60 men in our two companies. Our full strength of two companies was over 200. In our advance we had missed an intermediate objective called Kintore and this was to cause problems for those behind, especially 'B' and 'D' companies who we expected to come through us on Braemar as well as the tanks and their mine clearing teams and move on to our final objective on Aberdeen. 'B' company for instance whose duty was to get the tanks forward, found an enemy gap in their minefields which our tanks refused to use: much frustration. The gaps of course being narrow were very dangerous. The enemy put much reliance on mine laying and it served them well. Fortunately later, in front of our objective on Braemar we were to find they had laid anti-tank mines NOT anti-personnel, so when you jumped on them you were disconcerted, but safe.

I can only describe our advance and attack as a jumble of fleeting incidents. Generally we kept up our steady advance through the shell fire until forced to go to ground when the shout would go up to keep going. Considering the amount of shells exploding among us it amazed me how light our casualties were at that stage, soft sand no doubt helped.

The dust kicked up by shell fire was so bad and visibility so bad and fleeting, my chief concern was to keep our lines straight and keep our boys from straying off course. I am ashamed to say on one occasion I joined the hands of two of my soldiers to impress them to stay together. A glance to my right in a shaft of moonlight showed me a section of Aussies strung out in the best of good order, very encouraging.

Suddenly our advance was halted in the centre by extremely heavy point-blank rifle, spandau machine gun and mortar fire causing heavy casualties and stopping us in our tracks. Fortunately my platoon was on the flank of the enemy's position and my right hand section with Corp. Dunlop and Pte. Neil to the fore, took them at the charge with rifle and bayonet and killed the seven occupants and took over their position. I immediately returned to company headquarters to find Cpt. James McNiel, my company commander, badly, and indeed, mortally wounded and our attack grounded. I covered him with my jersey, told him the attack had succeeded and tried to compose him. We were clearly in the killing zone of the enemy platoon's position with the sections over the ridge bringing down accurate mortar fire on us and causing more casualties. We had to put a stop to it, so I told acting 'C' Coy. Cmdr. Lt. Harry Gordon, to give me a short burst of Bren fire on the enemy position we could see and I would attack it from our flank forthwith. It was quite straight forward. I threw my grenade on target and my section rushed them with rifle and bayonet. At the last minute one or two attempted to surrender but it was too late for them and the position was taken without further casualties. This improved our position with less fire coming in from mortars in their rear section. They were clearly cowed but would have to be dealt with sooner or later.

As senior surviving officer in the two companies it became clear to me that being in a tank minefield on the enemy's forward slope, we would have some protection in the event of a counter attack. Thus we followed our drill and started digging in to await the dawn. None of us felt very good taking such casualties to achieve so little, but getting down to a familiar routine helped to relieve the stress.

Our close formation advance, which had got us on our objective so accurately had closed up our ranks and needed dispersal urgently into a normal company defensive position. This was easier said than done as all ranks were thoroughly shocked: some who were short of weapons or ammunition were reluctant to take it off the dead and wounded. All weapons had to be cleaned of sand or blood and made ready for action. Much shouting and admonishing was handed out and taken in good heart. Fortunately as far as I can remember digging conditions were not too bad and we were reasonably well dug-in by dawn. We had forgotten about 'B' and 'D' companies not coming through us by this time, but not about the relief of our wounded who had to stick it out until mid-day. At dawn, as was my habit then and later, I moved forward out of curiosity, its called a recce. I found a small enemy artillery piece unattended. And stupidly I thought I should turn it round, facing the right way. Unfortunately it stung a response from their rear section and reminder me they were firing with real bullets. While I was thinking what to do next, such as bringing out two inch mortars into action, manna from heaven our artillery officer popped up beside me and within minutes put down a salvo near enough them to make up their minds to surrender to us – maybe a dozen, only one wounded. Unfortunately Sgt. Stevens from 'C' Company came up to help bring them in and was immediately killed by a burst of enemy spandau fire from the flank, which also wounded one of theirs. Someone fired from our ranks and an altercation sprung up about finishing them off. My view prevailed and they were taken prisoners.

A harsh clanking noise announced the arrival of a large German tank, stopping within ten yards of my forward position. Out of sight I dived into the nearest trench we had taken and feigned dead, which I thought I would be soon. More manna from heaven, with a great thud it was struck and went up in flames, its crew scattering. Our tanks which were supposed in the Plan to be forward of us and which I'd forgotten about had struck in time from the rear. Thus by 1000 hours we had taken control of the enemy platoon position of the 164 Mountain Division and were unobserved by ground fire, though our whereabouts was signposted by their stricken tank which attracted sporadic fire during the day.

My military dictum 'The winner is the one who makes the fewest mistakes' was laid on the line even if at times it cruelly exposed our human errors that had caused our casualties, there was no flinching. We believed in the survival of some of the fittest, with a lot of luck.

The first morning on 'Aberdeen' we were relieved to see we were well positioned with a good forward view of the hollow within the so called 'Kidney Ridge'. The first excitement was the sight of 20 plus panzer tanks withdrawing across our front at a distance of 500 yards. I got our Forward Observation Officer up quickly but too late. We had no 6 pounder anti-tank guns with us. We spent the night attempting to wire in front of our position, not a popular job, no mines available.

I marked the position of a Panzer tank which had been knocked out previously 500 yards to our right flank to prevent its recovery by night, their usual routine. I set up our Bren gun on a fixed line to affect this. I was overruled by the new Battalion Commander who ordered we send out a fighting patrol that night to prevent its recovery. My mistake was to order my platoon sergeant to command this two-man patrol. I failed to realise he was too shocked to leave our position. He refused my order. Then I had no option but to repeat the order. I then ordered him back under close arrest to Company Headquarters. I took out the patrol myself with Cpl. Dunlop, whom I made up to sergeant. We got out and back without too much trouble, but achieved nothing. The tank was missing the next morning. I learned that never in future to order patrol leaders, but to lead them myself and to choose members more carefully. Effectively I would have to do this myself.

Third night on 'Aberdeen' we suffered artillery casualties when a botched night attack by 4th Royal Sussex planned to pass through our position, mistook us for the enemy before getting forward. Two of our soldiers at Battalion Headquarters were killed. One Royal Sussex Fusilier was killed on my position by shell fire and died in my arms. As a Lorried Division the 44th had not had our thorough night attack training. They were not lacking in spirit and did not deserve their failure.

My morning recce observed 400 yards on my right three khaki figures running to the rear. When I got over alone (a mistake), I discovered a 6lb anti-tank gun in prime position aimed to its right overlooking a melee of our infantry (approximately 30) drawn up to surrender to five Italian tanks, swanning around. I got into an aiming position behind the gun with a tank in my sight, before second thoughts took over. How quickly would I reload and get the second shot in? What would happen to the men who had given up? Perhaps the gun crew who had deserted were right. I returned to my platoon in low spirits. There was a lack of control on 'Aberdeen'. That night I think we had a German half track run into our wire in front, much to our surprise. A voice shouted 'hello'. An Italian I thought. I repeated it but a long silence followed so I ordered my left-hand section to get behind it's back. All had their heads down and didn't hear my voice. Thinking I heard it's occupants getting out of the vehicle I hurled the grenade at what I hoped was its rear. All I succeeded in doing was to set it alight and illuminate my position for the rest of the night. In it were the rations and comforts for our enemy.

A loose cannon in the shape of a small scout car crossed our position at speed. Unfortunately the left-hand section was asleep. Pte. Connelly was killed in his slit-trench and his mate Pte. Buchan badly shaken.

Our last night. It was my turn to fall asleep on duty. The plan was to vacate our position in case the artillery fire-plan misfired and shelled us again. There was every reason to stay awake. The next thing I was being woken up by an excited runner from Company Headquarters to say the barrage was due down. We all belted out in a disorderly squad behind the runner. We joined in a long route march to the rear, near knee deep in desert dust, like white-coated ghosts we seemed to be walking for miles. No doubt some were asleep. When we finally halted and stood-down most were in such a state of exhaustion what when beer war offered as far as I remember only four of us joined in. Next morning, the 4th November, we heard the enemy had gone and the battlefield fell silent. Somewhere rear echelon troops stirred. No doubt searching for loot and going up on the odd mine, much to our amusement. The last thing I remember was Sgt. Dunlop calling my platoon and bringing them smartly to attention for my inspection. Of the two lines drawn up in the desert only the front line of six had made it through the ten day battle with me. They looked slight figures, tired and grey, but amazingly smart and proud. A chirpiness returned to the ranks and Pte. Edwards I think called out 'We did it then Sir'. He was not being boastful and I choked.

A more graphic description of death at Alamein is given by Roddy MacLeod:

My section commander was a corporal Morrison and he got killed at El Alamein. He lived for about quarter of an hour and he said to me 'Roddy, don't let this happen to those other young fellows that's with you'. I say's 'I'll try my best'. He asked me for a drink of water and I gave it to him. He say's 'what's my mother going to say when she hears this'? Then he conked out. It was a Sherman tank went up in front of us got a direct hit and I sheltered behind it because there was machine gun fire, that's what got the other boys. The fucking thing got a direct hit, and inside the turret of the tank was incendiary shells for setting places on fire and they fucking lit up in the tank and they all got burnt to death and I was lying beside it, and I could hear them screaming blue murder.

Then big Alec MacLeod, a big strapping fellow, a good six foot one I would say, a finer bloke never walked shoe leather, and he got wounded so myself and Roddy turned back to see if we could do anything for him. He says 'no I'll be all right. The stretcher bearers will take me back'. 'You fellows carry on before you miss the rest of the boys'. Because there was smoke and cordite everywhere, Christ, you could hardly see ahead of you. So we carried on and didn't go 25 or 30 yards when a shell dropped beside him and killed him. If we had stayed there another one minute, boy that was us too. Too bloody close.

Part Four

Europe

Unfinished Business

Ian Rintoul was taken prisoner while serving with the BEF in France and began the long march into a captivity that was to last five years:

> There was no mention about meals. I don't know how we kept going, as we hadn't eaten for days before the Germans captured us, and it was days on the march before we were taken into a field, a horse was brought in and the next thing we heard was a shot, but we had a lovely stew that evening then back on the road marching again. We didn't have watches and didn't know the time but after marching for some time, someone said, 'that looks like a river about a mile further on'. The lad was right, it was a river, and there were quite a few little boats sailing there. We thought we were going on a boat, but all we saw were barges, about a dozen of them. We were herded on to these and they were filthy. My army pal heard someone say the people on the little boats were having a picnic. He said, 'wait there Ian, and I'll

see if there are any sandwiches being handed out'. It was then I realised this was Dutch water we were anchored on. The barges were almost full and one of the guards shouted to us to sit down. We were moving and when he returned he could not get back on to our barge as it had gone. Well, it was 40 years before we met up again, 'what a reunion that was'. We had then marched from the borders, been on barges and again walked into Germany and taken to a prison camp. This took us approximately six weeks and a journey of over 200 miles.

Ian discovered that in the prison camp you were expected to work:

In the prison camp if your number was called you were allocated a certain job. I was working in a Sugar Beet Factory, unloading railway wagons filled with coke and various other jobs. We worked a twelve hour day during the week and an 18 hour day at the weekends, we didn't get a big meal just a piece of sausage and three potatoes which hadn't been properly washed, I thought I was lucky one day, I had an extra potato but it turned out to be a stone. So much for hygiene!

Stalag 9C was the camp to which I was allotted. Stalag working camps were run much the same way. In the morning you were all called out on parade to be counted, if they counted correctly and the total was OK, no escapes overnight. After roll call we had to listen for our POW number, my number was 717. I will give you an example of one of the jobs that you didn't know about until you arrived at it. Someone was having a bungalow built. Two lads and yours truly were sent to dig the trench for which had been previously marked out. It was a nice change of job, rather than being sent down to the railway yards again. We didn't manage to finish the drain digging, so got another day to complete the job ending in the afternoon. The boss on the job was quite pleased with what had been done. We were nearly three years captive by now and were all wondering how much longer we were to stay in captivity.

After three years in captivity Ian was transferred to an officers' camp to act as an orderly:

Well, one morning about six of us had our number called out and the rest dismissed. We were told we were being moved to another camp. We were sent back to our billet to collect our belongings. We were put on a lorry and taken to our destination, quite a journey, this time to Bavaria, but it was worth it. The camp we entered was Oflag 7B a British Officers camp and we were to be their orderlies. Life started to get better from then on, regular meals and exercise if you cared. Next morning we went to the officer in charge of orderlies, who directed us to the room where we were to work. A few of the officers in the room were from our own regiment. The senior officer in the room told me what I was expected to do. Sweep out and collect rations from the cookhouse.

There were rumours going round that the Americans were pushing forward. One morning being counted we were told to get our kit ready, we were moving out. As we were marching, we heard planes in the area. Then all at once, this American plane started firing and I didn't hang about, I got behind a house, unfortunately there were a few wounded. The pilot thought we were Germans on the move. We were then taken back to the camp. The next morning all the guards had gone and the gates were left wide open.

What a sight it was to see the Americans streaming in and what a reception they received. In a few days lorries arrived to take us to an airfield where we were fed and told we were being flown to France (RUEON) and from that Dakota we waited for the Lancasters that took us to England. On arrival there, we were transported to billets. We were told to go for a walk and to shake off the thoughts of a guard walking behind us. We thought that way for some time, it was very hard to do so after five years imprisonment.

Iain MacAuley also spent time in captivity:

During my service I became a prisoner of war of the Japanese in Java and I ended up in Sumatra. From there I helped to bury 1800 of the 2000 men that I went to Sumatra with. I sat with most of them at one time or another and we held hands and I eased their passage into eternity. Strangely enough, all of them died with a belief in God.

There didn't seem to be any atheists there. War sees many faces and many things happen.

After his capture in Belgium Charlie Smith was taken to Poland:

I was captured at a place called Lauvan. We were taken to a railhead and put in cattle trucks and transported for a couple of days to a place called Thorn. That was in Poland. And we were put in marquees in Poland, they had no place to put us. They just took some of the Highland Division boys there.

And this German officer came round the camp, he spoke as good English as we do. He says 'It's very unfortunate you have been taken prisoner of war but you must remember that you were up against the might of the German Army'. Ha says 'We're just about in Paris and after we take Paris we're going to make our way across to Britain'. And this is how sure they were. He says 'If you've any letters to deliver to your loved ones we would only be too pleased to deliver them'. As I said, this German officer gave us a dressing down. We were on the march for about ten days without food.

The British officers said 'now if the Germans come along and want you to work, by all means go and work, because that way you'll get food'. So I went out on a Commando, it was a building Commando, just stacking bricks. Then the farmers were needing men and I went on farms and I went in a sugar factory in Danzig. Making sugar out of sugar beet. We were paid hundreds and hundreds of Marks, worthless money. That was Marianburg, that was the major camp, camp XXb. There was a thousand of us in that camp. Poles, Serbs, French, Belgians and British. In the same camp but separate huts. We had the guards with machine guns all the time. At night, for sanitation, they used to put a barrel outside the hut and you done your business in that, in the barrel. We were watched all the time because the searchlights were going round. You got your role call twice a day to see that everybody was there. They used to come round counting everybody, the whole lot of us. Then they would dismiss us. In the afternoon you got a piece of bread. We started off with four to a loaf. When you got the loaf the other three men were with you and you measured it there and it was cut. By the end of the war it was eight to a loaf. You got a bit of sausage, a bit of margarine and that was all. It was all cooked for you.

And of course by going out with the commandos you ate with the German civilians. You were trusted to leave the camp, maybe about ten men, and it was all small hamlets round about, one prisoner to a hamlet. That was alright. We used to be taken down to the German farmer, and I sat at the table with his wife and his kids and ate the same as them. I went from there to a railway, on the sleepers, on the track. My mother used to knit woollen socks and sent them over through the Red Cross and I used to go to the German civilians and ask them if the wanted to buy them. I used to ask for a loaf of bread and a dozen eggs for them. Then I went to forestry work. Digging out big boulders out the ground and rolling it down to the road because they were helping to make the Berlin/Danzig road. We noticed while we were digging out these boulders, women walking about amongst the trees with baskets. They were looking for mushrooms but they weren't just looking for mushrooms, they were burying food for us. You would watch these civilians and you would say to the guard 'can I go to the latrine'? and you would to the tree and there would be something there. Then I went to a sugar factory in Danzig. My job on that Commando, all I had on, I had on a pair of short pants on, no vest, nothing on my legs, nothing on my feet. All I done was keep the sugar, it used to come down the chute, it used to stick, and I had a sort of a scoop and I used to keep the sugar running all the time. You got good food for that. It was eighteen hours work at the weekend. When the snow came we were sent out to clear the streets and keep the traffic going.

The Germans at this time were falling back. The Russians were shelling them. That was the second forced march. They moved the camp altogether. It was another forced march just like at the beginning. It wasn't a march, it was a straggle. The guards knew the war was over for them but they couldn't desert. At that time we could hear the American guns and that night we were in this big shed on straw and that and in the morning there was a lull, the guns had stopped, and we came out and all the guards were gone. And then the Americans took us back. April 1945.

The Med'

After his specialist training with the RAF, Ian Cameron was posted to the island of Malta and suffered the deprivations of the 'Siege'. He experienced the air raids and the food shortages and understood what created the spirit of the 'George Cross' island.

The system there [RAF Wigan] for picking for overseas was 'last in first out'. So, the squadron had been asked for so many recruits for overseas. There was an English boy greeting because he had to go overseas so we tossed and I went. Landed in Malta. The officers were hopeless there, literally, the admin – they put us in this chateau type of place, 250 of us, two toilets. The older boys said 'to hell with this'. Everybody had dysentery – the place was overrunning with shit everywhere. Nobody did anything. So we went up to the village and just disappeared for a while. It was cruel the way they did things. Petrol came in four gallons and there was an old railway tunnel in Malta and they filled it with these tins. When you went in there you could hardly breath for fumes. We got up in the morning and you were supposed to trundle all this stuff into the tunnel and pile them up, so we did one shot and then disappeared. Come back in the evening. We just disappeared to the boozer or someplace. Just disappeared for the day. Everything was comic, it was like comic cuts kind of thing. We used to go to the same place for fish and chips with three retired prostitutes from Malta and they were all like Michelin adverts and their boyfriend was a homosexual with purple piping round his jersey. A thing I'd never seen. We went along quite regular so they invited us up for Christmas. We didn't know what was going to happen to us. We went along and certainly they fed us and then the three dames jumped us. Great big women, God we were terrified, scared out our wits and the boyfriend wanted McNamara to go upstairs with him. They gave us a treat, God it was terrible. We made our escape. They would have eaten us alive actually.

It was quite good. There was air raids but nothing special. And the airfield had been flattened the previous April. There was nothing standing. All the hangers, everything was smashed. There was no tower, they just conducted it from the ground. The Germans arrived, everybody had been expecting them back. God it was hell. I was caught in the middle of the airfield. I was worried, not so much about the bombs coming down – it was all the shrapnel and nose caps and everything. So I sheltered in a place thinking 'this will do me' never knew where I was, and in the morning I found it was a dump of anti-aircraft mines for putting out on the airfield, you put them out on the runway to prevent enemy planes landing. There were plenty of air raids and every body ran away, literally. But by that time you always carried your knife, fork and spoon in your side bag – they were getting scarce. So Jock Gluckman I think it was, from Glasgow, when he ran he forgot to take his side bag with knife, fork and spoon. So he went back and was throwing things around looking for the bag and got his name taken. He thought 'God, I'm on a charge', no, he got mentioned in dispatches. All the wee boys are always very brave let me tell you, the smaller they are the braver. He got excited when you were firing. You'd be in the slit trench and he'd jump out fighting. There wasn't anything of course. You couldn't hit anything with a rifle. Him and a chap Brendan, from Motherwell, were always beautifully dressed. They went over, hitched a lift to Sicily, and the Yanks were there, so they took on the Yank army, landed in jug, there was an air raid and they escaped, so they caught them again and took all their clothes away, then they flew back in a pair of shorts, lost their boots. They lucky sods, they got put on a aircraft going home.

You never saw an officer. When the blitz started in earnest it was bloody hell. You got bombed five, six, seven times a day, every day, all night and the weather was foul. You were still getting food, you couldn't get sleep. The boys started sleeping in the deep shelters, slept in the sewers, all sorts of places. Discipline slowly went, never saw an officer. Folk didn't bother coming in, boys were staying in the deep shelters 24 hours a day. Frightened to come up. One air raid was 24 hours. I has claustrophobia, I couldn't go down there – it was a killer 'cause when you were down there you didn't see anything and the noise was terrific. A bomb dropping a mile away would make you think it was next door. So I stayed on top. I lay on my back, funnily enough, and looked because you could see what was going on and you weren't so frightened, you could see the bombs dropping and everything – see them coming. You never saw anybody, our sergeant was yellow. So he used to want to run to the deep shelter. We wouldn't let him go. Used to stand with our back to the shed. He used to beg us to let him go. Then we would let him go and he would run like a bloody hare. Then after he would say 'go and have a look at S43' or something and they would just say 'fuck you, do it yourself'. Then he would plead. The Scots boys were a lot of show-offs, naturally, so he would turn to us and say 'jock, your bomb group, will you do it?' 'cause there was the bomb happy that wouldn't do anything and the bomb group that could do things. When you walked round the field you kept your eyes open for every rut that you could jump in, you went in pairs. One boy stood outside and was supposed to tell you what was going on while the other boy went inside. But the place was littered with bomb holes and unexploded bombs and eventually we couldn't cope and were short handed, even the aircrew had to go out with pick and shovels and then the prisoners came out from the jails and the women came up as well – Maltese prisoners. Brave folk. Our lot were so demoralised, the Maltese labourers would be jeering at them fighting their way down the deep shelter. It was a bit disgusting.

They sent out clapped out aircraft, bloody shame. So they sent out MK 1 Hurricanes against the ME and 88s. Clapped out Hurricanes couldn't even catch the bombers. It was horrifying. They would send out 20 and a day later you maybe had four or five, shot down, blown up, strafed, everywhere, they never learnt the lesson. Sent more and more, totally useless. Then they sent Spitfires, again, they would ask a Squadron to send planes and they sent their worst of course. Guns weren't lined up, they would land and we were supposed to do them over. 50 came in one day, twenty-four hours, I think there was only 5 left. The Germans came down like a ton of bricks. They never learnt their lesson. The rumour went round that the aircrew mutinied, we never knew anything, no radios, no papers, no information, no officers. We never had pay parades because you never had money to spend. Nowhere to buy any bloody thing. Then there was rows about food. You got about 9 – 10 ounces of bread a day, which you needed because there was no potatoes. So, hell to pay, so an officer sat with scales and you all walked up and he measured out your bread and that was your days ration. You just put it in your battledress. Then the food went scarce. Half a sausage for breakfast. half a tin of bully beef, or a slice of bully beef for lunch, no potatoes or anything. The same for tea. It got so bad they issued ration cards. Everybody got a ration card. You had to produce this when you went for your breakfast or whatever. And the cook marked an X on it. So naturally the boys went back and rubbed the Xs right off. Went round twice. The next step was they pushed a hole through and the boys would go back and tamp it out with the back of a spoon and go back round again. Then some bright spark decided to cut a hole and folk were going round collecting the wee circles that were punched out. Eventually some brilliant intellectual in the cooking department decided what they would do was number from the bottom up and they would cut it off. But you could still go out for the day if you wanted. You had to get a leave pass and this allowed you to go to the Maltese kitchen and get bread. Naturally the boys pinched those passes, wrote them out, then sent scouts out to get bread. That soon stopped, then you had to have this censors stamp on it, what they did was get the linoleum and carved it but they decided they would have to get the real censors stamp which was no problem, someone stole it from the safe took the impression and put it back. All the young boys were greeting when they got their food, next to nothing, a handful of peanuts. At the end of the evening, this is the sickening bit, all the scraps, like cabbage stalks and all that was boiled in the evening and if you were on night duty you could get a cupful of this stuff. But there was so many folk congregated that weren't on night duty at all – they filled up the zinc baths and slid them into the middle of the canteen floor, it was really sickening, boys were taking handfuls, others more or less dived in these things, some of them would carry a handful down to someone who was sick, like animals fighting for scraps, unbelievable – absolutely sickened you.

Night duty, you couldn't sleep. There were air raids all night, sleep was almost impossible. There was always folk trying to land at night. There was no electricity, we had to place goose necked flares down each side of the runway. And at each end of the runway was a long slit trench with armour plating on top and you went in there with some officer who was controlling everything. And the one I was on with went trench mad, he pulled it back when our lot were coming in and he would fire flares to try and get the Germans to come in first – they followed our lot in you see, shot them up as they landed. When our lot were coming in we had to run down and light the flares and when they had landed we had to put them out again. It was cruel.

There was no transport you felt like a beast of burden. You had to put oxygen in the aircraft and it was 8 bottles, you couldn't carry eight bottles for a mile or so, they weighed about 120 lb. You slung a rope round your neck and you got two on the rope, two with your fingers and someone would tuck another two under your arms and you wandered across, always an air raid when doing this, totally exhausting. Some brilliant bloke decided that they would use big cylinders, 250lb, on a donkey cart. You had to put 2 of them on the donkey cart. The whole thing was chaotic. They were sending new officers out all the time to try and cure moral. The first thing any of them did was Parade. Blokes would turn up on parade in sandals and cut downs, lost kit, torn shirts, some wearing topes back to front to keep the sun of their faces. The new morale officer would end up ranting and raving. Then they would out you on training – folks just issued each other forged chits to say they were on essential duties. I went on one which was really bloody stupid. The Germans were threatening to invade, went down with the Irish Fusiliers, charging about for a fortnight with bayonets and all sorts of bloody rubbish. There were five or six air raids a day and the officer wouldn't let you take shelter, it was supposed to harden you up and everybody was terrified. An ME dropped three bombs right in the middle of us but they didn't go off, they bounced. The next time the officer let us take shelter. Another newly appointed bloke came out and decided to have pay parade. This time there was no soap on the island and hardly any paraffin and there was a plague of fleas, literally, every man had at least 20 or 30 fleas on him – round your waist and round your ankles. So this new bloke was standing there, eventually he gets fleas to, so they stopped the pay parades. There was always somebody coming out with new ideas, there was one who sent all the boys on cross-country runs when they had barely enough food to keep themselves alive. You had 25 cigarettes a week, no drink.

The last Spitfires they sent out it was organised. The guns were properly lined up, everything. There was blast pens with about 20 army boys, it was army boys that guided the aircraft in towards the blast pens, the army whirled it round and shoved it in backwards, then the army rearmed it, poured in Glycol, did everything. The bloke that flew it in was a rookie from home, he was just tossed out and a Maltese pilot stepped in. Off they went. They didn't bother about runways, it was so important to get up in time cause the Germans would be over, 100 aircraft, 200 aircraft within minutes. They didn't line up or anything, they just went straight out the blast pen across the airfield. Two or three of them met head on in the middle. They shot down about 100 Germans that day, God it was a braw day, it was smashing. The Germans were over every hour, strafing up and down. I got a bit through my tin hat and never knew. The wagon came round with food for your breakfast and dinner and gave you water, but there was nothing to clean your plates with and the place you could hardly see for stoor. I got dysentery then and just lay in the tent. Passing blood, laying in the tent getting weaker and weaker and the boys were bringing me down a cup of tea but eventually they carried me up to the MO who put me in right away, just looked at me and stuck me in the hospital. When you went in there you went in with your tin hat on your chest and your rifle down the side. Went in there filthy and you got no food. They put you on Epson salts six times a day, no tea, nothing, just water. Never felt so bad in my life. Backside was raw. I counted the times – I was sitting on the commode 48 times the first day. The second week they put you on jelly, then chicken soup. The Germans were marching over Italy so all the walking wounded and sick were paraded in the centre of the hospital which was a big square with a red cross on it. We were issued with bren guns and mills bombs and all sorts of rubbish and put in places to defend. But the Germans had a continuous relay of aircraft going round every day, 24 hours a day just went round and round, MEs, so they saw this farce of a parade in the square. They bombed the place the next day. The stupidity of it. They put me to a convalescent camp.

The raids were still going on. You got to know when the convoys were going to run so you knew they were going to bomb the airfield first so you went and slept in Valetta, down in the red light district, you got a bed for a shilling. You flitted back when the convoy was getting close 'cause they then bombed the docks. The one I stayed at was the White City boarding house at the docks, ex navy men ran all these places, very clean, you went in there you got a bed for the night, in the wire cage, and you got a black market bully beef sandwich for tuppence and they cleaned your boots for a ha'penny. The bed was a shilling.

The food got worse and worse, never saw an officer except the flying boys. I was in Malta for three years – I was away with the fairies when I came back. What got me was the total incompetence of the place. You hardly knew whose squadron you were on. There was a recognisance aircraft which was shadowing the Italian fleet and which was nothing to do with me. Couldn't find anybody else to work on it so I went myself, running across the runway, next thing a jeep screams up, our new station commander. Hauls me up, crossing the runway, everybody in Malta crossed the runway because there was no transport to go round. It made the difference between walking a mile and a quarter of a mile. I tried to explain to him I was going to go over this aircraft that was shadowing the Italian fleet, he wasn't interested. I had just come off 24 hours emergency duty so I was pretty scruffy looking. He charged me with not shaving. Flight sergeant took my name, I was furious, literally. I went back and walked out of camp, went to see a Maltese friend. When I was out some officers passed me and I gave them a cheery wave while I was sitting on a wall. They must have been newly out from Britain. They sent out the sergeant major to take my name and number. So he came and said, 'I want your name and number'. I said, 'what the bloody hell do you want my name and number for'? 'oh, they sent me out because you didn't salute'. Next day I was paraded, crossing the runway, unshaven, breaking out of camp, breaking in to camp, not saluting, and I thought I was one of the best airmen that ever walked the face of the earth. 'Cause I always did what I had to do. I thought I was for it. By this time I was so war weary I couldn't care less. A lot of folks ambition was to get into the glasshouse because you were safe there – they put you into shelters when there was a air raid. So, he said I could be charged with mutiny and said, 'what do you think about that'? I said, 'well, I'll have to give it a bit of thought'. Anyway, he gave me a severe reprimand.

There was a dance thrown by the Knights of St Columbus, nae weemin, just Ausies and Scots. So, a fight started, an Ausie sergeant said to one of our sergeants, 'stand to attention when I speak to you'. And then the fight started, Ausies and Scots against the English.

Another fight was at the Union Jack club, this was a serious one, there must have been about a hundred blokes in. You see the booze had come back after the siege and slowly but surely folks started separating. All the English at one end, New Zealanders and Canadians and Scots at the other. Then somebody threw a bottle, then the chairs went, the place was wrecked, it was a shambles, they broke everything in the place. I carried two books with me during the war, one of them was Plato's Dialogue and the other was McGonagall. They were both difficult to read so to speak. After one air raid there was a Maltese policeman and there was a bomb lying on the edge of the quay and he lifted it and threw it in the water, I thought, what a brave man, I couldn't believe it.

You couldn't buy bread, of course, but you could wrap a blanket round your waist and go into Orme and just stand in the shadows somewhere. Somebody would pass, you would follow them round the corner and swap the blanket for 14oz of bread, a small brown loaf, and the girls made clothes out of the blankets.

If you lost your mug you had to make one out of a beer bottle. If you lost your knife, fork and spoon you were in trouble. You had to steal them or make them. If your mug went you had to borrow a mug from someone. Nobody would lend you anything. You went to bed with your small pack and your tools, you never let it out of your sight.

I was put on the ration wagon, going round all the wee places, giving them half a pound of tea here and there, sugar, bread ration etc.

I was a good watcher. The Germans came in V formations of five planes. If you were good at watching you could tell roughly where they were going to drop the bombs. So the cookhouse, everybody ran, so I went in the back, crawled on my hands and knees and got a loaf of bread. Crawled out and lay, the bombers just arrived then, I was lying at the back of the cookhouse, watching.

I was always divorced from it, I was there but not quite connected.

I got promoted sergeant and at that time I thought all the senior NCOs were yellow. I went to headquarters and they threw me three stripes, I said, 'what's that for'? 'Just get them sewn on, you're a sergeant'. I said, 'but I don't want to be a sergeant, you should have asked me first'.

There wasn't much rank among the old salts, we were in the same trouble, but the new ones coming out were a bloody nuisance.

We were losing so many aircraft. There were three clocks in a Baltimore, wireless operator, observer and captain. So I just took two of them out, I had a pile of them, 'cause if they got shot down you only lost one clock instead of three, and then they wouldn't get pinched if I had them. I used them for bribery and corruption.

You were underfed, no beer, no fags, they eventually gave you fags you couldn't smoke, they gave you Indian fags, Victory V they were called and they had weevils inside. You couldn't draw them, they had so many holes in them and every now and again there would be a 'pop' as the weevils exploded with the heat. I'm sure they were made out of dung.

So stupid, I went down one day and there were six Baltimore's out on dispersal. They had left them in a line. I went out to service them. Germans arrived, MEs come and strafed, one went up, back they came, another one was gone, another one, then another one. There was none left at the end of the day. They slowly learnt to build blast pens, hundreds of them.

A.L. Forbes spent the early part of the war years stationed at Gibraltar:

We were taken on strength of 33 (L) Company RASC. (L) meant Local. We were quartered in Rosia Barracks, opposite the entrance to the South Mole and dockyard. We were responsible as a unit for the supply of transport to other units although each unit, depending on its size, had its own transport. In addition we were responsible for a WD fleet of five ships, a tug and four motor launches.

I remember being a little disappointed as to the military strength of The Rock. One could see that life had hardly been disturbed although we had been at war for about six months. Every Saturday there was horse racing at North Front as usual. We could wear civilian clothes if we liked but they had to be of a reasonable standard – any old clothes would not do. All in all we had nothing to grumble at but then came the fall of France. We had no airfield. The race course was the only part of the Rock which could accommodate one and work was started there and then.

About mid 1941 supplies were coming out quicker than we could deal with and I was taken off transport duties and given the job of searching for certain commodities which the O i/c Barracks urgently required. By asking the master of the ship for a look at the ships manifest I tracked down some of the items but often the stores had been moved to another shed of wharf. The unloading of ships must have been time consuming to say the least.

About the end of 1942 it was clear that we were preparing either to attack or be attacked, besieged even. The Canadian Tunnelers had opened up the rock interior which could now support thousands of men and supplies. It was about this point in time that EXERCISE CASTLE was served on us. The idea was that in the event of action we would man the vulnerable points, fight fires, etc. my station was by the telephone, in the transport office, and of course one can imagine the remarks of the others at my having drawn such a easy number. The army never lacks a humorist if the need arises.

I do not know how many times we were turned out under CASTLE but about 2nd November we were turned out for real. The sight that met my eyes as I opened up the office was one which I will never forget. The bay was covered with ships. It must have been a feat of seamanship to get them all into the bay. The rendezvous must also have been something because some ships being slower would be less manoeuvrable. It all happened during the night. The time I looked at them was about 7.30 am.

Of all the operations of the war, TORCH, I think, must have been the most efficiently carried out. No sooner had the ships arrived than came the airborne force. There was one minor accident to which we sent an ambulance. Other than that everything seemed to go right and many of the ships which had conveyed the force from Gib to Africa were coming back empty. This prompted the question: Why can't they take us home? Especially those of us who have served over three years overseas. Some good fairy supported us and in January 1943 I was once again on a troop ship; this time bound for home.

Also serving in the Mediterranean theatre of operations, John MacKenzie was involved in RAF Air-Sea Rescue operations, rescuing downed pilots:

I was in the RAF Air, Sea Rescue. In the Mediterranean. Any aircraft that went down they let us know. There were 11 in the crew. Quite a big boat. The boats were made of wood and they were very fast, 40 knots. They had petrol engines, I was a fitter and I had to fix them.

I enjoyed it very much. It had guns on board but we never had to use them. It was aircraft mostly that we attended. We never came under fire ourselves. We had a doctor on board and it was just a case of going out and rescuing them, you just dragged them on board.

Keith Hodgkin's diary for the end of 1944 and early 1945 recalls his service in the Mediterranean:

Told I was to be transferred at sea to [HMS] Atherstone. Packed everything up in about an hour and was ready for transfer. Good to sea the Atherstone come steaming up from the stern and then work gradually closer. Both ships going at about 8 Knots. Curious to see the people with whom you are going to live with for so long becoming clearer as you got closer.

The method of transfer was to stand you in a basket and after having attached a line to the basket across 15 yds of sea, both destroyers hoist you and the basket up on ship's derricks and swing you out to sea. As the destroyer crew heave on the line, the derrick lowers the basket and one is pulled aboard the destroyer. All under the eyes of about 1,000 troopers. The crew realised that something was up and rushed to look over the side, thereby causing a list so that I was dunked in the water.

5th September. Typical day at sea. Hot, lazy, no land, no birds. But Oh Boy what lovely nights. Cool with the most glorious moon and a lovely transparent haze below it. Steaming gently into the moon light with the convoy dimly visible on the starboard bow, another destroyer ahead in the moon track and the constant musical pinging of the ASDIC apparatus.

9th September. 4 Alsatian puppies brought on board making a mess everywhere with much running of water. Very sweet though. The thought of 4 fully grown Alsatians dashing and leaping about makes me laugh every time I see them.

21 September. Dealt with various hangovers. Got to know two nice nurses who were keen to come sailing in the whaler. Very pleasant sail. Drinks and supper at the officers club. Supper was annoyingly Cornish pasties, roast pork, tart – might as well have had it on board but Mount Carmel hock was pleasant.

22 September. Spent morning ferreting about for fresh veg and fruit for crew. 30 cases of bubonic plague in hospital. Tried to see these but failed.

Party. RAF there in force. RAF takes dancing very seriously sticking its bottom out and placing the feet in the careful way of him who is a good dancer but hasn't got beyond the desire to give that impression. Other parts of the RAF gloriously drunk and studying the local brandies, singing lustily and driving the waiter to distraction.

4th October. Arrived Port Said to find we were being packed off early for secret hampering operations Aegianwards.

After censoring a whole pile of letters, manage to get ashore with Mid for supper. Find a really 'woggy' bit at about 10.30om with all the streets lit up with stalls and packed with 'wogs'. I didn't see a single non 'wog' while walking about there and, from the way we were stared at, it seemed rather unusual for the navy to be walking here. We gradually collected an increasing number of children until we were walking very much on our dignity with an amusing train of children in a melee behind us.

I find the annoying thing is, if you look at the interesting sights and people, someone immediately rushes up to you and tries to sell you something only here it was rather more on the lines of, 'I find you French girl, Yes?' 'You fuck my sister for 50 francs, yes?' 'Feelthy pictures?' all absolutely as one had been told would happen.

This didn't happen in Palestine, only Egypt. In fact in Palestine one small boy said, 'You English, Yes?' and on my saying 'Yes' he replied unexpectedly, 'Keep it up, fellah! Keep it up!'

5th October. Up in the middle of the night to GQ (general quarters). Progressed to rendezvous with the Farndale at 26 knots. Apparently the trip may be quite interesting, certainly a change from convoy routine. Looks like we'll be up all night at GQ. General feeling of suppressed excitement partly because of the unusually fast speed; we're on our own with one other destroyer.

A night a GQ was had by all. Sweet FA happened except some lovely views of Greek islands by moonlight. They all looked gloriously mountainous.

6th October. Early hours were spent looking for a certain target (Rhodes) which did not appear to be there. Later on we went into Piskope bay to find some Jerry troopers. It was an odd feeling being fired at. Farndale was holed slightly just above the waterline.

14 November. As I joined the ship, MacDougall, a taciturn, moon-faced, good natured Scot reeled up the gangway. About 10 seconds after passing me he let out a yell, 'Ah know thaaaat man!' At a guess I should say Muscat. This has a delayed reaction with a very deceptive taste; after drinking a lot without effect – it really hits you hard.

18 November 44. A young, new rating came up with a cut lip and when asked how he did it he said, 'Fell in the hoggin, sir'.

'Well, Sir I was throwing the gash bucket over the side and I didn't notice the railings were down and I followed the gash into the hoggin Sir'.

4th December – Island of Veli Rat. Apparently the Partisans and a few Russian communists are in control but are wanting to liberate their country themselves so that they'll be in complete control of it when the time comes for a government to be set up.

On the other hand though they're excellent gorillas?? When equipped as at present with British uniforms and guns and equipment, they've not enough experience to fight a straight battle with the Germans or enough sea power to oust them from the islands. At every step the same thing seems to happen; the Partisans try doing without assistance and then are forced to ask for help to save their own skins. On an island recently, they landed with the help of the navy but they failed to hold it when the Germans landed reinforcements and eventually we had to help them again. Again they will not allow us to use their ports until they discover that they want something from us through those ports.

On the other hand all the civilians are very pro British and said to be Royalist. I think they just want to live in peace and quiet. They are very friendly but tend to freeze off if they see a Partisan because the latter disapprove strongly of fraternising with the British.

Partisan men and girls all wander about in uniform together, carrying rifles and hand grenades with little difference between the sexes. They have attractive faces and take a lot of trouble to make their hair look nice.

7 December. We passed a Yugoslav cruiser that Captain Evoe had commanded in the last war but had been taken over by the Germans in this. It had been accidentally run aground during an MTB action a year ago when the German Lieutenant had lost his head. It looked so lifelike that I remarked that it must have given many ships a nasty few moments before they realised it was a wreck. He gave a lovely mime of a skipper holding up his hands in horror and going into a panic. Later he gave a wonderful fishlike imitation of guns going 'pough, pough' at him when he had been under fire.

Later on after nosing about in the coves for German explosives or boats we came out into the open and started shelling the big six inch battery that was reputed to be out of action in order to finish it off completely. After about 4 shots, fire was returned by 2 guns quite accurately enough for my liking. Curious feeling being fired at – seeing a flash and know that sometime in the next few seconds, a shell that has been carefully aimed at you is going to explode.

Firing at a target makes me feel that I'm throwing darts. I suddenly woke up to the fact that I was much more akin to a dartboard in this case. We cleared out after a little while, making smoke and firing out of range.

D-Day Dodgers?

A lot of ill feeling is the British fault for one hears of drunk ratings or soldiers reeling about yelling at the tops of their voices, 'These fucking Italian Bastards'. The Italians are probably doing the same thing only I've not learned Italian for that particular phrase. (Keith Hodgkin)

After serving in Africa Ernest Jamieson took part in the allied landings on Sicily:

We sailed into the Med and one of the crew told us we would head towards Crete then change course for Sicily. Ate in the ships galley, good food, beautiful white bread. We had a calm crossing during which we had safety drill and watched the Oerlikon gunners at practice and finally arrived at Syracuse where they were already unloading LSTs. The captain of our ship lowered a motor-launch and headed for the beach. He must have had a disagreement with the Beach Major who wanted him to stand off but he took us straight in between two other LSTs. When I started up my truck I found the gaskets on the exhaust manifold had perished probably due to the salt air so I puffed all the way up the beach and had a new one fitted later. The landing was easy and there didn't seem to be any opposition. Later we found out that there were just Italian Coastal defences whose troops withdrew with the capitulation. The Herman Goring Division came in later. The 'Height' of my experiences in Sicily was toward the end of the campaign when we travelled up and over mount Etna and at the top we were looking down at clouds and small villages where sometimes you had to double cut to get into them before arriving at Santa Maria at the foot of Etna and from there pushed on to Messina arriving on 17 August along with the Americans.

Like Ernest Jamieson, Bill Edgar was also in Sicily but quickly moved over the Messina Straits to participate in the invasion of the Italian mainland.

We were only in Sicily for a fortnight or ten days. Went right round the back of Etna. We had the First Canadian Division with us. We embarked at Mesina and went round the coast to Bari. We personally were put with the paratroops and we went just across the Messina Straits and landed at Rogia Calabria. And we went across country to a place called Fogia. The Para's had no heavy engineering, that's why they sent us. And Fogia was a ghost town. I don't know if you've ever seen those funny clips of chasing up and down main roads and streets. Our paratroops were in jeeps, the Germans were in their Volkswagens, the flat fronted things, and they were chasing one another round the streets. We landed in the technical school, a big technical college, we got up on the first floor, bedded down there, and from the top of the college we watched it happen.

In preparation for the Italian campaign, Pal MacLeod was also posted to Sicily,:

We landed in Sicily, which is a marvellous place, we were camped at the foot of mount Etna. You didn't have camps you didn't have anything, you slept like the animals out in the field. We were there while the initial invasion was going on in Italy and when we crossed into Italy we had the same work there as we had in the desert, just keeping things going, keeping machinery going. Following the front and taking them back for repair, what had broken down. We went as far as Naples then they took us home for the invasion of France, of Europe. And we got one weeks leave then.

Ernest Jamieson also crossed over to the Italian mainland but was transported in a more holiday-like atmosphere:

Crossed over to Italy at the straits during which we were overtaken by small landing craft who were having a race to see who could make the most crossings. The Navy boys had a huge board marking them off.

Landed at Regio di-Calabria, stayed the night and next day travelled round the boot of Italy reaching Taranto where we stayed a few days before heading up the east side of Italy. Arrived at Foggio where there was a large airfield then to Cerignola arriving at night and bedded down. Next morning woke up to find most of the population round the trucks. We breakfasted at the cook house but didn't enjoy it, seeing all the hungry faces, however the cooks gave the youngsters biscuits with jam.

Posted from England to the Italian campaign, A.L. Forbes recalls that not everyone was enthusiastic at receiving an overseas posting:

After generous leave I reported to the Holding Battalion and was with hundreds of others billeted in Nissen huts in the grounds of the home of Lord and Lady Liverpool, near Lincoln. I was warned that there were violent would-be escapists among them and that I had to be vigilant when it was my time for guard duties. I later learnt that there was a group who would do anything to avoid going overseas. They broke their dentures, spectacles, etc. Eventually they were put aboard ship under escort. The date would now be Xmas/New Year 1943/4.

The Italians were out of the war but the Germans in Italy still carried on. We had no idea as to where we were bound but after much checking of names and numbers we were transported to Grimsby/Humberside to embark for destiny not known. The troopship was crowded and a notice went up on the notice board to say that we were bound for Italy. We were all glad to get of the boat which had berthed in Naples harbour despite bombed ships and other debris of war. We were then entrained for a large military camp comprising barracks, tents, etc. On the walls of the main barracks were engraved fascist slogans, a common one was 'crederi obedieri combatteri'. A feature of the camp was that there was no glass in the windows. We were told that the Bersaggliare had to climb up ropes to the windows to get their food. Those failing would get no food. This may have been fine for hardy Italian soldiers but it was too much for me and I went down with pneumonia.

Ernest Jamieson had mixed feelings about his time in Italy:

I never enjoyed my stay in Italy, seeing all the poverty and hunger around you. Maybe the desert was the best place to fight a war. I experienced the same feeling all across Europe. Sunny Italy was a bit of a myth, especially in winter with heavy snow, bad roads, and with the railways badly damaged heavy supplies were brought up the coast by flat bottom boats manned by RASC personnel to Vasto where we loaded up and set off to several units. Each driver was given a route card with names of towns to help find your destination. On one journey we set off with an officer and sergeant. We passed through several villages then we came to a stop. The officer got out his route card. There was a large sign on the road reading No Entry with an arrow pointing for diversion. The officer asked the sergeant if we were on the right road as he couldn't find the name 'No Entry' on the map. I wonder if he was taking the mickey?

Thinking he was on his way home, Bill Edgar suffered the disappointment of returning to Italy:

We went from Casino to a place called Lake Troterino and then they took us back to Toranto, put us on ships, we thought we're coming home, and then we landed at Alexandria in Egypt and went into camps there. Bloody awful it was. Next thing we know we went back to Italy, straight in the Apennines, in the mountains and spent the winter in the mountains in Bologna. It was a hell of a winter. Then we went in the Poe valley with an Italian Division. Then we kept going until Venice.

When the allied army advanced through Italy, the local Italian population were not always fully co-operative. Ernest Lovett was given the rather unusual task of tracking down a missing train and its contents:

We were stationed in Perugia. I was told to report to the C.R.E. He said a train carrying a Bailey Bridge in sections had been missing for about 5 days, and a forward Field Company R.E. urgently needed it. He gave me the train number, destination, and the last reported location, and told me to find it and get it to its destination.

I collected my driver and my platoon sergeant, as the latter was a fine Italian linguist, due to his many female conquests. We arrived at the railway line a day later, and asked at a signal box if they had seen this train, and the signalman confirmed that it had passed some days before. We then took a road in the same direction of the railway, and when we started up a hill and turned a corner, I shouted to the driver, 'Mine on the road'. I had recognised a teller mine lying on the road. My driver swerved the car past the mine, and went round the corner. I shouted to my driver to stop, and grab his tommy gun and shoot anyone who appeared. The sergeant and I rushed back round the corner – he with his rifle cocked, and I with my pistol drawn. There was no mine on the road. We realised that someone was trying to un-nerve us to say the least. We went back to the car and proceeded on the road. We eventually arrived at a country station and there was the train standing with the driver and guard sitting near the locomotive and smoking.

I told the sergeant to ask the guard if the train was carrying a Bailey Bridge. The guard's reply was non-committal. I told my driver to open some of the trucks. He shouted that the bridge was on board. I told the sergeant to tell the train driver that I would shoot the guard if the train did not move out in 5 minutes, and that I had shot many Italians and that I was a sadistic killer. I drew my pistol and looked at the chamber to show that it was full of cartridges. The guard and train driver exchanged glances and the train driver mounted his cab. I told the sergeant to tell him that if the train did not arrive promptly at the correct destination, I would search for him and shoot him. The train left immediately.

The Italians standing around were suitably impressed. The sergeant spoke to them and discovered that they had no idea that the Germans were in retreat and that the Italian Army was co-operating with the allies. We told them that the allies were well forward of their village and that if there was any nonsense like putting mines on the roads, the British Army would arrive and deal with them, they appeared to be chastened. We left with no trouble. When I reported to the C.R.E. he told me that the bridge had arrived.

Ernest Lovett also unfortunately experienced the seedier side of military occupation in Italy when he shared quarters with the Soviet OGPU, the forerunner to the KGB:

> We had some interesting interludes, but the most interesting were our experiences in our flat. We occupied one floor of a modern luxury block of flats. On the floor above us was a Russian O.G.P.U. office. When we went up in the lift we occasionally had foreigners going up as well and sometimes they would breakdown and weep. We tried to pacify them. We found out that they had come from Eastern Europe. Now the O.G.P.U. had located them and had ordered them to come to the office for 'repatriation'. They knew full well that was really 'removal to Russia and execution'. The C.R.E. used to get angry and sometimes he ordered us to go down to the basement car park and lift our vehicles in front of the Russian cars so that they could not get out before ours. The Russian sentries did not interfere. Maybe this was petty but we felt better.

The Italian campaign was not all grim, as Bill Edgar found out, there were lighter moments:

> We had a dog called monster which we swapped for a sheep. We swapped the sheep for a quarter barrel of wine. The dog, monster, was later run over and killed by a dispatch rider. We gave him a military funeral, firing shots over him, someone shouted out, 'has war broken out or something?' We were crackers.

Posted to a Petrol Depot in Taranto, A.L. Forbes found himself with the job of resupplying the 8th Army as it moved up the Italian mainland:

> As ever in the army you had to study the notice board daily to see if you were selected for duties, posting, etc, and sure enough about the first week in March 1944 my name appeared and I was posted to 118 Petrol Depot, Taranto, right in the heel of Italy. I found the unit in a collection of wooden huts which the Germans had left behind

when they retreated. The 118 Petrol Depot had recently come over from Africa and were preparing to go into operation with 119 Depot. The system was that one of the depots would operate forward while the other would stay behind, making good stocks and replenishing generally. There were about 30 men in each depot. We had four or five Fire Fighters whose job it was to advise and see to it the stocks were diversified in location, etc. I soon realised that I had come to a good unit. They were very resourceful. For instance they carried a large white bath with pipes (hot and cold) and fitted the whole to a water supply so as to have hot baths, one a week per man, until the proper bath unit came with a shower unit.

It was not long till we carried out the leap-frog manoeuvre which ensured that 8th Army troops were never short of petrol and derv, also engine and other oils. On our third leap we arrived at Rimini and set up for operation. I applied to the Town Mayor for Italian labour and soon had a hundred plus booked for all sorts of duties, such as filling jerry cans with petrol from bowsers. They were mostly women and had a good attendance record; the men were not quite so good. Drivers calling for a fill-up were given the quantities they asked for without check-up or questions asked. Judging by discipline notices it seemed that blankets were the sought after items and units sometimes had to have a guard on QM Stores. Of all the places in Italy that we operated from Rimini was the one we stayed at longest. We could swim in the warm water or sun ourselves on the beach, not to mention a bit of footballing, but it did not please everyone: Lady Nancy Astor, Parliament's first woman M.P. called upon the War Cabinet to bring these D-Day Dodgers home. She said we were having it too good; drinking too much vino, etc. Soon a record was made by some parodist using the melody of Lili Marlene with his own words. It kept Nancy Astor quiet for the rest of the war.

Ernest Jamieson was on his way home at last:

Travelled by train to Taranto then after a few days got on the train again heading for Naples. Arrived in Naples and marched to docks to board old P&O liner Almazoora (In Gods Keeping). The captain never left the bridge. He had a camp bed there. In all its wartime service the only damage it received was when part of an enemy aircraft that was shot down struck the bridge. The Brigade was homeward bound. Arrivederci Italia.

D-Day: The Longest Day

The invasion of Normandy, codenamed Operation Overlord, was four years in the planning and culminated in the biggest seaborne invasion ever undertaken. It marked the beginning of the end of German occupation in Europe. The allied high command had decided the beaches of Normandy offered the greatest chance of success for the operation. The landings took place on five beaches: Omaha and Utah were assigned to the American forces, Juno was assigned to a predominantly Canadian attack force, and Sword and Gold were designated as British. The amphibious landings were supported by Airborne landings on the flanks of the beach landing area and further inland behind enemy lines. Over 6,000 vessels were used in the operation.

On D-Day itself some 61,715 British troops were landed on Sword, Juno and Gold beaches. British casualties for that day stood at approximately 2,600 dead, wounded and missing.

Murdo MacLeod recalls sailing with the invasion fleet:

All the ships were congregating along the south English coast, Portsmouth and all along there. I always remember the Monday night, how the hell there was no collisions because when you could see, when the light came, there were thousands of ships, as far as the eye could see. And we were in front, the only thing ahead of us was the minesweepers to clear a path. You had big merchant ships, big liners loaded with troops and then you had the LTAs, Assault landing Craft, slung over the side and they filled them up and of they went and we escorted them, we kept on their flank all the way just in case there was dive-bombing, shelling from the beaches. There was quite a lot of them drowned too 'cause some of them landed in deep water and they were heavy loaded, they just went down like a stone.

Everything was that black near the shore, the night was all lit up with shell fire and tracer bullets and god knows what. You would get shot you know if you showed a cigarette end even on board, all the portholes were shut, blacked out, everything was blacked out.

At 7.25a.m. on 6 June British commandos attacked Sword Beach. John Forfar landed in the first wave with the rest of his Commando. However, from the beginning things did not go smoothly:

In the weeks prior to D-Day we were based near Winchester. On the 4th of June they decided to re-locate the troops and I was on a cross channel ferry called the Princess Josephine Charlotte and they decided the medical section should go on another old tramp steamer called the SS Victoria. So we moved over into a very, a much less elegant ship but it was a perfectly good ship.

We set of in the evening, that'd be the evening of the 5th. There's a number of things one remembers: this enormous number of aircraft passing over, a kind of general, well naturally a certain air of appre-hension. The troops were all getting ready, and we were getting our medical stuff – not that it wasn't carefully packed but you wanted to go over everything just for the third, fourth, fifth and sixth time. And just waiting and watching to see what was happening.

A medical officer in that kind of unit is very limited. Really, your main function is just to patch up wounded soldiers as best you can and make such attempts as you can to get them evacuated.

There were some chaps got sea-sick they had hardly started. They got sea-sick, they felt so miserable, I think they were quite glad at the thought of landings. We all had bags, you know the naval 'bags vomit' which every chap had. It's not so bad on the big ship, on the SS Victoria, but once you were in the landing craft you were jammed together under a kind of overhang thing, at least the Marines were. It's not the best place to be vomiting because of the chaps immediately in front of you so you have to have the bag with which to deal with this problem.

The parent ship the SS Victoria took us to about 8 miles off the French coast. And, of course, they'd been practicing this for months. The landing craft takes about 36 men: the Commando itself consists of 400 men. The landing craft can either be lowered into the water empty and you go down a scrambling net into it or, as happened in some of our ships: on our ship, they lowered some of the landing craft already loaded. They don't normally do this but they did this on D-Day with some of the craft. They're always frightened that if something goes wrong they'd tip all the troops out into the water. But anyway, they lowered them down loaded, some of them, about half of them; and half of them went down the scrambling net.

It was astonishing I mean the amount of ships around. There were so many ships around, I mean if you looked away to the left you could see battleships, cruisers, landing craft, tramps and parent ships, there was almost a queue of ships all striking away to the left of us. During the night of course there were cruisers which were bombarding the French coast. There was a great booming going on all night: right close beside us was the Orion, which was like a cruiser, it was blasting away most of the night.

One of our craft was hit well out, you could hardly turn, well out, a mile or so. And when this craft got hit we saw the chaps all jumping into the water and one of my medical orderlies was killed there, there was quite a lot wounded, some drowned. And then we went along parallel to the coast and then of course we saw a beach which wasn't where we were supposed to land in – the one which we obviously had to because it already had troops on it – we turned in towards the beach, and hopefully we would get in dry. But unfortunately 5 out of the 14 landing craft never got ashore dry. The one I was in was sunk. I don't know if you know a tetrahedra: tetrahedra were Rommel's sleepers [railway lines]. Rommel had them hauled up and he stuck them into the sand, well out, and if the tide was out you could see them all. Of course the tide was not out because the idea was to get as close to the beach as possible, not to go advancing across long stretches on open sand. But unfortunately when the tide was in or rising then you couldn't see the ends of them, loads were about. There was a great scraping noise, grinding noise, then the whole thing tipped over. Then there was a resounding bang at the back, blew the back of the machine and killed another of my medical orderlies, Kinloch was killed, and a few other people. But anyway, I jumped into the water.

A Mae West is a remarkable thing, because it holds you up. I mean I had boots on and I was not a terrific swimmer but I'm allowed to carry an automatic pistol with me – the medical officer carries that for his own protection – but that's pretty heavy and the boots were heavy and of course the Mae West was excellent at floating.

My remit was to do what I could. All this idea of landing dry and forming up and going inland. We were scattered across kilometres, the whole commando was scattered all along the beaches.

The other thing I remember too was the awful mess, you know you had a ration of chocolate, you know you had a big pocket in the battledress here, you'd get a great slab of this chocolate stuff which was supposed to be – nobody ever tested it in water as far as I could see! This great slushy, gooey mess started extruding out of my... I mean I was soaking wet, to be added to it this... gooey mess.

Hordes of troops were coming ashore at this time, the whole thing was chaotic. There were people lying on the beach. It was a very narrow beach because the tide was coming well in and there was a wall, it was pretty narrow beach they had to land on. And there were tanks manoeuvring, bren carriers, there were men doing things, and among other things there was a beach dressing station. My job of course was not to hang around beach dressing stations. I mean we got the chap, brought him along and then we left. Our job was to look after our own unit. And indeed you weren't even allowed to pick up anybody in the water, you were not allowed to pick them up on the way in from the landing craft because that would have meant the landing craft stopped, it would've meant that it was much more easily hit by the enemy who were up on the headland ahead of us. The second wave coming in would have been held up and therefore it was a strict border 'Nobody was to stop on the way in'.

Meanwhile, Jimmy MacKenzie was also landing on day one with his Commando:

We set off on the sixth of June and sailed across the channel.

We landed up off Normandy, I think it was about seven miles off the coast when the ships stopped then we were put in little landing craft. We lost about a hundred shot killed and drowned, a lot of the boats ran into underwater obstacles. Some were shot at. In spite of the fact that there were warships blasting into the coast there for hours, the amount of shells that were fired, we were in our own boat watching it and we couldn't believe that anything could exist. The Jerry was a little bit smarter than we were. He had most of his defences well back from the sea. He knew what would happen at the front but he would have his pillboxes at the back. Anyhow, we had a job to do ten miles down the coast to take a small port, Port Bessongne I think they called it. They needed it for landing supplies, ammunition, that sort of thing before the big Mulberry harbour was installed. So that had to be taken, do or die. We set off and so many things went wrong. The weather was wrong, and the landing was wrong. There was another unit should have landed and cleared the way for us, ahead of us. We couldn't afford to get involved in any fighting. There wouldn't have been enough left to do the job. One of the English regiments were supposed to be ahead of us to clear the little villages but they never got there so we had to scramble our own way through. It was practically midnight before we got to our objective, and it had to be postponed to the following day but that gave the Jerries a flying start. The following day was the attack on the port and that was really a horrendous affair.

I fell asleep lying down. We had sorted out the town and there was a hundred yards between us, that was the front line, a hundred yards between each man.

It was a long day, well they called it 'the longest day'.

As part of a Combined Operations force, Murdo MacLeod found himself closing with the beachhead to give close fire support to those soldiers on the beach:

The landing craft, the Combined Ops was separate from general service like cruisers and destroyers and that. We had our own flotilla of landing craft, gunboats and flack ships. We were there to protect the assault infantry boats, landing craft, anything going into the shore or the beaches. We could go right into the beach with them. We were lucky, we seen three others getting blown up when they hit these obstacles. There were whole rows of these cross things with explosive tied to them whenever a boat hit that it would blow them up. That was Normandy.

We got in close and when the assault landing craft touched the beaches the front dropped down and the men rushed ashore and the tanks went ashore. Well we were covering them all even from the Germans ashore. We could train our guns on them and give our boys a chance but even then they paid a price.

We stayed there and we saw the 6th Airborne, the Dakotas with the gliders, hundreds of them passing over the beaches, the boys were in a bit by that time and you could see the parachutists coming down.

Charles Devlin was surprised to learn that he was part of the reserve in the event of a failed landing:

We went across to HMS Glendour which was another Butlins camp. We were in Glendour when D-Day was coming on. My training was from March 1944 until the end of May. D-Day was coming off so all leave was cancelled, normally when you ended training you went on leave and then down to Portsmouth, but we didn't get any leave. We went to Collingwood and were issued with rifles, bayonets and ammunition pouches. I said to one of the chief's 'navy doesn't get rifles and bayonets and that'. And he said 'son, there's a bloody great battle going on across that channel, if things start to go wrong you're the reinforcements'. I didn't like it at all.

Murdo MacLeod had taken part in a number of practice landings in Scotland:

It was cold and at Invergordon, the place was covered in snow when we went in there. We were up there for invasion landings before the actual real invasion.

Bill Edgar felt sorry for those who were to land in Europe, calling them 'amateurs':

> When we heard about the D-day landings we felt sorry for them, they were only amateurs. The 51st Highland Division went from us, the 50th Tyne Tees went from us and then the 7th armoured, Desert Rats, went from us and they were the only really good divisions that had been in action. And of course we were just knocked out of it straight away because we had taken the first capital in Europe the day before, Rome, and of course that kyboshed it all then, we just disappeared from sight but we were still fighting up the Italian peninsular. We used to sing the song 'One more river, one more river to cross'.

Ernest Jamieson was one of those for whom Edgar was expressing sympathy. Fresh from the North African campaign and the invasions of Sicily and Italy, Ernest returned home with the 'Desert Rats' in time to take part in the D-Day landings in Normandy:

> Arrived in the UK and sailed up the Clyde to King George IV dock. Hail Caledonia. We boarded a train in Glasgow and stopped long enough in Edinburgh for to get a letter posted by a porter, then the long tiring journey to Goring-on-Sea and billeted in a school. Leave passes, pay and Ration Books were given out. I got a train to London and the Flying Scotsman to Edinburgh and home to my wife and son, who was now three years and five months. Our Brigade HQ which was in Worthing was inspected by Brigadier Currie. We had now taken over our new Brigade sign, the black desert rat. The Brigade was now an Independent Support Group and was almost as large as a Division. We took over our Fordson four wheel drive trucks and picked up our waterproofing material at Bicester and distributed it round the other units. We were on standby from the beginning of June, loaded up with Compo ration boxes.
>
> Set off for Gosport but my condenser burnt out and returned to HQ. saw the Airborne flying over. A few days later switched to Tilbury and loaded onto LST; flying bombs coming over. Arrived off Normandy in the evening and next morning the battleship Ramilles

fired broadsides alongside us. Went down the ramp and saw the water creep up to the top of the radiator and then the wheels gripped the beach and then it was up to the road and met up with the company. Heard the stories of some of the lads who landed earlier. Our CO Major Pollard and CSM Garfield riding a motor cycle were blasted off when a shell landed near them and a chap called Lennox who was in the first truck to go off sunk out of sight into the water with a load of 25 pounders. Seemingly it was a bomb crater he went into, however he was OK.

For Murdo MacLeod it was not the action itself that caused the greatest concern. It was the waiting:

> The worst thing is not the actual action, it's the waiting, 'cause your insides are, you know, it's the adrenalin I suppose, it's the waiting to go in. You don't know what to expect. You know they're firing at you. You see maybe one of the other landing craft hitting an obstacle and exploding. You feel the support of your mates, you've got to have that, you're in a unit.

Serving in the Burmese jungle, Bill Cochran was surprised to hear that large-scale landings had taken place:

> We didn't know about D-day until a fortnight after the event. Nobody envisaged anything like that, we were just thinking about small boats taking men across, not large scale landings. Nobody ever thought it was going to be that scale.

Landing in Normandy, James Hogg drove straight into the nearest German minefield, but his luck held out, although not with his commanding officer:

> The whole of the south coast was more or less blocked off, nobody was allowed in or out. All I can remember is I was then in Portsmouth and we waited to go on the tank landing craft in the docks. We went on there because they rose us to the top and then they put the heavy stuff

underneath. And when we landed it was the same procedure, the heavy went out then we came down by night. Came out and I took a wrong turn and went up the minefield. The commander was doing his nut.

The Colonel, he went over first to Normandy, he was to see where his unit would be put, his driver was a young lad, he was only 21, he went with him, the armoured car went as well. And seemingly, he was only there a day when he walked into a minefield, gone, killed, killed outright. And I thought, 'my God' He was there the day before, you know. The following day we were told, 'the boys been bumped off'. Walked in to this minefield. See, that's what I did, when I landed I went into this minefield, they did their nut, because the commander then told me how to get out, just went back the way I came in. But I was just very lucky I got away with it.

When I was heading to Normandy, you never seen anything like it in my life, the bombers, you could'na see the sky for bombers, they were chock a block. They had already been there, they were coming back. Sights that you would never see in your life again.

On the landing craft, on the top deck, there were these caps, and there were sort of a bar across them, and you had to get your armoured vehicle and strap it down on to these. I got mine strapped down and I went down, got myself, my head down, it must have been about one o' clock in the morning and we were heading out to sea then. Came over the tannoy, somebody in charge of this whatever, you had this number, I hadn't done mine right and my car was practically hanging of the side of the boat. Believe it or not, the gunner was sleeping up in the turret. He was sound asleep. I says, 'the cars sliding of the deck'. He wasn'a long in getting out of there. We got out and we got it strapped back in, I hadn't done it properly.

Posted to an American vessel, Keith Hodgkin was given the task of setting up a hospital deck. He recorded the preparations and the landings in his diary:

Letter May 1944
I have been posted to an American LST (Landing tank ship) with an American crew who have done all their training on the Mississippi.

The ship is a huge flat bottomed tub with a hollow centre. They can be beached and the bow opened and a ramp let down so that the cargo can be discharged through the nose of the ship. Quarters are comfortable but crowded – 3 doctors to one cabin. Food consists of a lot of tinned luxuries I haven't seen for years as well as a lot I've never seen. Exactly the same food for officers and men served on a cafeteria system so no separate messes. The whole ship is dry i.e. no alcohol on board.

Came aboard in the Solent onto USS LST 493 which was about to set sail for target practice. It had to be converted into a semi hospital ship. There was much to organise and improvise to convert the dirty tank deck (300 by 30 ft), which had no water, heating and drainage, into a hospital ward.

There were many fruitless visits. Visiting NSO, one got referred from office to office indefinitely until you'd spent the day accumulating stores' papers but no stores. Suddenly one could get the stores and then find that there was so much that you couldn't manage them. On several occasions I was reduced to pushing a trolley round Southampton.

Work was interesting and it was pleasant to have a little responsibility for a change. Fortunately there was a lot to do for at times I was very lonely. Americans were very pleasant but I found right up to the end that it could be a strain talking to them simply because one had so little in common.

Discipline was not what we would mean by discipline in a British ship. I felt that what they meant by discipline, we would simply call cooperation. No Captain Bligh stuff and a minimum of spit and polish. Very pleasant provided you weren't at sea or in any kind of emergency situation. Because of this, if officers were good, you probably got a more efficient unit but when they were weak or inexperienced, their form of discipline was lacking. And you could be in real danger. Generally speaking this was not an efficient ship and you rarely knew exactly where you stood so it was not an ideal example of a American ship.

D-Day begins. Everywhere one went one could feel the tension of the invasion with all its hundreds of preparations. No one knew anything very definite but everyone was speculating hard. One got the impression that all the arrangements were completely haywire (SNAFU) and disorganised but if you went into any particular matter and got the correct dope on it, you found that everything was remarkably under control.

Later we loaded up with our cargo of tanks and pongos (soldiers). They were crack troops and we are promptly 'sealed' up. We wondered whether this was the real thing but no one knew exactly how long we were going to remain like this. Gradually, as we were sealed, people began to talk and we learned where we were going and what we were going to do.

The D-Day programme for the invasion forces, run by the Germans, told us that it was going to be Monday. Sure enough on Sunday we were briefed. It looked like Monday but on Sunday evening nothing happened. It had been cancelled because of the weather. It was an appalling decision to have to make. It was hard on the pongos who by now were very keyed up. The tension became extremely marked wherever one went. Add to this the strain of being overcrowded and cooped up.

Monday 5 June 1944. The weather is appalling but everything was apparently on. Everyone depressed because the obvious inference was that they couldn't wait for the weather and were going in regardless.
Monday evening. Our little group of ships steamed out of the Solent around the needles. I wondered if we were perhaps the only group that had not received the cancellation order and we would arrive to find that we were the only ships there. I think that the same thought occurred to the others but no one said anything.

However as dusk fell, on the horizon all around us, there were hundreds of lights flashing and little hulls just showing. At least we weren't the only ones going and the weather was a lot better, though we were wallowing slowly in the remains of the sea.

On going on deck in the morning, we found that the convoy was wallowing along – the same, but instead of being alone there were hundreds of ships around us gradually converging on a single point.

An upturned LCT floated by and we wondered what was going to happen to us in a little while. Gradually, as the line of France came into view, we heard and then saw the guns of the warships shelling much more spasmodically than I'd imagined. Then gradually the beaches and shells became visible and everyone was topside 'goofing'. In fact it was more like a football match or a grandstand view of Blackpool.

Pongos getting very anxious because they weren't going shore – poor devils. Rhinos had their hands full and everyone was getting very depressed by evening with no chance of getting unloaded that night. K rations for supper because the galley staff had been goofing all day and did not cook anything.

Wind got up that night. The anchor dragged and after drifting and dragging we ran on to a British hunt destroyer, who only got away by a very nice bit of seamanship. Then we got involved with another United States LST stern cable, managing to twist ourselves once completely round the other cable by drifting out of control. LST 439 did not shine here either. Eventually freed.

Everyone was very much on edge because one felt that your own cargo was essential to prevent the bridgehead being pushed back into the sea. We received orders to beach that evening. We got the cargo ashore and everyone felt better. There were no casualties and so we went ashore.

I went through the taped minefields to Vers sur Mars. By now there were 100's of supplies going in trucks, ducks, etc, streaming by filled with troops. There was some rather frightened French villagers, a lady gathering a bunch of radishes and scuttling home.

We went back and forth several times over the next few days. We went to Juno beach twice and Gold beach twice. Once to the American beach at Omaha. Here we picked up sixteen casualties and had a little difficulty with the Americans over the various questions of responsibility.

On one occasion we went over to the other side but couldn't land because of the storm and came back. On our last trip to Courseille, we ran over someone else's stern anchor and took a 6ft hole in the bottom. The duty officers who were supposed to be on the bridge were playing poker in the wardroom!

French people were by no means friendly. Natural I suppose if you've had your homes blasted to bits.

Through out the period of operations discipline was lax. No sentries at the doors of the ships, everybody wandering all over the place. French children coming aboard and joining in the captain's food queues. A lot of ill feeling as a result.

On D-Day James Kerr was put ashore on Sword Beach to provide artillery support for the glider troops of the American 6th Airborne:

I was one of the British assault troops landing on D-Day, day one. I was a wireless operator/driver in one of the non-firing communication Sherman tanks.

It is a little known fact that the first tanks landed in Normandy at SWORD beach early on D-Day 1944 were six non-firing Assault Command Communication tanks of the 3rd Division, from the Dundee and Fife batteries of the 33rd Field regiment Royal Artillery (ex 76th Highland Field Regiment). We were also the artillery for the Glider troops of the 6th Airborne.

After a rough crossing in flat bottomed LTCs low clouds made it impossible for the gliders to come in on schedule – they landed miles away, many hours late – almost too late. In consequence a 'touch and go' situation developed as our Assault Observation Party was wiped out, and our other vital Observation Officer was in the gliders.

Our guns – American Howitzers – each with their own wireless operator on open Sherman chassis were given fire orders from their own command Sherman tank. Command wireless operators had to have a good memory as no code signs were allowed to be written down, plus the fact that he also had to operate two frequencies at the same time.

We held the Germans back with sheer fire-power until other Airborne units eventually arrived. Initially our guns were firing while standing still in the sea. We lost two of the six non-firing Communication Sherman tanks which reported the situation to 'Monty' every hour for the first week (and I had volunteered for this stressful task!).

The beach had to be cleared of casualties before any tanks could land. All other divisions, including a tank division, came in after we could move forward from the beach. Tragically, some of our urgent initial casualty replacements (signals) lasted only 24 hours. If our reports had been as freely given out to the public as per the Falklands war, I'm sure we would have lost the war that first week in Normandy.

As Murdo MacLeod discovered, it wasn't only the initial landings that men had to contend with:

After the first initial landings we had to get in and clear the beaches, to dig in waiting for the German counter-attack and after a heavy day you were tired and they were giving you Pithedine, Pithedine I think it was, tablets to keep you awake, a stimulant to keep you going. I mean, you didn't get any sleep the first couple of days. But when the effects of this wore off you were just like a wet rag.

They were booby trapping the bodies. They took some of the men of the ships and sent them ashore as burial parties gathering the bodies. They had to take ropes, they had them booby trapped, that's a fact.

Thomas Yates and his crew were serving in one of 'Hobart's Funnies', a variety of tank designs created by Major-General Percy Hobart to overcome the obstacles of D-Day, obstacles such as mines, soft sand and ditches. The crew were happy to be held in reserve for the big event:

So this seemingly endless training brought us up to D-Day. Luckily, the Lothians and Border Yeomanry were drawn out to be in reserve for the actual landings because we knew there would be heavy casualties and nature comes to the fore – survival.

Murdo MacKenzie recalls crossing the Channel with 23 Casualty Clearing Station to deal with the aftermath of the landings at Sword Beach:

It was stormy, but not too bad. I wasn't seasick. We were full of apprehension, we didn't know what was going to happen.

He recalls his role collecting the wounded:

> Enemy troops were lying next to our boys, so we treated them the
> same. We hoped they'd be doing the same for our lads on the other
> side.

For Murdo MacLeod, the Normandy invasion was not a brief experience:

> We stayed there for two months. What we done was every night we
> went out and from the Normandy beaches at intervals of maybe
> quarter to half a mile between each boat did a semi-circle facing
> towards Le Havre. The army never took Le Havre right away. It was
> that strong an area that they just passed by it and went straight on
> further into Belgium.
>
> After Normandy we were ten weeks without ever going near land,
> ten weeks in the English channel and we weren't even allowed to go
> into Aramanches or even Mulberry, we needed provisions. We were
> down to sea biscuits and they exploded a mine and the fish were
> stunned and we were over the side scooping up fish. Our skipper
> signalled a merchant ship going in and they gave us a couple of sack
> of tatties and it wasn't until then that they let us in for provisions, and
> ammunition of course.
>
> I was on two flack ships, LCF 42 I was on and I was only off it a
> fortnight when she was going alongside the cruiser Belfast when she
> was hit. The Germans were shelling from Le Havre, anti-personnel
> shells massacred about 50, they were trying to hit the cruiser but it hit
> her mast, LCF 42. I had only just left her to go onto her sister ship
> LCF 39. Somebody was looking after me that day.
>
> We picked up these 50 odd survivors from that destroyer that got
> sunk, The Swift. A lot of the men were in the sea, on Carnie floats
> and some were on corked scrambling nets and we went as close as
> we could to them and the marines tried to haul them on board. They
> were shocked. It must have been some explosion. The ship was in two
> halves. Just one hit. A torpedo.

On To Germany

The period between D-Day and the end of August 1944 became known as the battle of Normandy, as allied troops fought to break out of the beachhead.

Ernest Jamieson was now on his fourth campaign – North Africa, Sicily, Italy and now the Normandy landings and the advance through Europe:

> On the second night [D-day plus one] at 2am I was ordered to dump the Compo rations and pick up ammunition and along with others headed for Bayeaux to supply the guns. One night (fortunately I wasn't on the detail) some of the lads were off loading at the guns while they were firing when a single German plane came over and seeing the gun flashes dropped anti-personnel bombs. Some of the lads were taken to hospital and I never saw them again. A chap called Whittle returned with his windscreen and cabin like a pepper-pot. Our Brigadier was killed at Bretteville by a shell, a great loss. We were alongside the Canadians trying to take Caen. At the aerodrome at Capriguet the Germans had dug in tanks and 'Typhoons' with rockets came over and blasted them. Quite a show; then in the twilight bombers flew over Caen. You wondered how anyone could survive.

Serving with his RAF recognisance unit out in advance of the main body, James Hogg recalled the 'race' across France:

> Once we broke through the Falaise Gap it was quite helter skelter, I was doing about 70 miles an hour. I thought, 'my God, where are they'. When they broke out we were there and we pushed on up, as far as I mind it was Arras. Pulled into this great big field and consolidated wirselves out a wee bit. We were there for about a couple of days and then we headed on up into Brussels. I thought the war was over, I really thought the war was over. The place was polluted with people, waving flags, shouting victory and all the rest. That was good that, I thought, 'thank goodness, I'll get away hame in a wee while'. We

then went through Brussels and stopped at a place called Vilbruog, just something like Birkhill to Dundee.

We were sent from Portsmouth to Normandy, about three weeks before we went out there, of course the beachhead was established by that time. When we landed there we landed at Bayonne and from there, once we had burst through at Falaise Gap, all the Germans just, we couldn't find them. I was doing about 70 miles an hour, wondering, 'where are these guys'? To tell the truth, we came to a stop at Arras, in France, and from there there wasn't much of a carry on there. And then we headed up and weren't long before we got into Holland.

Ernest Jamieson was also part of the breakthrough at the Falaise Gap and recalled the devastation that met the advancing allied troops in the aftermath of large-scale air attacks:

After the breakthrough we travelled on the main road and saw a sign Paris 60km. We headed into the Falaise Gap (also known as the Falaise Pocket). Falaise itself was badly damaged and many civilians were killed. When we went through many women turned their backs on us. No cheering there. The devastation was terrible, horse drawn vehicles and men bulldozed to the side, bodies in the fields, guns and half tracks. One vehicle looked like a personnel carrier with dead all round with one body, arms outstretched, one knee up as if sunbathing. A sad sight was a farm cart with two dead horses and the old grey haired farmer lying between them.

In contrast to this, Keith Hodgkin found his tank landing craft back in England:

Back in England too, no official liberty but everyone took it. Most unsatisfactory. One evening we shipped a British colonel with our troops. Two of the US officers came in really tight. One was hurriedly put to bed, the other we rather foolishly warned to be on the lookout for the colonel. He marched into the wardroom and said at the top of his voice 'Where the hell's the fucking colonel.' As he was sitting about two feet away there wasn't much doubt.

At one point in London the whole crew went on a blind in the dock area. Our next load of ships stores arrived with only a couple of hours before we sailed. The American watch were unrousable. They told their American duty officer to 'Fuck off'. Eventually our 30 SBA (Sick Berth Attendants) volunteered for the job. The British navy had saved the day.

In August 1944, in his role as medical officer, he was called to witness punishment:

Had to go and witness a whipping in the cells. Everyone very stern and all seemed so unnecessary. Didn't feel disgusted so much as feeling that it was entirely pointless. Came away thinking that if I'd been given the choice of having a day's leave docked or twelve strokes of the cane, I'd choose the latter every time.

Before they could get into their first action, Thomas Yates and his crew were wounded:

Early July 1944 saw us at last in France, on the outskirts of Caan. Up to this time we had not done any flailing. Moving up to the area where we were going to do our first flailing in action – we were halted and naturally all dismounted – wondering what time we would move ahead, and looking at our maps when a salvo of mortar bombs straddled us. Each member of my crew, including myself, got hit by shrapnel, but only one seriously. We were 'walking wounded'.

Roddy MacLeod took part in the fight for Le Havre. After the fall of the town, Roddy had a strange meeting on the street.

We captured Le Havre in France and on the Sunday the fighting was over and I went for a walk and I seen an old Frenchman with a black beret on coming down the street and he says to me 'it's a fine morning', in Gaelic. I thought to myself 'Christ'. I quizzed him how he spoke Gaelic, he married a French lassie during the Great War. So he asked me was there any Gaelic speaking men in the unit and I says 'aye, plenty of them, come and show me where you live.' So he showed me this underground cellar on a main street and I went back to the unit and I used to take my turn on guard, the NCO in charge of the guard in the underground tunnels in the mountain above Le Havre. I went up there with a 15 cwt truck and half a dozen of the Gaelic speaking boys. And mind the big Ceylon boxes of tea you used to get, well got one of them and bottles of brandy, cigars, tins of cold ham, tins of bully beef and we loaded the bloody lorry and went to see him, we took all this stuff into his cellar underground and we had a Ceilidh, I tell you, there was plenty Gaelic songs. The tears were running down his face.

However, Thomas Yates and his crew had recovered in time to take part in the operation to clear the Channel ports:

We were preparing to clear the Channel ports – Le Havre being the first. Stroke of luck again, my squadron was to be reserve, and although we suffered some long range shelling, we were not called on to assist in the actual assault.

The next port of call to be liberated was to be Boulogne, more heavily fortified than Le Havre, and more open ground overlooked by the German gunners 88s and very heavily impregnated with land mines. Prior to going into action, we all had to attend a scale model of the objective – where the enemy guns are sited, and tank traps, hazards, etc. I got a decoration for my action, but it was not until I was again in hospital in Eindhoven that I got the letter from my C.O. informing me of the award. The reason for being in hospital was failure of the flail to explode a mine, this time because the ground was frozen.

Thomas was awarded the Military Medal for his actions at Boulogne:

On 18th September 1944 at Boulogne, this NCO was in command of one tank in 1 troop, C Squadron, 1st Lothians in support of 8 Canadian Infantry Brigade.

During the breaching operation in which his troop were concerned, all the other tanks of his troop were knocked out and his, only,
was left to complete the breach. This he did by making two sweeps up
and down the lane all the time under heavy fire. On completion, he
immediately found and directed the infantry through the lane which
subsequently, became the main axis of advance.

That the operation was successful was largely due to L/Cpl. Yates'
skill, initiative and determination in continuing a task in which 4 other
tanks had already been destroyed.

James Hogg continued to play a recognisance role as the allies
advanced across France:

Although we had the RAF flashes on, it was just battledress, the
armoured boys did as well. We were the first unit in the RAF to be
organised in that manner. We did assault courses, all that as well. We
were with the 11th Armoured Division. We were only part of them.
We did a bit of reconnaissance and that, did a few night patrols. Out
into no man's land, see where they were and what not. Three in an
armoured car. The gunner, the commander and the driver.

Thomas Yates continued to participate in the operation to 'roll up'
the remaining enemy-occupied Channel ports:

After Boulogne, it was the turn of Calais to be freed. The previous
night to our assault on the fortifications on the high ground overlooking the town, a 500 bomber raid took place which we witnessed from
only a couple of miles away. Sadly we saw a few planes come down
in flames. At first light we formed up and made our way to the hills,
and surprisingly we didn't get any hassle from our objective, but the
big guns at Cap Griz Nez got our range and we were lucky not to be
hit. When we – the flails at the forefront of the assault team – reached
our 'Start to Flail Line' we couldn't. the ground was completely cra-
tered by the previous nights heavy bombing raid. Our instructions
were then to support the infantry as gun tanks. This was a nightmare.
Many landmines had been tossed in the air around the bomb craters.

It really surprised us that the land mines could survive the bombing and lie around unexploded. The ones you could see were alright – as far as it goes, but no one knew if there were any lying beneath the surface. I weaved about round the craters, the tanks would bog down in the holes, guiding my driver until I could not proceed any further. I informed my team leader and he told me to withdraw. What a problem. No place to turn round, the only way out was to reverse my tank out, in the self same tracks I had made on the forward journey so as to avoid blowing an unseen mine. This was a distance of 500 yards and believe me it felt like 500 miles, speaking to my driver over the intercom, stood well out on the turret hatch, remembering that we were going in reverse – left a bit – right a bit – right a bit more, etc. So it went on until we were clear of the minefield and craters. I don't think I have sweated so much in a short time.

Back to our forming up place where we were told to dismount and the usual thing was to get a bite to eat, and a brew. Each tank crew was a little unit on its own and carried our rations, mostly a 5 man–3 day pack which contained all the necessary items of food, including chocolate and cigarettes. Routines to be carried out on all the tanks before bedding down for the night. Tarpaulin on the grass at the side of the tank, a blanket to lie on, and pull the tarpaulin over, and pray it doesn't rain, or that the enemy feels like dropping a few mortar bombs or shells over.

After what seemed to be about 1 hours sleep I was awakened by our squadron Sgt Major who told me to wake my driver and take our tank back up to where we had been the previous day, and have a flamethrower tank (Churchill) along with me. Actually, this was about 5 am and just beginning to show signs of dawn.

Off we went, me and the flamethrower. By the time we had reached the outer edge of the minefield, I stopped and signalled the flame-thrower to stop. We both dismounted and after I had explained about the previous day we had both walked in tank tracks to the crest of the hill. Lying down and easing forward we peered over the top of the crest to look down on to the foreground and forward to Calais.

What a beautiful sight to behold. White flags were flying from every pillbox and fortification we could see. I was so elated I could

have ran the whole distance back to our camp. On return, reported to
Sgt Major who took On to the Squadron Leader – made my verbal
report, and then was whisked away in a jeep for a couple of miles
where I had to make my report to the G.O.C. myself. Not bad for
a L/Cpl really.

Back in the UK after the excitement of the Normandy beachhead,
Keith Hodgkin found himself returned to the boredom of regular
medical duties at Chatham:

A whole morning of lamp inspections about 200 in all.
'Over here Jack – Give me your card'
'Slip your gear down. Any complaints'
'Arms out'
'Now put your hand in front of your mouth and cough'
'Your mouth I said, not your privates'
'Turn round'
'When were you last with a woman?'
'Here's your card – Carry on'
Amazing variation of form and physical characteristics and types.
Then a whole afternoon of inspections for the army. The worst part of
this was the foot inspections in a hot stuffy room with no ventilation.
There were 63 of these in the afternoon.
'Ever been seriously ill? Pneumonia, diphtheria, T.B.?'
'Ever had VD, trouble with your ears?'
'Look at the bridge of my nose' Test their pupils.
Then down to their feet – get this done quickly.
'Up on your toes'
Then up to the genitals.
'Any varicose veins? Piles?'
then up to the chest and finish off.
So much for preventative medicine. After a day of this one would give
anything for a good clean disease.

The task of clearing the remnants of German resistance in France
was coming to an end, as Thomas Yates was glad to discover:

After Calais, the last of the big guns which had threatened Channel shipping since Dunkirk, were at Cap Guiz Nez and would be the last of the Channel ports to be liberated. Once again an early morning start after a night time bombing raid. We had some fire directed at us as we began to flail but in ¼ mile we didn't encounter any mines, and we were told to halt and give covering fire. We fired a few shells at the openings towards the top of the large concrete gun emplacements which housed the 15" and 18" long range guns. Some of our shells went into the holes and later when we went into one of the large gun emplacements, we found that quite a lot of damage had been caused. Luckily, these guns could not fire inland, otherwise it would have been a different story. This position fell with not too many casualties.

Ernest Jamieson crossed into Belgium:

On into Belgium and stopped at Renai where we saw a V1 rocket site which had been destroyed by the RAF. House on top of the hill where Germans were billeted was destroyed. Germans cut road further up and the people started taking in flags again from windows. Road opened again and many prisoners taken, I was sent up to collect prisoners and take them down the line, I carried a load of Mongolians fighting for the German Army. Brussels is free and there is a big parade by the Guards Division. We were given a days leave in Brussels which we enjoyed very much and given a great welcome by the citizens.

The German last-ditch effort in the Ardennes was recalled by James Hogg:

We were just reconnaissance, that was all we were used for. When we got into Holland, Eindhoven was our headquarters. We were doing reconnaissance for the armour that was coming in back of us, we were just poking aboot. That's all we did, and of course we just went on bomb dumps and things like that. Believe it or not we were stuck there for about six months and we had to take our turn in the front line just like everybody else. As a matter of fact, one of the particular things – the Ardennes where Von Runsted pushed us out, the Americans were getting battered to hell in there – when that happened we were shoved into a place called Best and we were put in the front line there and the 15th Scottish Division was taken out of there and by all accounts, as far as we were concerned, that's what we were replacing in the front line, to let them away down to the American sector, and as far as we believe the 15th Scottish took up position behind the Americans and when the Americans were coming back they filtered through the 15th Scottish line and when Von Runsted came up against the 15th Scottish, that was the end of it, it was all over. To me that was about the finish of the war. Because that was their final push, their idea was to push through there and come round the back. I've often wondered why that's never been in the history books. And that's really what happened, the 15th Scottish Division, all little fellows too.

Thomas Yates is adamant his Scottish unit was the first 'British' armour to cross into Germany:

At the end of October the fighting had moved almost up to the German border. Part of our action here was actually in Germany and I don't think I would be far wrong if I said 'C' Squadron 1st Lothians were the first British armour on German soil. Since our first involvement in the fighting we had been in support of a Canadian Division, but for the first time we were in support of an American unit in the vicinity of Waldenrath. The objective was to take a wooded area which was approached by open land and suspected to be heavily mined. The time was towards the end of November 1944, and after a wet period the ground was very soft. On this occasion I was the only flail involved, no other armoured vehicles either.

Once the allied forces broke out from Normandy the German defences crumbled and the allies advanced across France faster than they had ever anticipated. The port of Antwerp was desperately needed to alleviate the supply crisis brought about by the speed of the allied advance and the inability to keep the forward sections of the army adequately supplied. However, although Antwerp was an important port as the allies pushed towards Germany, holding the port itself was not enough. The allies needed to gain control of the area to the north-west of Antwerp known as the Scheldt.

John Forfar was involved in the landings at Flushing in an attempt by the allies to clear the seaway to Antwerp:

> The Americans were clamouring for a decent port so the British captured Antwerp with hardly any damage. And then they said they couldn't use it. It was terribly urgent to clear the Scheldt. So they sent the Canadians to clear the south bank of the Scheldt and they sent the 5th Scottish Division and four commandos. That was No 4, which was an Army Commando, No 41 which was a Marine Commando, No 47 a Marine Commando and No 48. And the thing was, the way it was to be done was: four commandos to attack Flushing along with the 5th Scottish Division, a much bigger unit. 47 and 48 were to attack a place called Westkapelle. The 4th Commando and the 5th Division were to go to Flushing. We trained at Wenduine for this and the training, we're talking about maybe two or three weeks in October.

He recalls the first use of American amphibious vehicles – these 'Buffalos' had been used to good effect in the Pacific by the US Marines but this was their first use in Europe:

> They were astonishing vehicles when you got into them. The track went round, it propelled the thing along and they'd never been used in the British army before, they were American. They were absolutely marvellous because you got into the, you were in a landing craft tank and inside this thing which was armour, and it went trundling out and providing nobody had shot at it by this time you moved into the water. Then you sank away down. You've only again got that amount of freeboard and you feel pretty safe stuck down in this thing, quite remarkable. Well we got into our, well we're already in these thing we called a Buffalo or various other names. But of course it was terribly susceptible to tidal movements, not much headway.

The commando attack at Walcheren left the allies in control. Life now became a series of dangerous patrols for James Hogg and his comrades:

> The Jerries took up position on the other side of the canal in Holland, we were sat there for about four months. It was pretty easy there until we got to Best where we got stopped, the Jerries were on the other side. It was just a case of night patrols, that's all I did, a few night patrols to poke about and see what was happening. You went out into no man's land on foot, there was only two or three, there was only the corporal, me and this other guy. We had to get a replacement at four o' clock and at eight o'clock he was dead. Shot right at my side. Flown out from the UK as a replacement from some of our boys that had fallen by the wayside. He was with us and how they killed him, he had the bren gun, the machine gun, and Gerry saw us before we saw them, we were going down in the ditch, getting into the ditch when they seen us coming in. They opened fire, the tracer started shooting and of course the boy was killed outright. He was only twenty-one. Four hours.

Civilians were the unfortunate casualties of war:

> Evacuation of civilians began on the banks of the River Maas. We moved people from Maaseyeck to the Phillips factory in Eindhoven. I had the village priest beside me carrying the silver chalices and other objects from his church as it had been damaged. Though the church was badly burned and the large crucifix was still standing. The wood of the cross had burned but the body of Jesus was intact, not a blemish and as it was raining heavily it appeared pure white. (Ernest Jamieson)

Unexpected piano music and prisoners. Ernest Jamieson encountered both on the same day:

> Called out on emergency trip to replenish County of London Yeomanry who were supporting 6th Royal Welsh Fusiliers, (quite a

number of trucks involved). It was dusk and raining heavily as we approached and the sky appeared red from the burning buildings. As we entered the main street the RWF were on both sides and warned us there was still some sniping going on. We reached the main square where three tanks were standing and started off loading the fuel. We heard piano music coming from a building and when we investigated it was one of our mates, a Welshman with the uncommon name of Jones playing this piano at the window. It had been damaged but he was still getting a tune out of it. He was playing, 'I'll be Seeing You in all the Old Familiar Places'. In the surroundings it seemed eerie and out of place. Moved out of Bocholt and onto road where concrete road blocks had been moved to the side. Came to a farm where we were to stay the night. We tried to get into field but with the heavy rain some trucks stuck so we kept to the cobble paths round the outbuildings. Billeted in a barn which the Germans had used.

I was part of a guard detail that night. It was still raining but there was a two wheeled cart that we tipped up, giving us some shelter. Next morning the old farmer came to us and said that there were three German soldiers in one of the barns. I think he was afraid something would happen to him if he didn't tell us. They were up in the loft and when they came down they all wore Red Cross arm bands, plain uniform, no insignias, no weapons, very suspicious. We held them until they were taken back down the line.

In a strange twist, Thomas Yates discovered that he and his crew were the only ones invited to the party:

After a short artillery barrage we commenced to flail as per instructions. To my surprise I did not encounter any land mines, although I witnessed several mortar bomb explosions quite close. I was sincerely hoping that there were no German gunners with my tank in the sights of an 88 gun, which was the most feared gun of all our armoured units. The armour piercing shots from these guns could penetrate the Sherman armour at more than two miles distance. On reaching my operational 'cease flailing position' at the perimeter of the wooded area I prepared to give supporting fore to the infantry which was supposed to be following my tank – at a respectable distance of course. It was hard to believe but there was not one soul in sight, nothing anywhere, just my tank and crew for miles. Only the CRUMP – CRUMP of mortar shells landing around broke the silence. So radio to H.Q. to find that the planned infantry attack had been cancelled at the last minute, but no one had bothered to send a message to my tank, and on returning, luckily unscathed, I made my anger known to my senior officers. By early February the fighting front had began to move again. Not many established minefields appeared to have been laid and we did very little operational flailing. And once the Rhine had been crossed we were virtually redundant and possibly around as a show of strength, doing patrol duties and whatever was required of us. I can't say boring because there was still the odd long range gun firing on us, and it was a great relief when the surrender was signed and hostilities ceased

George Morrison was involved in the fierce battle for the suburbs of Goch:

> The Black Watch had made a night attack into the town, and found it lightly held with a few old spandaus. We came in the next morning to clean up on the right of the town. But during the night the Germans had reinforced the town with two fresh battalions and the situation had radically changed. The leading company commander was killed in the first five minutes by a sniper from the school. That was my company's objective, so we had to change the plan and I attacked from the right flank. We were sniped continually from the houses, but the lads dashed in with grenades and firing their automatics, and we routed them out of the school, taking about ten prisoners.

The next morning they attacked the German positions in the village of Thomashof:

> We were heavily mortared and under fire from 88s so we decided to clear one group of houses on the right flank to get a firm base for

the attack. One platoon went in with the flamethrowers, and took 23 Boche prisoners from those houses. I got the company in position and had a look across the field. In the main group of buildings I could see hundreds of Boche walking around. Their snipers were very active, and I had no sooner posted one chap at a window than he was killed by a spandau. To reach the main group of houses we had to cross 300 yards of open ground. Six spandaus were firing across this field, and it looked a pretty grim job. I told the tanks and flamethrowers to go in with the infantry, and they set off under cover of smoke. One of the flamethrowers got right across the field with the leading platoon, and they got into a group of buildings and took twenty Boche prisoner. The young officer in charge had just joined us two days before. He walked right through those spandau bullets, with a grenade in each hand, and as one of his chaps told me 'you couldn't help follow that man'. He walked back across the bullet-swept field, escorting ten German prisoners – three of the Germans were killed by their own bullets coming back. I found the officer was wounded in the hand, and had three spandau bullets through his ankle. He nearly wept when I wouldn't let him go back.

There was as much danger from your own side, as Ernest Jamieson found out:

The first night was on guard in a farm cottage near a large farm house which stood on the other side of the road. The cottage was bare except for a large picture of an elderly woman on the wall. About 2am there was a large bang from the farm house and what was left of the glass in our windows came flying in and the picture dropped of the wall but another guard came running in saying some 4.5 guns were across in the farm and at that another shot went off. The gunners said they were just a nuisance gun, firing across to keep the Germans awake. I was put on the bread run going back to Tilburg where a bakery had started then going round the units.

Bill Edgar was not impressed with the inability of the allied Sherman tank to stand up to the firepower of the Tiger:

The next one was Germany and there was a bit of a shindig there. He got his Mark VI tigers there, the first time we had seen them. It used to take two Shermans or four Shermans to get one Mark VI. No messing, if you hit a Sherman that was the end of it. We were trying to get them across the rivers, get the bridges across, pontoons, anything, boats. We used folding boats, paddling them across and coming back for more.

James Kerr found himself on the wrong end of a German self-propelled gun:

In the street fighting of Venrai I was in an OP party observing from and attic skylight. My wireless set was on my back as usual but I felt I needed a better aerial to get a stronger signal. I raised the aerial. Unfortunately, an SS officer in the courtyard below saw my aerial and fired 3 rounds impact shrapnel into the attic, knocking out my wireless and me. On our officers order we played dead (we had no real alternative) and the German self propelled gun withdrew satis-fied. I was badly concussed but was not listed as wounded. That was a nasty experience.

William Marks witnessed the allied airdrop on Arnhem:

I was in Holland, just came into Holland when I saw all these planes going ower, going to Arnhem. The roads were blocked. We were going one way and the Germans were coming the other. I said, 'some battle been going on here'. We got into Arnhem anyway and we got them oot o' there.

Crossing into Holland, Ernest Jamieson was also a witness to the drop:

Crossed into Holland and saw the Airborne Division fly on to Arnhem. One of the Dakotas was hit by ack-ack but managed to release its glider before it crashed.

James Hogg's recognisance unit was on the way to Niemegan:

> When they dropped the 6th Airborne at Niemegan and Arnhem we
> were on the way up to Niemegan and they were all dropping back, the
> Yankees as well. A Yankee said, 'God knows what your guys is doing
> over there, they're getting battered to hell'. Seemingly there was this
> tank division, German tank division, resting and our intelligence knew
> nothing about it. And our lads were dropped on the other side.

Also involved in the advance to Niemegan was James Kerr's unit, as
it rushed to the town to provide artillery support for the American
airborne forces:

> My unit (C troop) of the 76th Highland Field Regiment, Royal
> Artillery (renamed 33rd Fld. Reg. for D-Day assault) was chosen on
> merit to be sent from Holland on a secret mission (unescorted) i.e.
> going back into Belgium and France – a days long journey – to get
> across the only bridge still intact. We were being sent to try to help
> American paratroops who had landed at Niemegan shortly after the
> Arnhem drop and had sent an SOS for artillery support (no doubt
> not relishing another Arnhem debacle). We were a Scottish troop of
> D-Day assault artillery of 4 guns (minus their Sherman S/Ps) compris-
> ing about 38 men including 2 officers, (no infantry support) and a lot
> of jerry-cans filled with petrol and three times our normal amount
> of shells. Remember, this was enemy held territory and there were
> no allied troops between the rivers Maas and Rhine at that time – an
> almost suicidal mission it appeared.
>
> We were met by a Resistance fighter at every village and told
> which direction to go for next village contact. We even sometimes
> slept in a house (an unheard of luxury) and guarded by a group of
> resistance fighters who helped to refill our petrol tanks. On leaving in
> the morning each house had a note reading 'good luck and give them
> hell'. Only our officer was allowed to speak to them, but the note
> convinced me that some of those were British agents – since believed
> to have been the late Colonel Buckmaster's brave agents of the SOE.
> Were telephone lines repaired and used to confirm which way ahead

was clear? How else? Our valiant Captain was not deemed necessary risk – was too valuable – I believe he was sent on well earned leave.

On final contact, a few miles from Niemegan, farmers asked us if they could kill a farm animal as they were starving (living on potatoes only). They must only sell animals to Germans (none for themselves) for Dutch notes which the Germans were printing and which they thought were worthless. As a perk for successful link-up Military Intelligence had told us that these notes would be honoured – instant barter deals followed for sheaves of valuable notes! Furthermore, if we allowed them to kill a farm animal, we could send back for a piece of meat and some for the Americans' contact unit as well. Instant agreement, of course – a big morale booster all round and only 10 minutes used up. In my double role of senior wireless operator/driver I had been ordered to contact the Americans in person (wireless only for listening watch) and tell them to look out for, and use any means to repel, underwater frogmen intent on blowing up the bridge.

Our four guns, with tons of extra shells, were able to cope somehow for the best part of a week until British troops fought their way to us. Thankfully our sleeping agents were not double-agents or we might not have survived, nor were we attacked on route (still unescorted). This was a wonderful achievement for the resistance fighters. Soon we were taking up positions and the officer and I went to meet the Americans as arranged. A brilliant secret mission (directed by London no doubt) and with all the hallmarks of Colonel Buckmaster's men (and women) of SOE I think. In typical British fashion no medals were awarded as 'we were only doing our duty' even although it was hailed as 'A useful victory' and saved lives.

R.A.H. Hearn joined his regiment, The Scots Greys, as they marched from Belgium into Holland. The regiment was engaged in the attempt to break through at Arnhem. A letter from home describes life in Blighty:

Dear Bob,

Just a line to wish you as happy a Xmas as possible. It will certainly not be spent under ideal conditions, but we shall all be thinking about you a lot and hoping you manage to find somewhere dry with a fire and good company, and may we all be together for Xmas 1945.

It is very nice to be able to get news of you. When Iris gets letters at Reading she sends them on here, so altogether we do pretty well.

The pictures were most interesting and we all like to hear as much as you can tell us.

Life with us is going much the same as usual. Some Americans are coming to do excerpts from 'Messiah' tonight and two of them are coming to tea first, so I must stop and be pleasant to them.

All the best to you and best wishes for 1945.
God Bless
Jay

Roddy MacLeod also recalls advancing through Holland and crossing the canals under fire:

They were towing boats with tanks up to a sort of river come canal in Holland and we were under heavy shell fire and the arrangements broke down for dragging the boats up. It was canvas assault boats we had. There was eight of us in it and we got this boat up and managed to cross the canal and the Germans were firing at us, it was like hailstones on the water, anyway, we got across and out of the eight of us, three of us got out of it, the other boys were wounded. We dragged the assault boat up the bank so that the boys who came after would get to them, would attend to them. I got up the bank and I could see the machine gun nest just ahead, and kept the head down and pointed to the boys down below me where the, they had hand grenades and they lobbed them over the bank into the trenches and of course the hand grenades exploded and the Germans got down in the trenches and before they could get up again I was up there with the Bren gun and that was the end of them.

The German paymaster was coming along with the pay for the whole battalion and I captured him I took the pay off him and I split it up with the three platoons in 'A' company. And I wasn't very popular with the other companies but I dished it out with my own mates.

Ernest Jamieson recalls meeting men from the American 101st
Airborne Division:

The US 101st division had taken the bridge at Graves and were at
Son. Later I was on detachment from 5 Company under Captain Hill
to the 44th Royal Tank Regiment who were supporting the 101st
Airborne. We passed through Son where the Americans had anti-tank
defences, then on to the village of St Oendrode. This road was shelled
regularly but we arrived safely at the brickworks outside the village.
The commander of the 44th RTR had his HQ there as the road had
been cut further on by the Germans. We parked inside the outer wall
near the commanders tank. I was on the ration truck, the others on
petrol (the tanks didn't run on diesel). Quite a number of wounded
passing down the road on jeeps with stretchers strapped on. After
the first day had to go back to Eindhoven to replenish. One day two
echelon trucks came by filled up and only got a few hundred yards
up the road when both were hit and went up in flames. The chimney
stack must have been a good range finder for the German guns. The
road was open for a while then closed again. One night, when on
guard with a tankie, (one of us at each gateway), I was leaning on
the wall with the sten gun when I heard traffic moving up. The first
vehicle to come into sight was a jeep with an American officer and
some trucks behind him. Across from us was a small valley with trees
round it and as the jeep approached the brickworks a machine gun
opened up from the trees and bullets ricocheted of the road. The jeep
braked and then we heard the bump, bump, bump as trucks ran into
one another. He shouted for them to reverse which they did and
there was no more firing and some time later they sped past, (mostly
black drivers). Next day up marched a platoon of American Airborne,
tough looking characters with grenades taped to them and bandoliers
of ammunition around their necks. The officer told them to squat by
the wall. I was cutting bread at the time and some of them came over
for a slice and jam. They hadn't had bread for a while, but the officer
told them to pack up and move out. They went across the road and
into the woods and then some shelling started. You'd think someone
was pulling the trees out by their roots and throwing them away. The

road was later opened and we moved back down the line to join the company. The road was full of troops moving up.

Under fire for the first time, Peter MacLeod was surprised at how he felt:

I remember the first time I was under fire, I was supposed to be a sniper you see. There were two of these machine gun nests up on the hill in front of us. Every time I tried to get my head round a tree, Boom. I was as cool as a pipe, that's amazing. I knew that I had to leave that place and my training came in, I had to zig zag. I was never hit.

James Kerr was instrumental in initiating the surrender of an SS Panzer Division, but in order to avoid disciplinary charges his action was not officially recognised:

We had been tracking an SS Panzer Tank Division and came across a British soldiers body which, it appeared, had been placed in the path of our advance. My impression of this was that they were trying to create a diversion. We had been warned in training to treat anything like this with caution – it could be booby-trapped. The first inquisitive soldier had one foot blown off, then his would-be rescuer suffered the same fate. I was utterly sickened by this nasty act of German brutality and reached entirely differently from the Sgt. Major who, with great courage and some luck managed to rescue both. Anger took over in my case, with realisation that the SS had caused this diversion. I was one of the overnight wireless operators who had been unable to contact our OP party who had been following the SS. I wondered why and thought that their set might be out of range. Some Germans were in front of us so if our OP is now out of range then the Panzer Division could be behind us. We were cut off! If I was correct then our Captain would send one operator (spare set on back) and hope that he could get back within range. I had been relieved and told to charge up batteries. As I appeared to be the only person to realise the significance of the booby-trapped body – the situation was, to me, most desperately urgent so I disobeyed the order (a Court Marshall offence) and took the wireless truck to a suitable position. In this new position I fixed the tall aerial on a long lead, unlocked my dials and searched the airwaves for our OP. This time I beamed backwards. Within five minutes I had located our OP's weak voice calling for fire orders on a map reference. This I believed to be his way of asking to meet there and please hurry (unrehearsed code to a mate operator) which was surprisingly not coded (a top priority indication). His batteries were weak and he could not hear me. I rushed to our Command Post with map reference and found that I had guessed correctly – so furthermore I ventured to suggest that no further attempts be made to use wireless and for secrecy rather send line signallers with new batteries and an officer so that fire orders could be silently relayed by phone to guns. It was urgent that 'Monty' had to be informed for entire approval. This was done and C troop controlled every gun in the British army and Canadian army within range, with systematically deadly firepower – our guns turned in opposite direction to our previous advance direction. The Panzer Tank Division was force to surrender after seven days and nights non-stop shelling. I had caused an SS General to surrender his whole division. I never received any award or appreciation. Three medals were awarded to the observation party. My exploits were suppressed as I was told to keep quiet. I had committed a Court Martial offence – but with such spectacular result. Penetration by the panzer division to the North Sea averted, so hundreds of our forces were saved from being cut off.

You didn't have to be in the front line to experience death at first hand, as William Marks found out:

My pal, well he wasn't my pal but he was a good chap, we were in Holland, on this railway line into Germany and there were mines there, just thin boxes full of explosives. They were hidden outside in the railway embankments and we were prodding for these mines, using a prodder. I said 'I'm going for some prodders'. We had a hut built and we kept all our stuff in it. And there was this boy called Norman Beckesley, he was a corporal and he should have known about it. Anyway, he had all these mines laid out and I says 'we're going for a prodder doon at the houf'. 'Will you bring back a pair of pliers'? he says to me. On the way back I never stopped, I just says 'there's your pliers Becks'. And I kept walking on to where I was going. I heard this bang and I says 'what the hells that'? What he was doing I don't know but he should have known better because we were always taught never to touch mines if they've been fought over. We were to explode them. We found three bits of him. The chippy made a wee box and we buried him there in the corner of the cemetery.

Not having learnt his lesson, Roddy MacLeod was still volunteering for dangerous missions:

The Marith Line, a big ditch twenty-five foot across and about twelve deep and the Germans were dead fly, they had bends in it. This ditch would stop any tank crossing. They had corners cut into it for sentries and three minefields in front. This day word came that The Black Watch tried to take a prisoner but they were beaten and didn't get the prisoner and there was two of us and an officer sent to try and get a German prisoner in this Marith Line because they knew they were patrolling along the bottom of this Maas Line, this large ditch. This bloke Johnny MacIntosh, a member of the Black Rock tug of war team on the Black Isle, it was between him and me to jump on this Jerry, and I lost the bloody toss. He says to me 'och, I'll no' be far behind you Roddy, if you get the bastard down'. You had to wait for a cloud to come over to make it slightly darker. I could see him. The sentries walked across maybe a hundred yards each way and met each other and away back again. I just waited until the bastard was right under and I stepped of the top of the twelve foot ditch and I landed right on top of the bastard and he got a knife out but I floored him but he got a knife out and split my shirt right up the side of my ribs but my mate, Johnny MacIntosh, he landed right on top of the two of us. Fucking near killed me! Never forget that. Stuck a revolver in the back of his neck and up the side of the ditch, through three mine fields and back to the bloody battalion. He was quizzed there and interrogated and we got all the information we wanted.

It was the apparent randomness of death that struck Ernest Jamieson:

> Tragedy struck the company while we were at Cleves. Another section of the company was parked on the outskirts of a field across from us and as the Post Corporal in the centre of the field called out the names of the lads who had mail, this one shell dropped as they went across, killing three and wounding an officer. One of the chaps, named Lawrence, had been with the company a long time, one of the others, a sergeant, had joined us just recently.
>
> It may seem insignificant when you take the casualties of infantry regiments but to us it was a great loss.

When Ernest arrived at the Siegfried Line he found both death and humour:

> Crossed the river Mass at Venlo on towards Tilburg, came to Siegfried Line and passed through the Riechwald Forest where we were attached to the Canadians. The Scottish Division had many casualties there. Large steel bunkers, gun emplacements disguised as houses. Corporal Morrison from Aberdeen who was in 5 Company learned later that his 19 year old brother had been killed there.
>
> Very bad track, made of logs and railway sleepers. The Canadians had a sign which read 'Liver Cure Mile'. We came on to the main road again where a line was strung up with long-johns, shirts and socks with a sign, 'This is the Siegfried Line and this is their wash'. Stopped outside Cleves where there was quite a bit of shelling.
>
> We got to the river Rhine and we were waiting to gaun across there. I said 'I don't know how we're going to cross there' because they were shelling us all the time. This sergeant o' ours came in, the Lance Sergeant he had to go with his company across there, and we've got to build a bridge across the Rhine, a folding boat bridge. (William Marks)

When Ernest Jamieson crossed the Rhine he came across a former forced labour camp:

Before crossing the Rhine the company took over some DUWKs, no volunteers required, glad I wasn't picked. Crossed the river on a pontoon bridge. Our company stopped in the town of Solingen and used the railway yards for parking. No one on the streets. At night heard wild singing and shouting then flames from a large fire. On investigating we found a large camp which contained people who had been on forced labour, Poles, Hungarians, all nationalities with a great bonfire in the centre. An official from the town said they were scared of them as they had been looting and taking drink. Next day everything quietened down.

On through town and villages, I can't remember names, until we came to the outskirts of Bremen and after it fell went into dock area to pick up German prisoners. On the way there, women were waiting in long queues to buy black bread and on our return journey the women threw the bread into the trucks for the prisoners as we passed.

Crossed the river Elbe and onto Hamburg. Stopped at Wedel on the outskirts where we were billeted.

Life wasn't all grim. Ernest enjoyed some happier moments with the civilians:

During November and December the line was fairly static and we moved to a little town called Hamont in Belgium near the border of Holland. I was billeted with a family called Bongers, along with two others, Corporal Judd and Bill Richards. The father, Jan, was a painter and glazier and had a large family and a little girl called Magna was born when we were there. Jan gave each of us a glass of cognac and a cigar to celebrate. While there we were bombed by two German jets (the first I had seen). One little schoolgirl was killed and some damage to houses, mostly blown out windows. Major Pollard sent a truck back to Brussels taking Jan along to pick up glass. Spent Christmas with the family then shortly after moved on.

William Marks met the inflexibility of the army system:

I got compassionate leave when the wife broke her leg. She was expecting at this time. I tried to get extra leave because she would be bringing this youngster up with a broken leg. I went to Edinburgh and they said 'see your doctor'. So I went to the doctor and he said 'No, there's nothing wrong with her, she's managing'. I said 'she's no managing at all, she's got a bairn there and a broken leg, and your telling me she's managing'. So I had to go back to Holland, I was in Holland at the time.

James Hogg found himself in Denmark:

We went up to Hamburg, it was just a case of consolidating, then we headed up to Lunenburg, that was where Montgomery signed the peace plan. We shot past that, we were away up into Denmark, the Jerries held us in Denmark because they hadn't heard any word about that at all.

   When Lunenburg was signed, we shot off into Denmark to pick up intelligence officers and take them out into the countryside and pick up any Jerry commanders or Generals or whatever the heck was out there, officers, high ranking officers, and we were protection for these people. When we got there there wasn't much for us to do, that's all we did when we were out in Denmark. It was like a wee holiday for us. That would be 45, I spent about six months in Denmark. I wrote home and says; 'believe it or not, I'm only three hundred miles from my house, Denmark'. I say's, 'I'm nearer hame than ever'.

Nowhere could be considered safe, as William Marks was to discover:

We were going to put a bridge across this river, and we were waiting for the bridging coming through, all the stuff, the Bailey bridge. On the river Elbe it was and there were houses there and me and my pal went into the houses to see what we could find of course. I just got in side and these bloody bullets came right in front of me. I says 'what the hells happening'?' I'll hae tae get oot of here'. I was near killed twa or three times but it did'na make nae difference, I got through it.

For Ernest Jamieson, the end of the war was as vicious as any other time:

> Just a week or two before the end of the war we lost another friend. Sergeant Kip Fuller from Kings Lynn. There were still pockets of German resistance Kip and a dispatch rider were sent to pick up messages from Brigade HQ as there was radio silence at the time. They never returned that day so the next day a search party set out and found Kip dead in a ditch beside his motor-cycle. The other DR's bike was there too beside a pool of blood. The other fellow had been wounded and taken prisoner. I served a long time with KIP, he was corporal then in the Petrol Section. The tragedy was he only got married when he came home from Italy. Sad to think it was so near the end of the war, he was regular soldier.

For men like Roddy MacLeod, comradeship was a tangible thing:

> There was more comradeship among the men who were fighting for their lives than you ever see nowadays. There was no comparison. They would help each other and if one of your mates was blown up in a mine field his mates wouldn't hesitate to go out and get him. In the end an order came out that if anybody was blown up in a mine field they had to be left there until somebody came with the mine detectors because they were losing too many going to help their mates.

For some men like Ernest Jamieson, who had fought from Africa, through Sicily and Italy, Europe was the final straight in a race to the finish:

> We were now heading towards Eindhoven following the Guards Division but the Germans bombed straight through Eindhoven and the small town of Volkesward. As we approached you could see the smoke and flames rising above the town. Next day we passed through and saw the devastation. Some of the Guards trucks loaded with petrol had swung over the pavement and caught fire spreading the burning petrol onto the buildings. Men were still fighting the fires

and the hospital had been damaged. Ambulances kept busy and many
civilians killed.

Although RAF, James Hogg and his colleagues fulfilled what was
essentially an army role:

> The armoured car was full of petrol in the back, jerry cans, four gal-
> lons of petrol in there, there were 16 gallons of petrol in the back. If
> we'd been hit by a shell it would have blown us to smithereens. The
> Humber armoured car, what they called the Humber Scout Car. Just
> had a bren on that. It was supposed to be a reconnaissance car. We
> went out first and noseied about and we gave them the all clear and
> the big heavy stuff came up. We did that once and the big heavy stuff
> got hit, the Jerries were hiding. That was at Kiel, Kiel canal.

> Christmas 1945 was one I will never forget. We were having our meal
> served by the officers in the local beer hall and as we were eating a
> group of youngsters were peering through the steamed up windows.
> Major Pollard said there would be no second helpings as the children
> were to be brought in and fed. After the meal all their pockets were
> filled with sweets and any food still remaining given to the mothers.
> When we left Depenau people were crying when waving goodbye. I
> think they would always remember the Schwartz Rattens [Black Rats
> – symbol of the Desert Rats]. (Ernest Jamieson)

As reported in a local newspaper:

> Dressed in their snipers uniforms of camouflaged material and wear-
> ing the close-fitting helmets rather similar to the German fashion,
> three men in a Lowland regiment of the 15th (Scottish) Division
> were sitting in a café during a rest period a few weeks ago enjoying
> a glass of beer and a chat.
>   They were L/Cpl William (Spud) Thomson from Galashiels, L/Cpl
> M Thornton from Edinburgh, and Pte S W Fairbairn from Berwick-
> on-Tweed, and as they talked their Scots voices created interest among
> their neighbours.

Suddenly they were rudely interrupted to find a 'Red Cap' standing over them demanding to see their papers. After scrutinising their identity cards carefully and questioning them exhaustively, he asked them to step outside for a moment.

Wondering what it was all about they complied. Then the 'Red Cap' apologetically explained. He had been told there were three Germans in the café disguised as British soldiers. Apparently somebody had mistaken their Scots tongue for a German attempt at speaking English.

'You must admit' the CMP had added, 'that you were not speaking English'. Delighted at least they had not been mistaken for Englishmen, the three Scots went back to their table.

L/Cpl William (Spud) Thomson's wife received a letter from his commanding officer:

Capt J. R. Barraley
6th K.O.S.B
BLA

Dear Mrs Thomson,
I thought I would like to write to you at this season and wish you a happy Christmas, though I know it will not be as happy as you would wish with your husband away. And I thought that perhaps you would like to hear from someone who has been serving with your husband during these long months.
I can tell you that he is fit and well and doing a grand job of work. He is always so cheerful and ready to help that we could not wish a better man to work with. I was very proud to see him receive his DCM from 'Monty' the other day. He richly deserved it and we are all proud of him. Of course we would all prefer to be home, but we keep pretty cheerful and hopeful that the war is not going to last for so much longer.

Meanwhile, don't be depressed by newspaper reports of present events, – after all if you give a dog enough rope he will hang himself.

So best wishes to you for Christmas and may 1945 be a happier year. God bless.

Yours Sincerely
J.R. Barraley

Just like in the movies, Roddy MacLeod discovered that being 'quick on the draw' mattered:

There was a gap about the length of this house that I crossed to join the boys and than I went about another 15 yards. I didn't like the idea of crossing this gap, I was wide open, but anyway I thought 'To hell, I better get and cover my mates'. I got across the gap and I got to the corner of this hedge, this German officer and me. Well I would say I was half a second faster than him. He got a burst right in the chest and he fell forward and he must have pressed the trigger falling forward and it went through my coat. I had my legs spread with the machine gun and it went through my coat.

Got him and the rest of the patrol in one go. The Bren was deadly if you handled it properly.

During the war numerous pamphlets were produced with the title 'A Soldier's Guide' to Italy, Sicily, Alexandria etc. One, however, was produced by the 51st Division with tongue firmly in cheek. On their return home:

A Soldiers Guide to Scotland
Men, as this little book flutters into your hands, you are about to invade a strange and unfamiliar country. Remember that, whatever historians with long memories may say about your descent from the Scottish, you are now physically and temperamentally an absolutely different race. You are 'White Wogs' and when you get among the wild, hard folk of the North, you will be stared at. Your arrival will be perhaps the greatest event in their long lonely lives. You must GET TO KNOW these curious people and change your habits to suit theirs however repugnant this may be. If offered, 'a half and half

pint' (roughly Scottish equivalent to your vino) do not refuse it. Do not rudely brush aside the advances of a pretty 'lassie' (sonorita, bint). Be polite and firm WIN THEIR RESPECT!

The Country
According to Shakespeare, poor and afraid to know itself. Scotland is a rugged mountainous region which even those energetic colonists the Romans, could not face.

History
A series of unsuccessful battles with their neighbours, the English, fought on the fields of Twickenham and Murreyfield.

The People
Possess a high blood pressure, principally because 'their blood leaps in their veins whene're they hear the bagpipe strains,' which is quite frequently.

Divided into two social classes: Lairds or 'Monarchs of the Glen' and Kerns and Gallowglasses (mercenaries dragooned from the Western Isles).

By reputation 'canny' and 'fly' but with your recent experience of the native trader, they will probably be putty in your hands.

Morals are rigid, but don't despair. The Scot is not well known for extreme jealousy where his women folk are concerned (contrast that bit of transparent propaganda in 'The Soldiers Guide to Sicily') and even in a crisis is not likely to resort to the Skein Dhu.

Customs
The night of Hogmanay is generally celebrated in what you might be inclined to regard as an over-emphatic manner. Be tolerant. Remember the adage, 'When in Sauchihall Street do as the Sauchihall Streetians do.'

What do they eat?
The Scots, you will find, polish off an extraordinary meal called 'high tea' around five in the afternoon. A people of stern Puritan outlook, they regard Dinner at night as a dangerous build-up to license and exercise.

Towns and Cities

There are several of these. If you are lucky enough to get leave and
don't want to spend it in your battalion leave camp, you may care to
visit some of them. A short guide is therefore given.

Glasgow: Round about closing time is known as 'dear auld Glesca
toon,' and everyone asserts he belongs to it.

Edinburgh: Then capital of Scotland and very pleased about it.

Aberdeen: Notable as a manufacturing centre for humorous anec-
dotes directed against itself.

Dundee: Has a depressed expression as the result of witnessing an
unfortunate incident to an adjoining bridge.

Inverness: Frontier town – most northerly point of recognised
civilisation.

Perth: Worth visiting to see the only place in Scotland with two
Inches of different size.

Fiesta

Not a particularly exuberant race, the Scots maintain a moody scowl
during most Saint's Day feasts and have no Battle of Flowers or gay pro-
cessions to which you are accustomed in the Mediterranean countries.

Finally – A Few Don'ts

Don't…

Knock on the doors of houses in small villages demanding 'blondie'
and proffering a 10-lira note.

Burn up two-gallon tins of petrol by the road side in order to 'brew
up'. This will only lead to ill feeling among a people rationed to one
gallon a month for motoring.

Expect a tin of bully to get the same results as a diamond ring with
a Scots girl.

Bother to swat flies. You outnumber them now.

The Aftermath

After five years in captivity, Ian Rintoul was finally released from prison camp and returned home:

> A few days later we were transported to the railway station, which was quite a few miles journey. On arrival there we were given travel vouchers and told to listen for the train going to Edinburgh and a connection for Alloa. My parents were told I was travelling on it, but they were given the wrong date of arrival. When the train pulled in I was looking out, hoping for a welcoming party. I gathered my kit and walked home and into the house, what a welcome I got. My father had gone to work not knowing I was home. Someone who worked beside him said, 'I saw Ian walking home', so he got permission to go home and that was another welcome home I got.
>
> After a few days leave, a card arrived from some Army Office with a travel voucher to report for Rehabilitation to the barracks near Edinburgh. It was very informal, eating and chatting and taken to Edinburgh and then taken on a mystery tour. Next day we were informed to report for kit but it was a change of kit. It was flannel trousers and jacket. It's not what I would have bought but it was a change.
>
> We hear so much about Dunkirk but nothing about the sacrifice of the rearguard action to allow this to happen. 500 killed or wounded and taken prisoners. I will never forget the hopelessness of it all – 5 years lost out of our young lives.

Norman Patterson returned home to the United Kingdom on the first of two occasions to find himself offered a regular commission:

Came back to the UK in October 1945. I was offered a regular commission. The choice was, you could come home by sea or you could fly. There was 6 of us coming home, so we went down to Karachi to catch a plane, we were a couple of days there, and, you say, catch a plane you think you are all in a nice seat, we were all in the bomb-bay of a Liberator. We flew through the middle east and stopped somewhere during the night and we went down to Tel Aviv. We found out we were stopping off at Tel Aviv because of acclimatisation – what a load of crap. We had a week there and we were told not to go into certain areas of the town, maybe get shot. Then we arrived at Borden, near Cambridge, it was drizzly and the WAAFs met us coming of the plane. We were told, 'don't bring anything on this plane because of the weight'. The RAF boys had booze and carpets. So anyway, when we arrived at Borden, once we had got accommodation one of the boys came and he said 'the nearest pub's three miles up the road' so we got washed up and something to eat, and marched three miles up the road to this inn, somebody say's 'there's a notice on the door'. 'Sorry, beer sold out'. However, we were going up to London the next day and one of the guys had phoned, he came from there, he had phoned and he said 'my aunts staying in the Cumberland Hotel, so he said 'we're all invited to a big party in the Cumberland Hotel'. So we went to this party, I remember being in this dungeon of a bar and there was so much whisky. By the time we left there we were on the train coming up to Edinburgh. The next day we were put to Redford barracks, on parade, and this officer, he came up to me and he said 'Patterson, you're improperly dressed'. And I said 'in what respect?' he says 'you shouldn't be attired as you are, you should be in number one' I said ' for your information sir, that's all I have, what I stand up in'. Oh. 'All my gear my batman's packing, it will probably take six weeks to come by sea'. We were allowed out that day, into town, Princess Street, we were all in this hairdressers near the railway station. We were sitting having a haircut and one of the guys he said 'what about the trains north? And the barber said 'oh, there's one in half an hour or something' 'Right, stop!' he says 'what?' I said 'that's enough for me'. Paid him. Christ, I ran down, in all my gear, I was coming away from the barracks anyway, all my gear in the left luggage, paid for it, got it out, and I was chasing the train up the platform.

At the end of the war, Douglas Kerr found himself almost unemployed within an RAF which was overmanned by specialists it no longer needed:

> The war ended and armourers were no longer required, they took the guns out, so we were no longer required, they had to find something for us to do. We were just working in the NAAFI, wiping tables, anything, delivering coal, anything for a while. Then we went down to Filton and demobbed.

For many, the end of the war did not mean the end of military service. Charles Devlin continued to serve in the Mediterranean on board HMS *Atherston*:

> The war ended and we started going over to Yugoslavia to haul off the British forces that were there because the Yugoslavs started turning nasty. It was RAF personnel and special forces. We went in with an American LST, we escorted it, it was under British command. I remember distinctly all the Italians. That area had been an Italian colony. The came running down the jetty with their suitcases and their wives and their daughters and everything, 'wait, wait, wait we're friendly'. Take them, we couldn't, we weren't under orders to take them. It was a bloody shame. We were only taking off British personnel not Italians, whether that would have involved another diplomatic row, I don't know. We took them back over to Italy. We went up to Trieste just after that and immediately we lined the forward gun turret on the city square and the after gun turret was lined up on a tank, a Yugoslav tank which was sat round the corner and that was us for about two months. The war was finished and we sat there, they were our allies and we were going away to have another go.

There was one night when half the ships company was ashore and we were alongside the customs Quay, where the liners came in, the gunners mate, the CPO, he came running down to my deck and he said 'could anyone here man the Oerlikon', we said 'what's happening?' He said' come and look outside'. We looked out and the hills were on fire 'oh for God's sake, it's started'. I mean I was a gunner, a loader on the guns, and I was standing there with a shell, waiting to put it in. The Yugoslavs had machine guns along these roads and they were trained on us. Of course, if they had opened up we wouldn't have stood a chance. Anyway, we were all standing there and three Kiwis came on board. We said 'get under cover, the bloody war's started'. They said 'what the hell are you on about, it's just the fireworks for Tito's birthday'. We starved them out in the end. The British authorities must have told the Yugoslavs 'you say it's your town, you occupied it, you feed the people'. I used to be in command of a truck that went up the local warehouse for fresh veg and whatnot and one day a carrot fell out the sack and fell off the truck and people descended on it like and they started running after the truck. I told the officer when we got back 'this job's getting dangerous, they'll have to provide us with guards, I'm going to get torn apart'. They put up barbed wire all along the docks, and guards and the food ships were lying out in the bay. So Tito must have given up otherwise he would have had the population. Trieste was untouched, they were well dressed but starving.

For many men, like Bill Edgar, the end of the war left a bitter taste:

On VE day we were going over the pass, the Schlossen Pass, and we went down into Austria and there was 40,000 Cossacks waiting for us. The last terrible thing we did. It was our brigade who put them on trucks and trains. They were committing suicide. There was one woman who threw her three kids in the river, and they drowned, and went in herself, and I think it was the Argylls that went in and pulled them out. A terrible thing.

Ernest Jamieson continued to be stationed in Europe, assisting with the resettlement of refugees:

The following year until I was demobbed on May 1946 was really horrendous and sometimes heartbreaking. Most of the time was spent carrying displaced persons into former internment camps. We brought in timber for heating and food, much of which we brought from Lubeck (mostly Red Cross parcels which were meant for our own prisoners of war).

Went on detail to Hamburg Zoo where people were camped, all Russian women and teenagers. They had been in forced labour camps. One young chap walked with two sticks, I took him in the cab beside me and we headed for Lubeck. Whilst waiting there a young dark haired girl came and asked me if they were Jews. I said no, she was a Jewess and spoke good English. All her family had been taken away, her father was a doctor and a German friend of her father, also a doctor looked after her.

She survived, I wonder if her father did?

When we reached Lubeck we handed the people over to the Highland Division. The young man with me said he had been pun-ished by straddling him over a fence gate and beaten with a stick, damaging his back. They were taken over a bridge where Russian soldiers took over. One of our soldiers said that shooting took place on the Russian side after each batch arrived.

Took rations through Flenburg into Denmark where some Scots Greys and KRRC were in the port of Kolding. We were warned by them to look out for Danish Communists who strolled the streets looking for trouble, they wore red stars on their lapels, only met them once and gave them a wide berth.

Billeted in a small village near Kiel and took over the local beer house. I got a good detail there going to Kiel to pick up beer at the brewery. Couple of old chaps loaded up the truck then in sign lan-guage asked if I had cigarettes and food. I gave them some and they gave me two cases of bottled beer. Cheers.

Went on detail to pick up German prisoners arriving from Norway with their Norwegian wives, some with babies. I had an attractive

blonde girl with her baby sitting beside me whose husband was in
back of the truck, she spoke good English. It was a cold day and as
we were driving along the Autobahn a mist came down so we all
stopped and started a fire for a brew up and give the women a chance
to feed their children. We dropped them off at a German barracks. I
hope they both survived.

Posted abroad for the second time, Norman Patterson was on board a
troopship bound for the Far East when Japan surrendered. However,
unfortunately for him he wasn't sent home. He was sent to Palestine
as part of the peacekeeping force:

> Of course it came through then that Japan hadn't chucked it in, they
> were still going at it so they took all the younger lads out and took
> us hame and put us on a ship for the far east, we didna ken where
> we were going but when we got on board the boat, the 6th Airborne
> was on board that boat as well. It was The Duchess of Richmond, the
> boat that I sailed on. Word came through that the bomb was dropped
> on Hiroshima and the Japs had chucked it, that was it.
>
> I was on the way to the Far East actually. We were in the Bay of
> Biscay on August 15th when the bomb was dropped on Hiroshima,
> they transferred me to Egypt because they were having problems in
> Palestine, between the Jews and the Arabs. Of course the problem
> then of course the Jews are supporting us here. We weren't allowed to
> do anything unless they did something against us. So we were sitting
> in Palestine all the time. We were on patrols from Haifa, all the way
> down the Bitter Lakes.
>
> Landed at Cairo, picked up the big Stag Hounds [American made
> armoured cars], so we picked up ten heavy, sixteen ton, armoured
> vehicles, they had a thirty-seven millimetre gun in. What they used
> to do, they had these petrol drums and you used to fill them with
> sand, and they used to put them over a bridge like a fence and we
> picked these heavy armoured cars up and I drove the officers car, I was
> the first to go over and they were eleven foot broad these armoured
> vehicles, and as I was moving in I hit one of these drums and of course
> it went off and into the river and as far as I believe by the time the

whole convoy got over there there were no drums left, they were all in they river. These Stag Hounds, they were due for the Russian front but when the Jerries capitulated ower here they transferred them to the middle east.

We went in to Cairo, we went to Cooke's Engineering, we had to get brackets welded onto the side of the armoured car. When we were there this little man came up and he said, 'what part of Scotland do you come frae, Jock?' and I didna ken wha was speaking. I looked and he says, 'hey, I'm speaking to you', as broad as you like. That's because there were so many Scottish divisions ower there. In Egypt we were just on patrols, it was just as I say, 'showing the flag' that was aw.

William Marks found himself posted round the Mediterranean at the end of the war:

I got posted back at the end of the war, thought I was going home but I went to various places, all the different countries. They had to get rid of us someplace, there were too many of us in the country. I was in Manchester and they had to get rid of us someplace. So I was sent back to France, up to Italy, and then we went to Greece. It was just bridge repair and various things like that. I finished up in Palestine. The Jews were just coming in then, from foreign countries. We got on fine with the Palestinians. But the Jews were beginning to come in and they began to kill us. I came home from there and they gave me a set of clothes, a demob suit they called it.

There were some prisoners, I wouldn't say they were prisoners, they were women, they had walked from different places and they were in this commandeered house and I said 'you've nothing to eat, we'll have to do something about this'. So this farmer had chickens and I said 'right I'm wanting a chicken'. 'No, No, No'. I says 'I'll shoot you ye bugger'. So he gave us this chicken and we gave it to the women and they plucked it and ate it. But we were telt then to keep away from them because of the diseases and various things that happened. I said 'we'll get help for you, but we couldn't do any more than that. That was in Germany – the women were refugees trying to get to the west I think.

James Hogg also found himself dealing with refugees but in a different manner:

> We were on the main road, we were heading somewhere and these two women came rushing across from one of the camps and they stopped at the officer and they spoke to him and seemingly it was two Russian prisoners and the were in pyjama suits, stripes, one was a tall fellow and one was a wee fellow and here they were molesting these two women, German women. The women, when they saw the armoured unit they ran over to us. The officer said to me, 'look, get the car, pick these two idiots up, take them away somewhere and dump them'. So I went away down and picked up the two Russian lads. Told them, 'jump up on top of the armoured car', and drove them away, a couple of miles away, something like that. About half an hour later the women were back again, the blokes had got back again. The officer said, 'how far did you take them?' I said, 'just a couple of mile'. He said, 'take them about five mile up the road and dump them'. I took them about ten mile before I dumped them. What a bloody shame, the poor guys were just from Buckenvald camp.

Returning from leave, Norman Campbell found his comrades had already left for home without him:

> By now I had got my first stripe and was working in the Orderly Room and in September was one of the lucky ones to be drawn out of the hat for 28 days LIAP leave in the UK. The Orderly Room Sergeant offered to get me another stripe if I would forego the leave, but I preferred to go. I had to travel from Dehra Dun to Cochin in Travancore, to get the ship. Why I couldn't have got it at much nearer Bombay was not disclosed and I didn't argue. Even the ride on India's finest railway seemed pleasant.
>
> After my months leave I returned to India on the Mauritania. Sailing into Bombay harbour we passed an aircraft carrier sailing out. I didn't know it then, that my unit was onboard en-route to Singapore, to where I followed them some weeks later.

I will not say that I would not have missed it for anything. Very few people would have volunteered for that show knowing the physical and mental privations which had to be endured and overcome. But having done it I am glad I had the physical and mental strength to cope with it and the Chindits have every right to be proud of their achievements, somewhat limited though they might have been.

After having served in four campaigns, Ernest Jamieson records an understated reaction to the end of the conflict:

Moved to barracks in Schleswig-Holstein where I was demobbed in May 1946. Fond farewells to 5 company whom I had served for over five years and of the comradeship of those served with. Now there is only memories.

Thomas Yates gives a more realistic view:

On reflection, I, along with many thousand other servicemen who had been in the thick of the action, wonder how we escaped with our lives [had his tank blown up three times]. It was an experience I will never forget. I am glad that I went through it, but would not do it again even if I knew the outcome would be the same.

Like many 'duration only' officers, Hugh Davidson was allowed to keep his rank after the war:

8th January 1946

Sir,

Now that the time has come for your release from active military duty, I am commanded by the Army Council to express to you their thanks for the valuable services which you have rendered in the service of your country at a time of grave national emergency.

At the end of the emergency you will relinquish your commission, and at that time a notification will appear in the London Gazette (Supplement), granting you also the honorary rank of Lieutenant.

Meanwhile, you have permission to use that rank with effect from
the date of your release.

Not all were desperate to come home. Many sought employment
with the new occupation authorities. Barrie Herbert was appointed
a Control Officer after the war:

Sir,

I am directed by the Secretary of State for Foreign Affairs to
offer you an appointment as a Control Officer Grade III in the
Civil Transport Organisation of the Control Commission for
Germany (British Element) subject to completion of the necessary
Establishment formalities and to your undergoing inoculation and
vaccination.

The appointment will be subject to the terms and conditions set out
in the enclosed memorandum CCB/40/4 and the commencing salary
will be £320 per anum; allowances will be paid in addition to salary
in accordance with paragraph 5 (b) and (c) of the mamorandum. The
appointment will comence on the day on which you report for duty,
and you will be required to serve for a continuous period of one year
in Germany from the date of your first arrival there, on the expiration
of which period your appointment will terminate unless specifically
extended by the Foreign Office for a further period.

If you wish to accept this appointment you should complete the
enclosed acceptance Form and return it to the address shown thereon
without delay, together with the documents, etc. referred to in the
enclosed Instructions.

I am, sir,
Your obedient servant

A.L. Forbes returned home to his previous job, but like many others
he was unable to settle down after the adventure of war:

With the ending of the war in Europe speculation regarding how
long would it be until we got home was the favourite subject of

conversation. A scheme had been devised on a points basis; you got so many points for service overseas, so many for marital status, number of children, etc. I came out quite well. My release number was 18 which meant I would soon be home. The notice board had to be watched every day and finally my name appeared along with a few others. I was to proceed to Brecia, thence via the Simplon Tunnel through Switzerland to Dieppe. Meals would be available en route. On arriving in the UK I had to report to Redford Barracks for overnight stay and processing in the morning. Again the organisation was good and we were all kitted out with civilian clothes – everything including shoes, suit, raincoat, hat, and neck tie. Added to this we were given three months leave pay.

Employers were obliged to take on personnel who had been in their employ before joining up, so I had a job to go to. I went to the job alright but could not stick it. After adventuring as I had done for about six years it was not easy to settle down into routine dullness so I replied to an advertisement for Control Commission of Germany requesting applications for civilian posts in the British Zone of Germany. I was accepted and posted to Minden in Nord Rhine Westfalen. My wife joined me and we had about ten happy years in Germany.

Pal MacLeod felt that war was justified:

It wasn't a waste of time because the Nazis were poised to take over everything.

Mind you the ordinary German troops were just like the troops here but the Nazis, they were fanatics.

These views were echoed by many, including Jimmy MacKenzie:

I'm not glorifying war and I don't believe in it really, but I can't say in regret anything I did and I certainly don't regret being in the marines and I'm certainly very proud of being in the marines. Although war is a horrible thing, there must be times when it is the only option.

Iain MacAuley also echoes the strongly-held views of many Scots:

> Although we don't like some of the things that were done on our
> behalf, they were successful. The French didn't do us any good. And
> the 51st Division were sacrificed. Not for any great glory that they
> could obtain or wear they could win but to appease the French. And
> when it came to the final, the French disappeared and left them.

And finally....

> See for being lucky, I was the luckiest man alive. I should have been
> dead dozens of times. (Roddy MacLeod)

> I wet myself a few times, well more than a few times, in the carry-on
> from 39 to 45 but I wouldn't have missed it for... (Bill Edgar)

List of Illustrations

Royal Scots Museum.
17   Assault craft. ADC, Royal Scots Museum.
18   Preparing for departure. ADC, Royal Scots Museum.
19   A gunboat sinking off the beachhead. ADC, Royal Scots Museum.
20   Tank landing craft heading for the shore. ADC, Royal Scots Museum.
21   One of 'Hobart's Funnies'. A British flail tank lands on the invasion beach from an LTC (Landing Craft Tank). ADC, Royal Scots Museum.
22   'Hobart's Funnies'. As a flail tank lands on the beach, part of another device can be seen rising from the body of the landing craft. ADC, Royal Scots Museum.
23   Caring for the wounded as they wait to be evacuated from the beachhead. ADC, Royal Scots Museum.
24   Washing day for RAF recon'. Courtesy of James Hogg.
25   RAF recognisance unit on the way to Denmark having a rest at the side of the road. Courtesy of James Hogg.
26   James Hogg and his crew with their Humber Scout car. Courtesy of James Hogg.
27   Time for a beer: just how many men can you fit on an old car? Courtesy of James Hogg.
28   Cleanliness is next to godliness: washing day in the field. Courtesy of James Hogg.
29   A Group pastime. Courtesy of James Hogg.
30   Scottish pastime – tossing the caber. Courtesy of James Hogg.
31   A squadron of British Shermans moving up. ADC, Royal Scots Museum.
32   A Bailey bridge and the original, destroyed by the Germans as they withdrew. ADC, Royal Scots Museum.
33   British Sherman tanks about to cross a Bailey bridge. ADC, Royal Scots Museum.
34   Tank landing craft lie off the beach and disgorge 'Buffalos'. ADC, Royal Scots Museum.
35   Buffalos heading for the beach at the Scheldt during the operation to clear the approaches to the port of Antwerp. ADC, Royal Scots Museum.
36   Buffalo coming ashore and climbing up the beach. ADC, Royal Scots Museum.
37   As the tide goes out, a line of Buffalos come ashore. ADC, Royal Scots Museum.
38   Troops wade ashore from landing craft while the Buffalo is already on the beach. ADC, Royal Scots Museum.
39   The assault craft are beached at low tide while the Buffalos can run

Index

TEMPUS – REVEALING HISTORY

R.J.Mitchell
Schooldays to Spitfire
GORDON MITCHELL
'[A] readable and poignant story'
The Sunday Telegraph

£12.99   0 7524 3727 5

Forgotten Soldiers of the First World War
Lost Voices from the Middle Eastern Front
DAVID WOODWARD
'A brilliant new book of hitherto unheard voices from a haunting theatre of the First World War'
Malcolm Brown

£20   0 7524 3854 9

1690 Battle of the Boyne
PÁDRAIG LENIHAN
'An almost impeccably impartial account of the most controversial military engagement in British history' **The Daily Mail**

£12.99   0 7524 3304 0

Hell at the Front
Combat Voices from the First World War
TOM DONOVAN
'Fifty powerful personal accounts, each vividly portraying the brutalising reality of the Great War... a remarkable book'
Max Arthur

£12.99   0 7524 3940 5

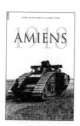

Amiens 1918
JAMES MCWILLIAMS & R. JAMES STEEL
'A masterly portrayal of this pivotal battle'
Soldier: The Magazine of the British Army

£25   0 7524 2860 8

Before Stalingrad
Hitler's Invasion of Russia 1941
DAVID GLANTZ
'Another fine addition to Hew Strachan's excellent *Battles and Campaigns* series'
BBC History Magazine

£9.99   0 7524 2692 3

The SS
A History 1919-45
ROBERT LEWIS KOEHL
'Reveals the role of the SS in the mass murder of the Jews, homosexuals and gypsies and its organisation of death squads throughout occupied Europe' *The Sunday Telegraph*

£9.99   0 7524 2559 5

Arnhem 1944
WILLIAM BUCKINGHAM
'Reveals the real reason why the daring attack failed' *The Daily Express*

£10.99   0 7524 3187 0

If you are interested in purchasing other books published by Tempus, or in case you have difficulty finding any Tempus books in your local bookshop, you can also place orders directly through our website

www.tempus-publishing.com

TEMPUS REVEALING HISTORY

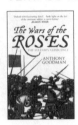
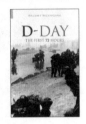

The Wars of the Roses
The Soldiers' Experience
ANTHONY GOODMAN
'Sheds light on the lot of the common soldier as never before' *Alison Weir*
'A meticulous work'
The Times Literary Supplement

£12.99   0 7524 3731 3

English Battlefields
500 Battlefields that Shaped English History
MICHAEL RAYNER
'A painstaking survey of English battlefields... a first-rate book' *Richard Holmes*
'A fascinating and, for all its factual tone, an atmospheric volume' *The Sunday Telegraph*

£25   0 7524 2978 7

D-Day
The First 72 Hours
WILLIAM F. BUCKINGHAM
'A compelling narrative' *The Observer*
A *BBC History Magazine* Book of the Year 2004

£9.99   0 7524 2842 2

Trafalgar Captain Durham of the Defiance:
The Man who refused to Miss Trafalgar
HILARY RUBINSTEIN
'A sparkling biography of Nelson's luckiest captain' *Andrew Lambert*

£17.99   0 7524 3435 7

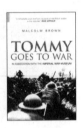

Battle of the Atlantic
MARC MILNER
'The most comprehensive short survey of the U-boat battles' *Sir John Keegan*
'Some events are fortunate in their historian, none more so than the Battle of the Atlantic. Marc Milner is *the* historian of the Atlantic Campaign... a compelling narrative'
Andrew Lambert

£12.99   0 7524 3332 6

Okinawa 1945 The Stalingrad of the Pacific
GEORGE FEIFER
'A great book... Feifer's account of the three sides and their experiences far surpasses most books about war' *Stephen Ambrose*

£17.99   0 7524 3324 5

Gallipoli 1915
TIM TRAVERS
'The most important new history of Gallipoli for forty years... groundbreaking' *Hew Strachan*
'A book of the highest importance to all who would seek to understand the tragedy of the Gallipoli campaign' *The Journal of Military History*

£13.99   0 7524 2972 8

Tommy Goes To War
MALCOLM BROWN
'A remarkably vivid and frank account of the British soldier in the trenches' *Max Arthur*
'The fury, fear, mud, blood, boredom and bravery that made up life on the Western Front are vividly presented and illustrated' *The Sunday Telegraph*

£12.99   0 7524 2980 9

TEMPUS REVEALING HISTORY

Scotland
From Prehistory to the Present
FIONA WATSON
The Scotsman **Bestseller**
£9.99
0 7524 2591 9

Flodden
NIALL BARR
'Tells the story brilliantly'
The Sunday Post
£9.99
0 7524 2593 5

1314 Bannockburn
ARYEH NUSBACHER
'Written with good-humoured verve as
befits a rattling "yarn of sex, violence and
terror"'
History Scotland
£9.99
0 7524 2982 5

Scotland's Black Death
The Foul Death of the English
KAREN JILLINGS
'So incongruously enjoyable a read, and so
attractively presented by the publishers'
The Scotsman
£14.99
0 7524 2314 2

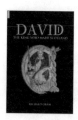

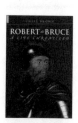

David I The King Who Made Scotland
RICHARD ORAM
'Enthralling... sets just the right tone as the
launch-volume of an important new series
of royal biographies' *Magnus Magnusson*
£17.99
0 7524 2825 X

The Kings & Queens of Scotland
RICHARD ORAM
'A serious, readable work that sweeps across
a vast historical landscape' *The Daily Mail*
£12.99
0 7524 3814 X

The Second Scottish Wars of Independence 1332–1363
CHRIS BROWN
'Explodes the myth of the invincible Bruces...
lucid and highly readable' *History Scotland*
£12.99
0 7524 3812 3

Robert the Bruce: A Life Chronicled
CHRIS BROWN
'A masterpiece of research'
The Scots Magazine
£30
0 7524 2575 7

If you are interested in purchasing other books published by Tempus, or in case you have difficulty finding any Tempus
books in your local bookshop, you can also place orders directly through our website

www.tempus-publishing.com

TEMPUS REVEALING HISTORY

William Wallace
The True Story of Braveheart
CHRIS BROWN
'The truth about Braveheart' *The Scottish Daily Mail*
£17.99
0 7524 3432 2

The Roman Conquest of Scotland
The Battle of Mons Graupius AD 84
JAMES E. FRASER
'Challenges a long held view' *The Scottish Sunday Express*
£17.99
0 7524 3325 3

An Abundance of Witches
The Great Scottish Witch-Hunt
P.G. MAXWELL-STUART
'An amazing account of Scots women in league with the Devil' *The Sunday Post*
£17.99
0 7524 3329 6

Scottish Voices from the Great War
DEREK YOUNG
'A treasure trove of personal letters and diaries from the archives'
Trevor Royle
£17.99
0 7524 3326 1

FORTHCOMING FROM TEMPUS

Culloden
The Last Charge of the Highland Clans
JOHN SADLER
December 2006
0 7524 3955 3

The Pictish Conquest
The Battle of Dunnichen 685 & the Birth of Scotland
JAMES E. FRASER
December 2006
0 7524 3962 6

Scottish Battles
500 Battles that Shaped Scottish History
CHRIS BROWN
November 2006
0 7524 3685 6